THE NEXT
WORLD

THE NEXT WORLD

WORLD

Extraordinary Experiences of the Afterlife

Gregory Shushan

www.whitecrowbooks.com

For information, contact White Crow Productions Ltd.
by e-mail: info@whitecrowbooks.com

Cover Design by Astrid@Astridpaints.com
Interior design by Velin@Perseus-Design.com

ISBN: Paperback: 978-1-78677-181-0
ISBN: eBook: 978-1-78677-182-7

Non-Fiction / Body, Mind & Spirit / Near-death experience

www.whitecrowbooks.com

In memory of Dr. Maya Warrier

PRAISE FOR *THE NEXT WORLD*

⁓

"Gregory Shushan is one of the brightest lights in the rising generation of scholars in psychical research."

> ~ Alan Gauld, author, *The Heyday of Mental Mediumship: 1880s – 1930s: Investigators, Mediums and Communicators.*

"This extraordinary book provides concise, clearly-written text describing important NDE elements: universal, cultural, and individual layers; revelations; geographical and historical perspectives; reincarnation; academic and popular hypotheses. Shushan provides abundant NDE narratives, illustrating his arguments. This book is both academically accurate and highly entertaining, a remarkable combination. A brilliant book – fun to read!"

> ~ James McClenon, Ph.D, author of *Wondrous Healing: Shamanism, Human Evolution, and the Origin of Religion* and *The Entity Letters: A Sociologist on the Trail of a Supernatural Mystery.*

"In *The Next World: Extraordinary Experiences of the Afterlife,* Gregory Shushan explores near-death experiences as inextricable from the cultures of the individuals who have them. As a comparative historian of religious and spiritual experiences, Shushan takes us beyond the usual arguments over the reality of NDEs, and shows that the true nature of NDEs is irrelevant to their ability to inspire and influence our views of life and death. Examining the relationships between afterlife beliefs and NDEs throughout history and across cultures enables Shushan to shed a unique light on what NDEs imply about the true spiritual reality and the possibilities of an afterlife, and to advance our understanding of NDEs and of our own nature as few other books have. This truly is a remarkable book."

~ Bruce Greyson, M.D., author of *After: A Doctor Explores What Near-Death Experiences Reveal About Life and Beyond.*

"This fine new book by Gregory Shushan encapsulates his decades of painstaking ethnohistorical research on Near-Death Experiences (NDEs) and various related phenomena, spanning a remarkable range of cultures and times. Examining these complex and multifaceted phenomena from his perspective as a scholar of comparative culture, religion and psychology, and paying close attention to both similarities and differences among experiences reported in different cultural settings, he arrives at a picture which avoids both facile universalism and facile cultural and psychological determinism. What emerges is a more complex picture according to which the underlying experiences, having much in common with mystical experiences more generally, end up being reported in terms which also reflect the influence of personal psychology and the cultural or doctrinal setting. A final chapter seeks to distill the implications of this impressive body of work for the possibility of postmortem survival, and for our nascent conception of what it might be like. Strongly recommended!"

~ Edward F. Kelly, Professor in the Division of Perceptual Studies, Department of Psychiatry and Neurobehavioral Sciences, University of Virginia School of Medicine; co-editor of *Irreducible Mind, Beyond Physicalism,* and *Consciousness Unbound.*

"What a breathtaking tour of the expanse of human experience! It left me with a sense of wonder and admiration - such a rounded, balanced, objective yet sympathetic look at the roots of our myths and beliefs, in a context grounded in evidence from just about every civilisation and period. A fascinating perspective on the multiple aspects of the relationship between culture and individual experience."

~ Zofie Weaver, Society for Psychical Research; Author of *Other Realities? The Enigma of Franek Kluski's Mediumship* and *A World in a Grain of Sand: The Clairvoyance of Stefan Ossowiecki.*

PRAISE FOR THE
AUTHOR'S PREVIOUS BOOKS

Near-Death Experience in Indigenous Religions

"... the most important scholarly work on near-death experiences in the last thirty years. ... This is a journey and an argument as fascinating and as engrossing as the social history of mankind itself."

~ Allan Kellehear, PhD., author, *Visitors at the End of Life: Finding Meaning and Purpose in Near-Death Phenomena.*

"... a uniquely insightful and provocative analysis of near-death experiences that documents their formative influence on worldwide beliefs about an afterlife. ... This book is essential reading for anyone seeking to understand NDEs and their role in society."

~ Bruce Greyson, author, *After: A Doctor Explores What Near-Death Experiences Reveal about Life and Beyond.*

"... a tour de force. ... Any future discussions of NDEs and the origins of religion will need to take Shushan's major contribution into account."

~ Fiona Bowie, PhD, author, *Tales from the Afterlife.*

"Interested readers will be amazed at the data reported by the author in this erudite and intelligent inquiry."

~ Gavin Flood, author, *The Importance of Religion: Meaning and Action in our Strange World.*

"A fundamental book for all those interested in religious expressions related to after-life and post-mortem, this volume will surely remain a milestone in the study of what Shakespeare precipitously called 'the undiscovered country from whose bourne no traveller returns.' After all, some travellers, so it seems, have trodden there."

~ Davide Torri, PhD, author, *The Shamaness in Asia.*

"There is a weighty poignancy to this [book], bearing witness to the value of studying historical records regarding the fundamental question "What happens to us when we die?"

~ Mary L. Keller, author, *The Hammer and the Flute.*

"Shushan has advanced the study of non-Western NDEs immeasurably. ... [He] has done the field a tremendous service, and his book is not to be missed by anyone seriously concerned with NDEs."

~ James Matlock, author,
Signs of Reincarnation: Exploring Beliefs, Cases, and Theory.

Conceptions of the Afterlife in Early Civilizations

"... a fascinating journey through ancient ideas about the afterlife.... the author brings them to life and makes them relevant to contemporary concerns about what has become known as near-death-experiences. ... This is a bold and engaging book." ~ Gavin Flood.

"... one of the most interesting and methodologically reflective examples of comparative work in the study of religions."

~ Michael Stausberg, ed.,
The Oxford Handbook of the Study of Religion.

"... a dense, rich, thought-provoking work. 9/10." ~ *Fortean Times.*

"a very well-written book by a consummate scholar.... a major contribution to the field of comparative religion and near-death studies.... a 'must-read.'"

~ Ken R. Vincent, *God is With Us: What Near-Death and Other Spiritually Transformative Experiences Teach Us About God and Afterlife.*

CONTENTS

ACKNOWLEDGEMENTS

~

I would like to thank the Perrott-Warrick Fund at Trinity College Cambridge, the Ian Ramsey Centre for Science and Religion at University of Oxford, the Society for Psychical Research, the International Association for Near-Death Studies, the Cedar Creek Institute, the Alex Tanous Foundation for Scientific Research, the Parapsychology Foundation, the Alister Hardy Trust and Religious Experience Research Centre, and the British Academy for various grants and other forms of support over the years that have helped enable the research distilled in this book. Thanks also to Jon Beecher and Judith Shushan for editorial comments and suggestions.

I would like to extend a very special thanks to those who have supported my work on Patreon, and those who continue to do so: Daniel Bourke, Jason Bugher, Rachel Carina, Wendy Dossett, The Daily Grail, Tim Hacker, Kristofer Key, Sylvia Kezele, Jeffrey Matthews, Pascal Michael, Eric Peterson, Denise Reynolds, Ayline Setaghaian, Chris Schelin, Space Lemon, David Sunfellow, Samantha Lee Treasure, Alex L. Tsakiris, Christopher Turek, and Edward Zukowski.

To find out more about my work, join my mailing list, or learn more about becoming a Patron, please visit my website: www.gregoryshushan. com. Some of the material in Chapter 5, in an earlier and very different form, benefitted from comments and suggestions from Paul Badham, Stephen Braude, David Fontana, and Guy Lyon Playfair.

INTRODUCTION

~

Death is one of the few unambiguous facts of life. Together with birth, nothing could be more basic and fundamental to the universally human path of our existence. Our knowledge of the inevitability of death helps define life, and even to give it meaning. As life's opposing state, death makes us aware of the finite nature of our time on Earth. This helps motivate us to act on our aspirations, providing a sense of urgency to *accomplish*, to create and procreate, to strive for fulfillment and contentedness in the brief time we're here, for on some level we continually carry with us the awareness that we won't always be. Though we may feel on an existential level that it is ultimately fruitless, we are preoccupied with leaving something of ourselves behind, some evidence that we *existed* – a gesture towards some kind of legacy that will act at least as an emblem of immortality: children who look like us and think like us, or material products of our creativity which we consider stand for who we are – a book, a poem, a painting, a photograph, a song, a favorite recipe – anything that attests to the fact that our individualities, our *selves*, were here and had some kind of impact and even purpose.

While most of us will never witness the violent destruction or physical decomposition of human bodies, it is common to intimately experience the death of a loved one. Their vision, their hearing, their engagement with the world slipping away, vital signs ebbing, color draining, and breath dwindling until that certain final whispery exhalation signals the end. The simple profundity of experiencing of another's death, of witnessing

1

their transition from *alive* to *not alive*, cannot be overstated. A human being once animated and dynamic, once so full of intention, action, and speculation, never to move, think, speak or smile ever again, never to interact with us again for the rest of *our* lives on Earth. The evidence of our senses confirms to us that every living thing will die, including our families, our friends, our pets, and ourselves.

And yet, the sense that our bodies are not entirely "us," that they are really just the things that carry us around, the machines that house our ghosts, is embedded in our very languages. We spend our lives alternately identifying ourselves with our bodies, and distancing ourselves from them. We say "I am hungry" instead of "my body is hungry," and "I am dying" rather than "my body is dying." But we also refer to our minds as being distinct from our bodies. We make up our minds, we change our minds, and we lose our minds.

Many of us – including atheists and agnostics – have vague, half-realized, or even wholly subconscious feelings that when deprived of our bodies we must still be *something*. If this body is not quite entirely "me," I am more than just my body, and something other than death must happen to "me" when my body dies. And of course, most of the 98% of the world's religious people firmly believe that they'll survive their own deaths, whether in some heavenly or hellish realm, through resurrection, reincarnation, or even liberation.

Experiments in cognitive neuroscience seem to show that we're hard-wired to believe in an afterlife, despite the evidence of death all around us. Very young children who have little conception of the metaphysical implications of death or afterlife seem to intuitively believe that physical death somehow does not entail the death of the "person." They naturally assume that it isn't *really* the end, and that "dead" people live on somehow, somewhere. At least since Freud, it's been said repeatedly that we're simply unable to imagine our own nonexistence. We haven't had the experience of being dead, and it's impossible to know what it's like to be wholly without perception, sensation, awareness, and thought.

Psychologists, philosophers, anthropologists, and sociologists of all description have weighed in with attempts to explain afterlife beliefs without reference to the theological or metaphysical. They hypothesize that they're due to either wish-fulfillment fantasy, to a yearning for justice in compensation for earthly unfairness, to observations of the "dying-and-rising" cycles of nature, or to the priests and kings who control the world through threats and promises of post-mortem punishment and reward.

These are all interesting theories as far as they go, and each has a place in explaining certain characteristics of specific beliefs in particular societies. But they all ignore two very important things:

The first is the existence of afterlife beliefs around the world that don't fit into such neat categories. Although virtually every society in nearly all times and places has some kind of belief in consciousness surviving bodily death, the conceptions are different enough that such generalizations are unfounded. For example, not all societies believe in moral judgement in the other world, meaning that their beliefs were unlikely to have been created by the elite as a tool of social control.

The second thing all these theories inexplicably ignore is the single human experience that is actually the most relevant to beliefs in an afterlife: near-death experiences, or NDEs.

NDEs were only popularly recognized in the mid-1970s, but people from the largest empires to the smallest hunter-gatherer societies have been having them throughout history. Accounts are found in ancient sacred texts, historical documents, ethnographic studies, and journals of explorers and missionaries. From a 7th century BCE Chinese provincial ruler to an 18th century British admiral, a 19th century Ghanaian victim of human sacrifice, a mid-20th century Samoyed Siberian, or a Soviet suicide attempt revived during government resuscitation experiments, NDEs can happen to followers of any religion, and to those of none.

Just as the evidence of our senses tells us that everything dies, NDErs seem to have another kind of evidence, inaccessible to the rest of us, leading them to the opposite conclusion: that we do not die. In both the historical and modern accounts, NDEs often lead directly to new beliefs, including that consciousness can separate from the body, and that it can continue after death. In my research for my book *Near-Death Experience in Indigenous Religions* I found dozens of examples of individuals stating that NDEs were the direct source of their "knowledge" about the afterlife. On the microcosmic level, the religious, agnostic, and committed atheist alike typically change their beliefs and worldviews following NDEs. Perhaps most famously, upon revival from his NDE, atheist philosopher A. J. Ayer told his doctor, "I saw a Divine Being. I'm afraid I'm going to have to revise all my various books and opinions." Many NDErs also undergo seemingly miraculous positive transformations as a result of the experience. According to his wife, A. J. Ayer "became so much nicer since he died."

Whatever their source (biological, psychological, or metaphysical), there's no question that NDEs are part of human experience. And while they share similar themes wherever they occur, as with any other experience, NDEs are filtered through our layers of culture, language, and individuality. One person reports meeting Jesus in the form of a centaur riding a chariot, another encounters a Hopi sky-god, and another an identity-less being that radiates light, love, and acceptance. Descriptions of afterlife realms and other details of the experience also vary widely, according to culture and individual. Nevertheless, the experience is virtually always understood as "this is what happens when we die."

Historically speaking, NDEs have played a major role in our beliefs about souls, bodies, and death. Typical NDE features such as beings of light and the evaluation of one's earthly deed and are also worth thinking about in terms of beliefs in gods and spirits, and the origins of our ethical systems. Indeed, NDEs and other extraordinary experiences may have laid the very foundations of religions *per se*.

Of course, it would also be monumental if NDEs were to conclusively prove survival after death – and many researchers believe they already have. Ongoing hospital experiments are seeking replicable evidence under controlled circumstances, with researchers placing objects up near the ceiling in hopes that a patient will see them while outside the body. It's no exaggeration to say that the success of such an experiment – proving both mind-body dualism and the survival of consciousness after physical death – would be perhaps the most significant intellectual and spiritual development in all of human history. But until then, we should recognize the other important thing about NDEs: they can help us understand how our very beliefs, and thus our very cultures, are formed, how they can change, and how *we* can change and become better human beings.

NDEs aren't the only kind of extraordinary experience that involve visions of other worlds. People who claim to remember past lives sometimes describe what are called "intermission memories" of the state between reincarnations. These descriptions can include the dying process, and they often correspond to NDE accounts. Similarly, alleged communications with spirits in the other world by mediums sometimes include descriptions of other realms, again with parallels to NDEs.

Shamanism is the closest parallel to NDEs – specifically the type in which shamans deliberately undertake a "soul-journey" to afterlife realms in order to gain knowledge or to rescue the soul of a person in danger of dying. These experiences are brought about by varieties of drugs, prolonged dancing and chanting, deprivations, and self-harm (such as being clubbed to "death") to such an extent that in some cases the shaman actually *has* an NDE. In any case, such experiences were often intended to rescue the soul of someone who was in danger of death, thus bringing about their NDEs.

All these experiences – reincarnation memories, mediumship, shamanism, and NDEs – are inextricable from the cultures of the individuals who have them. Understanding these relationships and taking them into account is essential to any theory of NDEs and the afterlife, though such understanding has been sadly lacking in books and articles on the subject. Materialist scientists and "true believers" alike are determined to believe that NDEs are "the same" across cultures. Overstating the case for similarities and universalism is essential to claims that NDEs are "all in the brain," as well as to claims that they are a true glimpse into a single human afterlife.

On the other hand, many psychologists, philosophers, anthropologists, and sociologists have a vested interest in NDEs being irredeemably different. Believing that people and their experiences are so essentially *unalike*, that cultures and beliefs are even non-comparable, is essential to the argument that NDEs are hallucinations – or even that there's no such phenomenon at all. Some of these scholars would have us believe that NDE narratives are entirely culturally created – nothing more than invented stories. Many of these prominent thinkers are sadly lacking in their knowledge of the history of NDEs and their occurrence across cultures, however. Some even outright deny the worldwide existence of these experiences, choosing instead to blindly see the phenomenon as a purely Western modern invention.

As a comparative historian of religions and related experiences, I've stayed mostly on the sidelines of the debate about whether or not these extraordinary experiences are evidence for an afterlife (incurring suspicion and occasionally wrath from both camps). My main interest is in understanding why afterlife beliefs and experiences are similar across cultures, and why they're different. The true nature of NDEs is irrelevant to the idea that they can inspire, influence, and even give rise to afterlife beliefs.

But as I've discovered in nearly every talk, interview, or casual discussion I've had about my work, when it comes to NDEs the question "But are they real?" eclipses all others. So profound is our desire to know what happens when we die that despite nearly 50 years of formal near-death studies, the cultural and religious aspects of NDEs have gone largely unexplored, trampled beneath the rush to debate their value or otherwise as evidence of an afterlife. There are, however, many interesting and important things about NDEs aside from whether or not they are evidence for an afterlife. They offer wide scope for further research from historical, sociological, philosophical, and interdisciplinary approaches as well as experimental ones.

Many excellent books and articles investigate the evidence of NDEs, mediumship, and reincarnation, outlining the pros and cons of their support for the survival hypothesis. While the present book will not cover such ground in depth, it will examine how the cultural dimension impacts the debate, both on empirical and metaphysical levels. It explores the relationships between afterlife beliefs and NDEs in history and across cultures, and in light of shamanic experiences, reincarnation memories, and mediumship. It contains both an overview and the conclusions of over two decades of research into cross-cultural afterlife beliefs, NDEs, and other extraordinary experiences. I've reached these conclusions by combining ideas and methods from a variety of disciplines, with a background in Eastern Mediterranean Archaeology, Egyptology, and the historical Study of Religions which itself is an interdisciplinary field, drawing largely on anthropology and sociology. Unlike any of these disciplines, however, I also cross over into metaphysics, philosophy, and parapsychology.

Only by taking such an interdisciplinary approach can we unravel the entanglement of experiences and beliefs, while also shining a light on what they actually mean for the survival hypothesis – that NDEs and other extraordinary experiences might be a glimpse into another world and a taste of the true spiritual reality.

I

NEAR-DEATH EXPERIENCES:
PEELING THE UNIVERSAL, CULTURAL,
AND INDIVIDUAL LAYERS

~

In mid-3ʳᵈ century BCE China, a man "sickened and breathed his last."
After several days, however, he revived "and said he had witnessed
all sorts of things relating to *kwei* [demons] and *shen* [deities] in
the heavens and on earth, with the sensation of being in a dreaming
state, and by no means dead" (de Groot 1892: IV, 127). This is just one
of over a hundred similar narratives from ancient and medieval China.

Over 700 years later and over 5000 miles distant in Greece,
Plutarch recounted the experience of Thespesius of Soli who, in
c. 81 CE, apparently died then returned to life three days later.
Thespesius claimed that his soul had left his body and traveled to
a place where stars radiated light "on which his soul was smoothly
and swiftly gliding in every direction." He "could see all around
himself as if his soul would have been a single eye." He met spirits of
deceased relatives, one of whom took him on a tour of otherworldly
places of reward and punishment. Previously wicked, avaricious, and
given to "lewd and illegal acts," Thespesius returned transformed
into an honest, devout man and "altered the whole course of his

life" (Plutarch in Platthy 1992: 74). At least a dozen such narratives survive from Classical antiquity.

Some 2,000 miles away and 500 years later, a Spanish monk named Peter apparently died and was "restored to life again." He described seeing men he knew suffering various torments in hell, then being rescued from the same fate by an angel. The angel sent him back to his body, instructing him to lead a better life, which he did after "waking out of the sleep of everlasting death." This is one of five such accounts found in the *Dialogues* of Pope Gregory I (c. 593/4) (Gardiner 1989: 47-50), followed by dozens of others from throughout medieval Europe.

Over 900 years later and more than 5000 miles away, Spanish missionary and early ethnographer Bernardino de Sahagún (1547-69: IX:3, II:498, 181, n.20) recounted the experience of Quetzalpetlatl, daughter-in-law of the 15th-century Mexica ruler Moquihuix. Quetzalpetlatl reported having died, then being led by a youth to the joyous land of the dead. There she encountered deceased relatives and the deity Tlaloc, and underwent a positive transformation when he gave her the ability to heal the sick upon her return to Earth.

Over 2000 miles across the North American continent and almost 150 years later, English astronomer and explorer Thomas Hariot (1588: 37-38) was told of two such accounts by the Algonquin people. The first, which was said to have occurred a few years prior to Hariot's arrival, involved a "wicked man" who had been "dead and buried," then revived. He described how his soul had journeyed to a hellish realm, but was saved by a deity who made him return to his body in order to teach his people how to avoid such negative fates. In the second, contemporary with Hariot's visit, a man left his body during his own funeral. His soul walked along a path lined with houses and abundant fruit trees. He met his deceased father, who sent him back to his body to tell his people about the happiness of the other realm. These are the earliest known of roughly 70 such Native American accounts up through the mid-20th century (Shushan 2018).

Back across the continent and midway in the Pacific, over 250 years later George Charter was a missionary working on the Polynesian island of Raiatea. In his journal of 1838-56, he recounted the experience of a woman named Terematai who had lain unconscious for a number of days. When she revived, she described a trip to a heavenly realm where she saw people she had known in life. She wanted to stay in the other world, "but God sent me back to exhort my family that they may be saved." She returned "in a very happy state of mind and appeared wholly absorbed in spiritual subjects" (Gunson 1962: 218). This is one of nearly 40 such accounts from across the Pacific.

Around a hundred years later, over 9,000 miles away across two oceans and a continent, in southern Africa, the missionary W. C. Willoughby (1928: 99) recounted the experience of a BagammaNgwato boy. The boy died, and "went away" to a place where he saw his deceased brother as well as his father and uncle. The uncle told him he must return to Earth because he should not leave his mother. The boy concluded, "they sent me back with great peace." He revived with "new life," fully recovered from his illness. Around a dozen such accounts are found from across Africa.

Spanning almost two-and-a-half millennia and originating in seven different parts of the world with seven very different religious traditions, these are all examples of a phenomenon that would later be termed "near-death experience" (NDE). Sometimes reported by individuals who are resuscitated from a period of temporary clinical death or near-death, NDEs were scarcely known in contemporary Western cultures prior to 1975 when named and popularized by the American psychologist Raymond Moody. Since then, however, examples have been identified from throughout history and around the world.

Although no two NDEs are exactly alike, and none contain all the defining elements, they are made up of a number of typical sub-experiences. These include out-of-body experience (OBE) in which consciousness seems to temporarily leave the body, rising upwards and seeing one's own "corpse" below, existence in quasi-physical form, entering darkness or a tunnel, emerging into bright light, meeting deceased friends or relatives, encountering a being of light or other spirit or deity, telepathic communication with other spirits, seeing or entering other worlds (usually idealized mirror-images of earth) which are often seen as one's true "home," a sense of moral evaluation or self-judgment, panoramic life review, exceptionally vivid senses and clarity, distortions of time, universal understanding or transcendence, peace and pleasant feelings, love and acceptance, having visions of the future or obtaining precognitive or other information or instructions, loud noises, music, vivid colors, reaching a border or limit, being instructed or choosing to return to the body, and lasting positive transformations following the return (Greyson 1983; Fox 2003: 100f).

Those who have such experiences almost invariably interpret them in spiritual or religious terms, and the phenomenon has been the subject of a great deal of speculation concerning the possibility of survival beyond physical death, mind-body dualism, religious beliefs in an afterlife, and our understanding of the nature of human consciousness.

Because one of the key issues in NDE studies is determining the degree to which it is a universal human occurrence, clearly defining the experience is important but has proven elusive. Since death and dying are obviously universal, the nature and meaning of NDEs should be universal as well. If the NDE is not the same for everyone, this requires explanation regardless of whether we believe the experience is simply the special effects of a compromised brain, or that it is an actual indication of what happens to human beings when we die.

While even the most skeptical researchers generally accept that NDEs occur (though see Appendix I), there is still no general consensus on which elements actually define the experience. Moody identified fifteen "stages" which have been used as the basis for nearly all subsequent NDE research (including the development of the widely used "Greyson scale") (Greyson 1999). In fact, Moody was describing a *composite* experience, for no NDE he recorded included all the elements, and only a few had as many as twelve.

Rather than a single experience, the NDE is best regarded as a collection of typical sub-experiences: a variable combination of a number of possible elements from an established repertoire, the details of which differ on a case-by-case basis for reasons which remain at least partly obscure. There is some evidence that the manner in which a person almost dies impacts the experience. Those who attempt suicide tend not to have a life review, for example (Ring 1980: 194) – though neither do people in indigenous societies. The duration of an NDE may also help account for differences (Stevenson & Greyson 1996). The life review may come at a later stage in the dying process. This is supported by the findings of some researchers (Sartori 2008), though it conflicts with those of others (Grey 1985; van Lommel et. al. 2001). There is also a human tendency to elaborate events into sequential narratives, so it is difficult to determine whether or not the order of the various NDE elements is consistent (Grey 1985).

The same year Moody's book was published, the German Lutheran minister Johann Christophe Hampe published a book called *To Die is Gain*, independently identifying the NDE and its main elements. Unlike the examples Moody cites, however, Hampe's NDErs returned to the body the same way they left it (through a tunnel). Hampe also reported only a few encounters with deceased relatives, and none of a loud noise (Fox 2003: 55ff). Even earlier, two popular books also independently confirmed NDEs for 20th century Western readers: Brad Steiger's *The Mind Travellers* (1969) and Jean-Baptiste Delacour's *Glimpses of the Beyond* (1973). The latter uniquely described accounts in which NDErs claimed the ability to control or influence the afterlife environment, similar to a lucid dream. These idiosyncrasies found in Hampe and Delacour suggest that some elements are experienced only in particular cultures (in this case, German and French), an idea supported by later studies of historical and non-Western NDEs as we will see.

Some NDEs are distressing, though they otherwise often correspond thematically to the more typical positive examples, in an apparently inverted way. Thus, the individual feels fear and panic during the out-of-body-experience, is filled with despair, enters darkness and a void, encounters an evil presence, and sees hellish places. It is unclear if there are, in fact, fundamentally different negative and positive NDEs, or if it is simply a matter of individual perception and interpretation of the same kind of experience (Greyson & Bush 1992; Serdahely 1995). The theologian Paul Badham (1997) – one of the first to look at the relationships between NDEs and religious beliefs – notes that in contrast to positive NDEs, however, negative examples are more dreamlike, they do not normally hold the same significance for the NDEr, and are not remembered with the same vivid clarity over time.

Like any experience, NDEs are also subject to the vagaries of memory and how people relate them. An OBE, for example, is not always explicitly reported, though obviously it is a journey of the soul, not the body, which is being claimed. It may thus be presumed that any individual who has had an NDE believes that he or she did, in fact, leave the body. Darkness is another element which might easily go unmentioned if the more interesting and memorable element is the contrasting radiant light.

It is also true that like any other narrative, NDE accounts are *literary* (Zaleski 1987; Couliano 1991). Like any literature, they are at least partly products of intertextuality, meaning that they are situated within a narrative genre and thus follow certain literary conventions. Ultimately, the extent to which interpretation and narrative – by both NDErs and researchers – affect conclusions regarding our ability to define NDEs is unclear and surely varies from case to case.

Neither sex, religion, degree of religiosity, nor other demographic factors have a significant bearing on the occurrence of NDEs (Ring 1980). Nor is there a correlation between the occurrence of NDEs and resuscitation technique, types of drugs administered during surgery, fear of death, foreknowledge of NDEs, or education (van Lommel et. al. 2001). The NDE is by no means a rare phenomenon. Thousands of books and articles have been written on the subject, and tens of thousands of reports have been collected from around the world. Nevertheless, it is estimated that they occur in roughly "10% of people who come close to death, or who survive actual clinical death" (Fenwick 2005: 2). Among cardiac arrest survivors, the percentage is somewhat higher, 12–18% (van Lommel et. al. 2001).

While these estimates are significant, so is the fact that they leave up to 90% who do *not* report having had NDEs. It is not clear whether the experience simply does not happen to everyone who nears death or who is clinically dead for a time, or whether some do not remember the experience or do not report it for other reasons, such as fear of being ridiculed or doubted. Conversely, NDEs (or at least very similar experiences) can occur in individuals who are not actually near death at all but believe themselves to be, such as when falling from a height or nearly drowning, though without being in any real imminent mortal peril (Stevenson et. al. 1990).

NDEs are complex, multi-faceted phenomena which can be approached from various different disciplines and perspectives, using diverse theories and methodologies. It is not simply a question of "are they real or not," but of the various ways in which they can be understood. As Carol Zaleski (1987: 181) pointed out in her book comparing modern NDEs with medieval otherworld journey accounts, "a comprehensive theory of near-death experience" would require a synthesis of "all of the medical, psychological, philosophical, historical, social, literary, and logical factors."

Theories integrating a number of such factors while still taking seriously the testimonies of NDErs have been put forth by McClenon (1994), Kellehear (1996), Badham (1997), Paulson (1999), and Shushan (2009; 2018), among others. In attempting to account for both similarities and differences between accounts, such theories present models which accept the idea of a structurally universal NDE, combined with a number of other considerations such as local cultural contexts and religious beliefs; cognitive, psychological, and neurophysiological findings; and in some cases (Badham, Shushan) philosophical and metaphysical speculations. This is the approach taken in the present book.

NDEs, History, and Culture

Accounts of NDEs can be found in purportedly documentary texts from ancient Greece and Rome (Platthy 1992), the ancient Near East, Medieval to modern Europe (Zaleski 1987), Ancient to modern China, India, and Japan (McClenon 1994; Campany 1995), Pre-Columbian Mesoamerica and modern Mexico (Shushan 2009), eighteenth- and nineteenth-century United States, twelfth-century to modern Tibet, modern Thailand and the Philippines (Belanti et al. 2008; Shushan 2009), and in the indigenous societies of the Pacific, Asia, the Americas, and Africa (Shushan 2016; Shushan 2018). There are also comparable narratives in mythological, visionary, and other religious texts ranging from the Mesopotamian Epic of Gilgamesh, to the Indian Atharva Veda (Shushan 2009), the New Testament (Paul's vision in 2 Corinthians, 12:1–4), and the Tibetan *Bardo Thödol* (*Book of the Dead*) (Badham 1990, 1997) (see also Chapter 2 of the present book).

Historical and cross-cultural NDEs are important in establishing the universality or otherwise of the phenomenon, a task made particularly complex by the fact that accounts vary not only between cultures, but also between individuals. Making sense of the similarities and differences is, in fact, the key issue in studies of NDE narratives from different times and places. Comparative research shows that while accounts of NDEs share many common elements worldwide, those elements are embedded in descriptions that are clearly culture- and individual-specific. This shows that NDEs begin as pre- or non-cultural *events*, which cause experiences that are both culturally distinct *and* cross-culturally thematically consistent.

The sociologist Allan Kellehear (1996: 28) stresses the sociological contexts of NDEs, suggesting that the variations between accounts in different cultures can be "accounted for by examining the way certain societies emphasize or downplay certain cultural images and symbols." Thus, while in the West individuals may describe moving through a tunnel, elsewhere people describe more generally moving through darkness. In other words, the key concept is not the tunnel at all, but the themes of transition and moving from a dark place to a bright one. Kellehear also argued that the lack of life reviews in small-scale societies was due to a corresponding lack of distinction between the self and that which is external to the self, and thus between the natural and supernatural. Individuals in such societies have no sense of *personal* guilt or *individual* moral responsibility, for correct behavior is encouraged by laws and fear of consequences within the social group, not by ideas of divine justice. One would therefore not "seek a life-review in evaluative terms or be impressed by a biographical review of their individual deeds" (Kellehear 1996: 38). While largely correct (see Shushan 2018), the suggestion does overlook the fact that NDEs are not sought, but spontaneous, and that individual evaluation and a reckoning of one's earthly life *have* been reported in NDEs and religious beliefs of some indigenous societies (Counts 1983; Wade 2003; Shushan 2016).

As Kellehear acknowledges, generalizing about NDEs in such societies is highly problematic, particularly as very few examples were known at the time his book was written. My recent research (Shushan 2016, 2017, 2018a, 2018b, and Chapter 5 of the present volume) explores how NDEs are culturally negotiated in the indigenous religions of North America, Africa, and the Pacific, prior to significant missionary influence or conversion. In Native North America, for example, NDEs were commonly valorized, and attempts were made to replicate them in shamanic visionary practices. In Africa, however, NDEs were often considered to be aberrational, viewed through the lens of local possession and sorcery beliefs, and were thus rarely incorporated into accepted afterlife conceptions. Furthermore, despite the cross-cultural similarities of these narratives to those found in other parts of the world, certain NDE elements do seem to correspond to social organization or scale. Aside from a lack of life reviews, only in small-scale societies, for example, do NDEs commonly feature an afterlife realm located in or accessed via an earthly locale, and which is reached by walking along a path or road.

Some argue that the NDE is not simply a matter of cultural and individual *interpretation*, but one of cultural and individual *perception*. In other words, *how* the experience is *experienced* varies by individual, including the use of local symbols to express ideas, feelings, and events associated with the phenomenon. As Kellehear (2001: 34) summarized:

> culture supplies broad values and attitudes to individuals and these provide individual orientation during an experience. In this way, cultural influences provide a basis for interpreting NDE content, and furthermore are crucial to shaping the retelling of the experience to others from one's own culture.

The cross-cultural evidence indeed suggests that certain elements of the NDE are thematically analogous cross-culturally, but experienced and interpreted in individual/culture-specific ways.

The reason for returning to the body is one example. In contemporary Western NDEs, the return is generally a matter of unfinished business: either the NDEr does not feel ready to leave family or friends, or has some important unfulfilled goal to pursue. In Chinese and Medieval European NDEs, however, the return is often due to mistaken identity: the otherworld entities got the wrong "Jane Doe" and she was sent back to her body when the error was discovered. This suggests socially and culturally constructed interpretations of a thematic universal "return" element. In other words, the rationale for the NDEr's return to the body is culture-specific, though being instructed to return (for whatever reason) and returning is cross-cultural. Thus, while NDEs are culturally and individually experienced and expressed (or "mediated"), they appear not to be entirely culturally constructed. If they were, accounts from around the world and throughout history would not share such core elements as leaving the body, seeing the body below, darkness, other realms, encountering deceased relatives, a divinity or other supernatural being often radiating light, conduct evaluation or life review, barriers and obstacles, the attainment of divine or universal knowledge or wisdom, and positive after-effects upon return.

In summary, like any experience, NDEs are rooted in the cultural environment of those who have them. They are processed live by an enculturated individual, then recounted in socially, religiously, and linguistically idiosyncratic ways. It is a symbiotic relationship in which culture-specific beliefs and individual expectations influence universal experiences and vice versa (McClenon 1994; Kellehear 1996; Belanti et. al. 2008; Shushan 2009, 2018). Local attitudes towards death and the afterlife affect receptivity to NDE phenomena and determine how the experiences are undergone and subsequently symbolically expressed. NDEs and OBEs clearly reflect established local beliefs *and also* share apparently universal structural similarities. Cross-cultural differences are attributed to the experiences being mediated, interpreted, and elaborated upon within individual and cultural contexts.

NDEs, Science, and Survival After Death

From the pioneering work of various psychologists and medical researchers (Ring 1980; Sabom 1982; Grey 1985), the field of near-death studies has evolved to focus on the key areas of obtaining empirical scientific evidence, cross-cultural comparisons, the relevance to philosophy and religion, and the implications for healthcare and psychology. However, for many the issue of whether or not the NDE constitutes evidence for survival after physical death remains paramount. While pro-survival perspectives are often criticized for conflicting with known laws of science and for drawing conclusions from unverifiable accounts of personal experiences, scientific-materialist perspectives are criticized for *a priori* reductionism, and for dismissing or ignoring the challenging evidence instead of adequately addressing it.

Various researchers have attempted to explain the NDE in materialist terms, though none appear to have fully succeeded. Some argue that it results from a deprivation of oxygen in the brain (hypoxia or anoxia) (Blackmore 1993). Opponents of the theory, however, argue that oxygen deprivation causes confusional states quite unlike the hyper-lucidity reported by NDErs, and in fact does not produce effects comparable to the NDE at all (Fenwick & Fenwick 1995). Excessive carbon dioxide in the brain (hypercarbia) is also enlisted as a materialist explanation of NDEs, and actually can produce NDE-like effects (Klemenc-Ketis et al. 2010).

There is, however, evidence that carbon dioxide is actually lowered during NDEs (Sabom 1982). The theory that the experience results from temporal lobe epilepsy is similarly problematic. Proponents of the theory (such as Blackmore 1993) argue that during life-threatening episodes the temporal lobe is stimulated in ways that could cause the typical effects of an NDE – for example, triggering memories resulting in a life review, and releasing endorphins causing feelings of well-being. However, the neuropsychiatrist Peter Fenwick (2005: 2) counters that "No epileptic seizure has the clarity and narrative style of an NDE . . . all epilepsy is confusional." Furthermore, in terms of memory and the brain's ability to construct mental models, "it should be quite impossible to have an NDE when brain function is really very seriously disordered, or the brain is seriously damaged" (Fenwick & Fenwick 1995: 205).

Still others have argued that NDEs are caused by anesthetic drugs, such as ketamine. However, it has been shown conclusively that individuals not under the influence of such drugs still have NDEs (Fenwick 2005), leading to a general loss of support for this kind of theory. A related idea is that the brain itself produces a ketamine-like substance, causing the effects of NDEs. However, a leading expert on ketamine, psychiatrist Karl Jansen (2001), pointed out that a similarity between NDEs and ketamine experiences does not indicate that NDEs are not genuinely "spiritual." Rather, the drug may simply enable access to the same spiritual "reality" as the NDE. Though while ketamine experiences can indeed resemble NDEs – particularly in causing out-of-body sensations and impressions of visiting other realms – such drugs are also known to cause feelings of disorientation and fear, the very antithesis of the clarity, peace, and joy reported by most NDErs. Conversely, other NDE features (darkness and light) are absent from ketamine experiences (Fox 2003: 145-46.

Despite decades of theorizing, the most comprehensive attempt to explain the NDE in reductionist terms remains that of psychologist Susan Blackmore (1993), who argues that the NDE is the hallucinatory result of a *combination* of neurophysiological and psychological events occurring in the dying brain. Some of her key claims are that the feelings of joy and peace are the result of natural opiates being released in the brain as it shuts down; the tunnel, light, and sound are a result of anoxia; the life review is due to "seizures in the temporal lobe and limbic system where memories are organized"; and the OBE is the brain's attempt to "model reality." All this is combined with "prior knowledge, fantasy, lucky guesses and the remaining operating senses of hearing and touch." The intense reality of the NDE is allegedly caused by the brain's attempt to retain the disintegrating construct that is the personality and consciousness.

Blackmore subscribes to the notion that the self is an illusion created by the brain, which attempts to maintain that illusion even in the dying process. However, though her theory rests heavily on the brain as a functional instrument, Blackmore does not adequately explain the purpose or function of this protective mechanism. From an evolutionary perspective, why would a dying brain make a futile attempt to maintain its delusional construct of the dying person's sense of self? Furthermore, in keeping with her commitments both to Western materialism and Zen Buddhism, she takes for granted that the self *is* illusory.

Blackmore also sees the tunnel experience as "neural noise" caused by a malfunctioning visual cortex, resulting in impressions of light growing increasingly larger and the sensation of moving through a dark tunnel towards that light. This is also problematic. As a supposed neurophysiological occurrence, the "tunnel" should be universal, though cross-cultural evidence shows that this is not the case. It is not reported in Indian NDEs or in small-scale societies, and indeed the tunnel *per se* is actually uncommon even in Western cases (Stevenson et al. 1994). Individual and cultural variations between NDEs should not occur if the experience is caused by a neurophysiological process, and this creates a serious problem for "all-in-the-brain" explanations such as Blackmore's (Kellehear 1996; Serdahely 1995). Blackmore has also been criticized for "massaging" her data into an erroneous claim that the tunnel is in fact experienced in India, in order to bolster her dying brain hypothesis (Stevenson et al. 1994; Kellehear 1996).

Another theory suggests that NDEs can be explained by "REM intrusion" – the activation of the dream state in the mind of the NDEr resulting in hallucinatory visions. This notion is easily countered by the fact that REM intrusion experiences and NDEs differ fundamentally: the hallucinatory, dreamlike REM state is simply inconsistent with NDE states. Nor can the theory explain "visual" NDEs in the congenitally blind, or in those who have the experience while under the influence of REM-suppressing drugs (Long and Holden 2007; Greyson et. al. 2009).

Yet another reductionist explanation for NDEs was proposed by Michael Marsh (2010), a Christian theologian and biomedical researcher. His "reviving brain" theory states that the NDE is a set of illusions caused by the disordered brain reorganizing itself upon returning from unconsciousness. His work, however, has been roundly criticized for failing to consider cases of NDEs in which the brain was *not* compromised, or which demonstrably did not occur during recovery; for a lack of serious engagement with competing evidence and recent research; for trivializing NDEr testimony; and for his arguments being deeply informed by his own Christian eschatological beliefs in resurrection via divine "re-creation" of the individual (Kelly 2010; Rousseau 2011). Opponents of reductionist theories such as those of Blackmore and Marsh also argue that they fail to explain the feelings of unconditional love and cosmic unity reported by so many NDErs, or why the experience would so often lead to positive transformations in the individual's values, a greater spiritual awareness, and a desire to help others (the "fruits" of religious experience in William James's terms) (Greyson 2006; Noyes et al. 2009).

Nor do reductionist theories explain cases of individuals accurately describing events they claim to have witnessed during OBEs. Fenwick (2005: 4) has shown that NDEs can occur in cardiac arrest patients while they are unconscious with a flat EEG reading, when there is "no possibility of the brain creating any images" and "no brain-based memory functioning." This means that "it should be impossible to have clearly structured and lucid experiences." Arguments in favor of the NDE as evidence for dualism and survival after death thus rest largely upon claims of veridical observations during such periods of brain inactivity. Perhaps the most famous such case is that of Pam Reynolds (Sabom 1998), who reported an OBE she had during brain surgery, while clinically dead, with her body temperature lowered and her head drained of blood for the operation. She claimed to have witnessed medical procedures from a vantage point outside her body, and accurately described them upon resuscitation, including details such as the design of the bone saw which cut into her skull and the pitch of the sound it made.

A recent international experiment led by resuscitation expert Sam Parnia, the AWARE study (AWAreness during REsuscitation), has apparently confirmed that consciousness can persist when no brain activity is detectable, actually during the period of clinical death prior to successful resuscitation. This was widely believed to be medically impossible, and has profound implications for the notion that consciousness can survive physical death. As mentioned in the introduction, researchers also attempt to verify OBE observations by positioning certain images at vantage points visible only from above, that is, by a person who had floated out of their body. While this has so far proved unsuccessful, one individual accurately described his own resuscitation which he claimed to have witnessed while out-of-body, including the sound of a defibrillator machine, allowing researchers to pinpoint the time of the event as having occurred *during* the patient's cardiac arrest (Parnia et. al. 2014). In a study conducted in a Welsh hospital, intensive care nurse Penny Sartori (2008) found that only those who had OBEs accurately described the resuscitation process (see also Parnia et al. 2007). Furthermore, OBEs (and indeed NDEs themselves, as mentioned above) have been widely reported in non-crisis contexts during dreams, meditation, shamanic trance, spontaneously, and in laboratory settings via artificial induction (Ehrsson 2007). Actually being near death is clearly not a prerequisite for such experiences, a fact that makes any "dying brain" hypothesis untenable.

The investigation of NDEs in the blind is another important area of research, for they report *visual perceptions* during the experience. Dozens of such cases have been published, including from individuals who have been blind since birth. This is significant because people who have *never* had the resources to "model reality" in the way Blackmore describes should not be able to do so during an NDE. Rather than simply impressions of light and darkness, their accounts include detailed observations of hospital rooms during OBEs, deceased relatives, and so on. This is in striking contrast to dreams of the blind, which are not visual (Ring & Cooper 1997, 1999).

Research into NDEs of children, as young as three or four, is important in determining the degree to which the experience might be due to expectation, for they would be less likely to have prior knowledge or understanding of the experience. There are, in fact, some differences between the NDEs of children and adults. For example, children do not commonly report a life review – perhaps unsurprisingly, given their relative lack of extensive memories and experiences (Morse 1994). There is also a higher incidence of encounters with animals, and even cases in which children report having met *living* friends, relatives, or teachers (Serdahely 1990), challenging the notion that the deceased individuals and other beings commonly reported in NDEs are "real." On the other hand, some children report encounters with deceased relatives *they never knew*, and are able to either accurately describe them or identify them from photographs. Similar cases are also reported by adults who describe encountering the spirit of an individual whose recent death was unknown to them (Greyson 2010). If confirmed, such cases support the theory that the NDE is sound evidence for survival, and that at least some of the deceased individuals encountered during the experience must be genuine conscious entities existing in some kind of afterlife accessible to NDErs.

Given the accumulated evidence, NDEs present a challenge to current reductionist models of the relationship between the mind and the brain (Moreira-Almeida 2013; Holden 2009). As with any area of scientific research, new explanatory models must be constructed to accommodate new information. In a recent development in the field, some scientists argue that NDEs are consistent with a "nonlocality" model of consciousness derived from quantum physics, meaning that consciousness is neither generated nor limited by the brain, but is a separate phenomenon which can survive the death of the body (van Lommel 2007).

The more materialist-minded scientists often dismiss the evidence as anecdotal, or explain it away by reference either to poor research protocol (such as leading questions during interviews) or to faulty memory and invention on the part of alleged NDErs. It is significant, however, that many who were initially confirmed skeptics actually altered their stances as a result of their own research, including the cardiologist Pim van Lommel, the psychiatrist Elizabeth Kübler-Ross, as well as Fenwick, Parnia, and Sabom. Ultimately, however, from the perspective of most scientists there has yet to be watertight, conclusive proof either way and much about NDEs remains mysterious. No reductionist theory has been able to adequately explain the phenomenon in all its forms and occurrences; and no empirical, replicable study has proven beyond doubt that NDEs are evidence of dualism or of life after death.

Philosophy, Religion, and NDEs

The existence of broadly similar narratives describing contextually stable experiences (that is, they usually occur as a result of being physically near death) from such different times, places, and cultural-linguistic backgrounds points to pre-cultural origins of NDEs. In other words, the experience must originate in something other than the culture-specific images and beliefs provided by any particular society.

Scholars such as Zaleski (1987), however, believe that there is no objective status to the phenomenon at all, writing that because experience cannot be divorced from culture, we must "renounce the notion that some original and essential religious experience can be discriminated from subsequent layers of cultural shaping." Again, however, cases of NDEs in children, atheists, and anyone whose prior beliefs conflict with their experience demonstrate that NDEs are not a product of expectation (see also Athappilly et al. 2006). An acknowledgment of "cultural shaping" as proposed by scholars such as Kellehear (1996, 2001) and McClenon (1994) does not indicate that there are no aspects of the NDE which are independent of culture. In other words, the fact that culture influences or shapes experiences does not mean that experiences do not also influence culture. This problem will be explored in greater depth in Appendix I.

When Zaleski (1987) compared modern Western NDEs with medieval European "otherworld journey" visionary texts, she found that the latter focused on punishment and the process of judgment, whereas the former were more concerned with education and rehabilitation. Zaleski (1987: 190) considered "the otherworld journey story" to be "through and through a work of the socially conditioned religious imagination." However, this conclusion does not explain the parallels Zaleski herself highlighted, for although the similarities are general and thematic, it is significant that the Medieval accounts share with modern NDEs numerous familiar elements: OBEs, tunnels and darkness, glimpses of other worlds, encounters with beings of light and other spirits, evaluation of one's earthly life, borders and limits, guides, reluctance to return to the body, and positive spiritual transformation upon revival.

While these similarities may not be surprising considering that Zaleski's Medieval and modern examples are both firmly rooted in predominantly Christian worlds, they also occur in cross-cultural examples. Indeed, Zaleski's conclusion implies the impossibility of cross-cultural consistency, unless we accept that different, culture-specific forms of "socially conditioned religious imagination" somehow lead everywhere to a similar kind of "story." This is not to ignore the numerous differences between accounts (also unsurprising given the cultural, geographic, and temporal distances involved), though difference neither negates nor explains away similarity.

Zaleski also argues that a supposedly neutral term like "being of light" is not only potentially inaccurate in characterizing what an NDEr may claim is Jesus or the Buddha, but is itself a culturally constructed term. However, this type of argument side-steps the issue that what is being described cross-culturally *is* a being that radiates light. Interestingly, this is explicitly supported in the *Bardo Thödol* which states that a "Clear Light" will appear in whatever form is most beneficial to the individual: as the Buddha to a Buddhist, as Vishnu to a Vaishnava Hindu, as Jesus to a Christian, or as Muhammad to a Muslim (Badham 1997). The description of dying in the *Bardo Thödol*, in fact, so closely corresponds to the NDE that it can effectively be seen as verification that the book genuinely is what it purports to be – a preparation for what happens at death. This is regardless of whether the experience has a biological or spiritual origin (Becker 1985; Badham 1990).

This raises the issue of the relationship between NDEs and religious beliefs about the afterlife, which has been explored by scholars such as McClenon (1994), Badham (1997), and myself. The notion that religious beliefs can be rooted in extraordinary experiences has a long pedigree beginning with E. B. Tylor and Andrew Lang in the nineteenth century, though it was fully articulated with David Hufford's (1982) "experiential source hypothesis."

In my book *Conceptions of the Afterlife in Early Civilizations* (2009), I compared afterlife beliefs in ancient cultures that had little or no contact with each other (Old and Middle Kingdom Egypt, Sumerian and Old Babylonian Mesopotamia, Vedic India, pre-Buddhist China, and pre-Columbian Mesoamerica). As well as expected culture-specific idiosyncrasies, I found cross-cultural elements to these afterlife conceptions which correspond thematically to the NDE. This will be explored in greater detail in Chapter 3, but it is worth stressing the overall conclusion that the authors of the ancient texts were familiar with the phenomenon of individuals who appear to die, return to life, and subsequently relate having undergone something very much like what we know as a "near-death experience."

This is reinforced by indigenous cases, such as those in many Native American societies, where NDEs were explicitly said to have formed local afterlife beliefs and even to have been the bases for particular religious movements (Shushan 2016, 2018b). These findings support the notion that while the NDE is both experienced and interpreted in culture-specific modes, it nevertheless has universal elements which in turn influence belief. These findings independently validate the hypotheses of Hufford, Kellehear, and McClenon: that culture-specific beliefs influence the phenomena, and vice versa.

In any case, the similarities between cross-cultural accounts clearly demonstrate that (1) the NDE is a common experience type that is regularly interpreted in religious terms across cultures; (2) these experiences cannot be attributed entirely to cultural expectation; and (3) they can lead to new beliefs and change preexisting ones.

2

REVELATIONS IN NEAR-DEATH
EXPERIENCES

~

Accounts of near-death experiences around the world often include claims of encounters with deities or spirits who impart information to the experiencer. These can be seen as "divine revelation" in the most literal sense. Other accounts involve the experiencer obtaining revelatory knowledge by other means, without the assistance of a non-human supernatural being. While some cases involve deceased relatives, the most prominent and memorable factor in others might be the person's perceptions of the body from a vantage point outside it, seeing or traveling to other realms, radiant light, having a panoramic life review, encountering the soul of a person not previously known to have died, prophetic visions, or more generalized impressions of universal understanding or transcendent union. In all these senses, NDEs can be seen as revelatory experiences, with profound information being conveyed to the individual through ostensibly metaphysical or "religious" experiences.

Because NDErs almost invariably interpret the experience in spiritual or religious terms, most examples can be seen as revelatory experiences. This means that multiple aspects of NDEs can conform to the experiential source hypothesis. This chapter explores how revelatory NDEs influence beliefs for individuals, communities, and entire religions, and also looks at the implications for the survival hypothesis of empirical claims about revelations.

Near-Death Experiences as Revelations for the Community

Examples from ancient China may be the world's earliest ostensibly documentary NDEs, and they feature clear divine revelations. The account of a local ruler named Jianzi (Kien-tsze) from 498 BCE also includes a brief description of the NDE of the ruler Muh of Tsin (658-620 BCE) some 150 years earlier, and both describe how the Emperor of Heaven gave the men prophetic information. In a narrative actually attributed to Muh, he told of a joyful visit to the Emperor of Heaven during days of unconsciousness caused by a serious illness. The reason for his prolonged absence, he explained, was that the Emperor had prophetic information to give him involving specific political events that would come to pass in the state of Tsin.

Jianzi's account of his own visit to the other world was also joyful and included details of the music he heard and the dances he saw in his spiritual wanderings. He, too, was given prophetic information by the Emperor of Heaven concerning forthcoming events in Tsin. Jianzi's NDE, however, detailed such unusual features as killing two bears, being given two baskets, and the Emperor of Heaven assigning a particular dog to Jianzi's son on Earth. Later in life, Jianzi met a man who recognized him from the NDE. This turned out to be a child Jianzi had seen during his NDE, standing at the Emperor of Heaven's side, who was now grown. The man correctly interpreted the events in Jianzi's NDE, all of which were verified (De Groot 1892: 113-15). By validating the information Jianzi had been given in the other world, the ancient Chinese historians affirmed their belief not only in the divine wisdom of the Emperor of Heaven, but also in the revelatory power of NDEs.

Perhaps the most common type of NDE revelation from ancient to Medieval times was a tour of the other world. Plato's Myth of Er (Platthy 1992: 68-73) from c. 380 BCE might be the oldest example of this genre, and perhaps the oldest surviving Western NDE if we accept it as documentary. What was meant by "myth" in this context is unclear, for in ancient Greece it simply indicated story or narrative, without specifying whether it was considered factual or not.

Plato describes how Er died on a battlefield, and his body was taken home by his people to be cremated. On the twelfth day after his death, he woke up on his own funeral pyre and recounted his NDE, describing how he had left his body and traveled with many other souls to a place of judgement. The good ascended to heaven, while the bad were subjected to various types of punishments before eventually being allowed to go to a happier realm. When Er met the otherworld judges, "he was told that it will be his mission to be the messenger to humankind" and that he should "observe well all that he could" so that he would be able to describe it to people when he returned to Earth. As well as the process of judgement, reward, and punishment, Er was shown how a prophet would help souls to choose lots that would determine their reincarnation into a new person or animal.

This rather lengthy narrative features many elaborate details, symbols, and concepts specific to Greek mythology and philosophy, including characters such as the Sirens, the Fates, and the soul of Orpheus who had reincarnated into a swan. The information Er was able to relate after reviving was thus not only about afterlife fates, but also complex material concerning the workings of the cosmos. Whether there was really a soldier named Er who had an NDE is impossible to say, though even if it was based on an actual experience the narrative is clearly elaborated with literary-mythological embellishments. Alternatively, it could be simply a myth in our sense of the word, but one that is grounded in a general knowledge of NDEs.

Zoroastrianism, the pre-Islamic religion of ancient Persia, also incorporates NDEs into some of its core tenets. In a narrative from the late 6th century, a man named Ardā Wirâz (or Viraf) was chosen by a council to test some Zoroastrian beliefs by journeying to the realms of the afterlife. As was typical of some shamanic practices in indigenous societies (Shushan 2018), Wirâz deliberately induced an NDE. He took poison, apparently died for seven days, then returned to tell of his spiritual experiences. As with the Myth of Er, it is a lengthy and elaborately detailed account full of Zoroastrian symbolism, indicating much literary elaboration. After leaving his body, Wirâz was met by the deities Srosh and Adur who took him on a celestial tour of purgatory, heaven, and hell, where people were being punished or rewarded according to their actions in life. He met the main Zoroastrian deity and creator, Ahura Mazda, described as a being of light. Ahura Mazda ultimately instructed Wirâz to return to Earth in order to tell people of what he learned on his spiritual visit in the other worlds, and to teach the truth of Zoroastrianism as revealed to him during his NDE. The account of his near-death journey became known as the *Book of*

Ardā Wirâz, which continues to be an important didactic text in the Zoroastrian tradition (Vahman 1986; Couliano 1991: 107-113).

It is interesting to compare the account of Wirâz's NDE with that of the Belgian Christian saint Christina Mirabilis (1150-1224), known as "Christina the Astonishing." In 1171, Christina died of a seizure but revived during her own funeral and told of how she had been taken on a tour of the other world before being sent back with a divine message to convey to humankind. Her biography quotes her own description of dying and being taken by "angels of God – the ministers of light" to "a dark and terrible spot which was filled with the souls of men." She recognized among them people she had known in life and saw the torments they suffered. She was told that this was only purgatory, where "repentant sinners atone for the sins they committed while they were alive," though she was also shown hell where she again recognized some of the people being punished.

Christina was then taken "to Paradise, to the throne of the Divine Majesty" who gave her two choices: to remain in heaven, or return to Earth and "suffer the punishments of an immortal soul in a mortal body" which would cause the tormented souls in purgatory to be freed. If she chose the latter option, her example would "incite living men to turn to me and to turn aside from their sins." After completing her mission of martyrdom on Earth, she would then return to the Lord "and will have earned a reward of much profit." Though she desired to stay in paradise, Christina decided on the second option, and was immediately returned to her body, saying "I am given back to life for the improvement of men."

Near-Death Experiences as Personal Revelations

Some accounts are more outwardly personal, concerning a transformation of the NDErs themselves rather than them being used as messengers to convey revelations to the community. The apparent literary elaboration of some such texts, however, indicates that they also had a didactic function and that their lessons would be shared with others as religious teachings. This is the case with a Chinese example from the mid-5th century CE, which includes direct revelations against killing animals and eating meat. A man named Yuan Zhizong apparently died, and when he woke up at his own funeral he told of how he had been bound and taken away by a crowd of a hundred people. They took him to a group of monks who were venerating an image of the Buddha, and one of them chastised Zhizong for enjoying hunting. The monk "stripped off his skin, and sliced him into thin cuts, exactly in the manner in which animals are prepared for sacrifice," then put him into water and hooked him like fish, then chopped him into mincemeat and cooked him. Zhizong begged for his life, and the monk washed away his sins with water. The monk then instructed Zhizong to refrain from killing even ants, told him that fish is the only kind of meat he is allowed to eat, and gave him ritual dress restrictions for vegetarian feast days. When Zhizong asked why he had to undergo such ordeals, the monk told him, "you, in your stupidity, were ignorant of karmic retribution, so you were instructed." After Zhizong revived, he no longer engaged in hunting or fishing (Campany 1990: 119-20).

Some NDErs claim that revelations they received during their experience are private, and even that they were instructed to keep them secret. An ancient Greek named Eurynous revived after fifteen days in a near-death state, and "relayed that he heard many wonderful things under the earth about which he was ordered to keep quiet." Whatever he saw, the experience led to a transformation in Eurynous, for "his conduct of life was more just after his revival than before" (Platthy 1992: 85).

Both Yuan Zhizong's and Eurynous's accounts exemplify one of the most common features of NDEs: that they can lead directly to some kind of positive transformation. Studies have shown that this is not due simply to the trauma of almost dying, but to the extraordinary aspects of the NDE itself. Revelation, or a sense of revelation, is one of the key spiritually interpreted elements of NDEs. While sometimes associated with a particular religion and sometimes with none at all, "changes in beliefs, attitudes, and values after NDEs uniformly include enhanced self-esteem, concern, and compassion toward others, sense of meaning in life, interest in spiritual matters, feeling close to God, belief in life after death, and decreased interest in personal wealth and prestige" (Greyson & Khanna 2014: 45).

Claims of Empirical Validation in NDEs

A concern for demonstrating the veracity of the experience is a frequent element of revelatory NDE accounts. In a Mormon example from 1913, a Canadian woman named Bertha had an NDE during an illness. When she revived she described leaving her body and seeing from above the nurse at her bedside. She felt feelings of peace and did not wish to return to her body. A woman appeared and led her to a room filled with the souls of people she had known in life; and then to another room where Bertha was shown the souls of two children. She was asked if she would like them for her own and she replied in the affirmative, saying she wished to take them back to Earth with her. The woman told Bertha that the reason for her visit to the otherworld was to meet her future daughters. Bertha returned to her body, recovered from her illness, and her next two children were the girls she had seen during her NDE (Lundahl 1993: 175).

In a second Mormon example, from 1923, a man lost consciousness following surgery. During his brief NDE, he was met by his daughter who had died 23 years earlier. She told him to go back to Earth because his six-year-old son must die first, followed by his mother, and then finally his wife. The man returned to life, and within a matter of months, both his son and his mother died. His wife followed six years later (Lundahl 1993: 177-8).

Claims of empirical validation are also prominent in another kind of revelatory NDE, in which the soul of an individual not previously known to have died is encountered during the experience (the so-called "Peak-In-Darien" experience). The death of that individual is then verified after the NDEr revives. In such accounts the revelation is a dual confirmation of an afterlife, validating both the encounter with the previously deceased person and the reality of the NDE itself. In an example from 1669, an English teenage girl named Anne Atherton had an NDE while in a coma during a serious illness. When her testimony of her NDE was met with doubt by her relatives, she recounted that "while she stood at heaven's gate, she saw several people enter in, and named three or four she did know, which died during the time she lay in this trance" (Atherton 1680).

Such accounts are also attested across cultures. In a Native American example from the Deg Hit'an people from 1887, a girl lost consciousness while out hunting with her family. She stayed in the otherworld for months, then one day while walking along a riverbank there she saw her father floating on a log in the direction from which she had come. When the girl returned to Earth and told her people of her experiences, her mother revealed that her father had died in her absence, providing evidential confirmation of the girl's experience of seeing him in the spirit world. Though the account is apparently at least partly legend, as a direct result of the girl's narrative new feasts and funerary offering traditions were instituted, indicating a change in religious beliefs (Chapman 1912: 66–7).

More recently, in an NDE from the early 1980s, a Kaliai man of New Britain, Papua New Guinea, apparently died of an illness. After entering darkness, he emerged in a field of flowers. Walking along a road he met "a woman whose death had occurred shortly after his and about which he could have had no knowledge" (Counts 1983: 119-20). Other examples of this phenomenon have been collected by Greyson (2010).

Revelatory NDEs and the Experiential Source Hypothesis

So profound are NDEs to those who have them, and so meaningful and spiritually resonant to those who learn about them, that their impact on religious beliefs can be dramatic.

Early Christians placed great value "on dreams and visions as revelations of divine reality" (Potthoff 2017: 73), and among those visions were NDEs. In a fascinating account from Roman Carthage, two Christian converts, Vibia Perpetua and Saturus, had a shared NDE while awaiting execution in a prison in 203 CE. Their "deaths" were brought on by suffering from prolonged deprivations, including starvation and being confined in constant darkness. Perpetua had experienced four different otherworld visions prior to this account, though a temporary death was not recorded in association with them. In Saturus's account, however, both the near-death context and the out-of-body travel to the otherworld are clear. Saturus is quoted as saying, "We had died...and had put off the flesh, and we began to be carried towards the east by four angels." They floated on their backs towards "an intense light" and arrived in a garden of many kinds of flowers and tall trees. They were greeted by four more angels who cheered their arrival. The angels led them down a road where they encountered the souls of four men they had known in life: three of whom had been put to death "in the same persecution" of Christians, and one who, like Perpetua and Sarturus, had died in prison.

The angels then took Perpetua and Saturus to "greet the Lord" at "a place whose walls seemed to be constructed of light." To the sound of voices chanting, "Holy, holy, holy!" four more angels in white robes led them inside where they met an "aged man with white hair and a "youthful face." He sat on a throne in the company of a number of other "elders." The angels lifted Perpetua and Saturus to kiss the man on the throne so he could touch their faces. The elders then told them to rise, and to "Go and play." Perpetua said, "Thanks be to God that I am happier here now than I was in the flesh." When they left this place of light, they encountered a bishop and a presbyter they had known on Earth, along with various other martyrs. Eventually the angels "seemed as though they wanted to close the gates," and Saturus "woke up happy" (Potthoff 2017: 44-5) despite the miserable conditions and doom that he faced.

While much of the imagery in this account likely originated in Biblical and/or Greco-Roman mythological or religious texts (ibid. 46-48), it is also generally consistent with NDE reports across cultures, including the thematic elements of OBE, traveling to another realm, bright light, meeting previously deceased persons and non-human spiritual beings, feelings of joy and happiness, returning to the body, and positive transformation. As historian Stephen Potthoff (ibid. 49) wrote,

> Like modern near-death visionaries who die and are reborn, no longer fearing death and yearning for the paradise they had just experienced, Perpetua and Saturus return to life, if ever so briefly, ready to confront, in confidence and without fear, their impending executions in the Carthage amphitheater, secure in the knowledge that death is but a passage into a far more glorious dimension of existence.

Furthermore, these experiences "transform not only the visionaries themselves, but the imaginal experience of the afterlife as embraced by the whole community," contributing to Christian conceptions of the afterlife, and affirming its reality to believers. Indeed, Potthoff (ibid. 210) goes so far as to state that "The shared, communal Christian vision of the afterlife as paradise emerged and evolved over time, drawing its inspiration and validation from the near-death otherworld journeys of martyrs, monks, and ordinary Christians alike."

Not only can NDEs be the basis for afterlife beliefs in individuals and even whole societies, entire religious movements are sometimes founded upon them. Such cases substantiate the experiential source hypothesis. Prior to the Western "discovery" of NDEs, the Swedish ethnologist and comparative religions scholar Åke Hultkrantz (1957: 235-37) identified NDEs as a discrete phenomenon in Native American cultures, and found that the indigenous people themselves distinguished between dreams, visions, and NDEs. Most crucially, they gave the NDEs the greatest importance and value. Indeed, Hultkrantz presented a great deal of evidence to support his conclusions that Native American afterlife beliefs were widely based on NDEs. When asked about such beliefs, informants from various tribes related accounts of such experiences, both to give a description of dying and the afterlife, and to lend their beliefs experiential authority – sometimes including claims of empirical validation, as we have seen. As noted in the previous chapter, my recent ethnohistorical research has unearthed dozens of further examples not only from indigenous societies in North America, but also in the Pacific, spanning the 16th-early 20th century (Shushan 2018).

In the late 19th century, the Ghost Dance revitalization movements originated with the NDE of the Native American Paiute shaman Wovoka (Mooney 1896: 701-02, 926-27; Shushan 2018: 53). Likewise, the Indian Shaker Church was founded by Squ-sacht-un, also known as John Slocum, following instructions given to him during an NDE (Ruby & Brown 1996: 7-9, 752). Indeed, although the Shakers considered themselves to be Christian, because Slocum returned from the dead with personal testimony of the other world, his word was valued as revelation while the Bible was not.

In another example of an NDE-based religious movement, around 1860 a Wanapum shaman named Smohalla was killed in a fight. He revived and proclaimed that he had been "in the spirit world and had now returned by divine command to guide his people." Having witnessed his death, his people believed him and accepted his teachings on the authority of his experience.

Smohalla's revelation and messages were consistent with those of many other revitalization movement prophets, and his new "Dreamer" religion – Washani – combined local beliefs and rituals with elements of Catholicism and perhaps Mormonism (Ruby & Brown 1989: 37). Washani spread to many neighboring tribes, introducing a system of hereditary priests, new dances, and ceremonies. The religion was sustained, in part, by further experiences in which Smohalla apparently died, left his body, went to the spirit world, and returned with additional revelations – and by the trance-visions of his followers via repetitive ceremonial singing and drumming (Mooney 1896: 718– 9, 723, 726– 8; Shushan 2018: 61-2). Many other examples of such movements originating in NDEs are known, not only in North American traditions, but also in South America and the Pacific (Shushan 2018). These examples substantiate ethnologist and psychologist Holger Kalweit's (1984: 70) generalization that individuals across cultures claim that they gained their knowledge of the afterlife "from the experiences of those who have returned [NDErs] and from shamans."

There is an important, even foundational connection between NDEs and Pure Land Buddhism in China and Japan, with many prominent figures in the traditions reporting them (Becker 1993a: 73-6). Indeed, the NDE of T'an-luan (476-542 CE), a founding patriarch of Chinese Pure Land Buddhism, was crucial in his conversion from Taoism to Buddhism. Though there is little description of his experience beyond seeing a gate of gold open before him during a grave illness, it was profound enough to T'an-luan that he was inspired to devote his life to spreading Pure Land beliefs, and developing new experiential practices for adherents in the form of repetitive chanting. McClenon (1994: 175-6, 182) cited numerous other Pure Land Chinese and Japanese examples spanning nearly a thousand years, and concluded that:

> The history of the Pure Land movement suggests that religious doctrines evolved in harmony with, and benefitted from the existence of, the primary features of NDEs. The patriarch T'an-luan's NDE was instrumental in determining the specific sutras granted importance in future Pure Land doctrines. Through the history of Pure Land doctrinal development, NDEs provided rhetorical tools for ideological innovation. Concepts supported by NDEs included the notion of karma, the superiority of Buddhism over Taoism, the prohibition against killing animals, the value of chanting, statue making, and sutra-copying, rituals for the dead. ...

NDEs also hold an important place in Mormon beliefs, featuring among the various visions and revelations of the church's early figures, including Joseph Smith and Brigham Young. They demonstrate to adherents that revelatory extraordinary experiences did not cease with the Biblical prophets, and that they continue even to the present day (Schlieter 2018: 79). This helps to validate the teachings of the early church leaders, and reinforces the belief that there are more revelations to come – and indeed that they are available to all who seek them. While Mormons may not have developed shamanic techniques to access other realms, the principle of a democratization of access to the afterlife for the living aligns with similar ideas in Native American and Pacific religious revitalization movements.

Not all NDEs lead to similar kinds of revelations and beliefs, however. Just like the experience itself, reception and interpretation of the phenomenon are very much rooted in preexisting cultural factors. In the early 18th century, the Kongolese prophet Dona Beatriz Kimpa Vita was both a Catholic and a medium in the local Kimpasi healing cult. Initiation into the cult involved a ritual death and resurrection, brought about by cutting off the circulation with tight bonds. Upon revival, or "rebirth," initiates were believed to be possessed by a friendly spirit who would stay with them throughout their lives. In 1704, Kimpa Vita died during a weeklong illness, then revived. She claimed to have met Saint Anthony, who told her he had "been sent from God to your head to preach to the people." He gave her religious and political instructions, then entered her body and remained in her thereafter, just as spirits did with members of the Kimpasi cult.

Subsequently, Kimpa Vita "died" each Friday in order to commune with God in heaven over the weekend. Her possession by the saint gave her the ability to perform miracles such as healings and controlling nature and the weather. It also led to the foundation of a syncretized religious revitalization movement called Antonianism. During a time of European religious and ethnic persecution, slavery, and political turmoil, Kimpa Vita taught a message of peace along with an indigenized Christianity that relocated the origin story of Jesus to the Kongo. The movement grew to have its own missionaries, some of whom replicated Kimpa Vita's experiences. The religion was also characterized by claims of an impending apocalypse, which alongside the NDE context and localization of foreign themes are all common features of religious revitalization movements across cultures (including the Ghost Dance and other Native American examples).

However, aside from meeting Saint Anthony, there is no description of any other elements of Kimpa Vita's NDE: it was her possession that held the religious import and significance. Nevertheless, two years after her experience, by order of the Kongolese Roman Catholic King Pedro IV (Nusamu a Mvemba), Kimpa Vita was burned at the stake on suspicion of being a witch possessed by a demon. This reflects the tendency in many African cultures to view with mistrust and hostility those who apparently revived from death (Thornton 1998: 57, 119, 131-2, 136-7, 148, 160; Shushan 2017; 2018: 122-24).

It should be emphasized that spiritual interpretations of these experiences are not confined to religious contexts. Staunch materialists and atheists have also had changes in beliefs following their NDEs. As mentioned in the Introduction, while publicly admitting only that his experience had "slightly weakened" his conviction that death is the end of consciousness, shortly after his NDE, materialist philosopher A. J. Ayer was so moved by his experience of seeing "a Divine Being" that he believed he'd have to reassess his life's work (Foges 2010). Likewise, prior to his own experience in 1983, mathematical physicist and psychologist John Wren-Lewis (1995) regarded mysticism as a form of neurosis. Not only did his NDE run contrary to his expectations, it also resulted directly in new spiritual beliefs, namely "that proponents of the so-called Perennial Philosophy are correct in identifying a common 'deep structure' of experience underlying the widely different cultural expressions of mystics in all traditions."

Theological and Metaphysical Implications of NDE Prophecies

Prophetic revelations "received" during NDEs demonstrate that even if some NDEs might have veridical content, others demonstrably do not. In the early days of NDE research, Kenneth Ring, an American psychologist and an important figure in the field, published an article called "Precognitive and Prophetic Visions in Near-Death Experiences." With data gathered from NDErs in the United States ranging from the 1940s-1970s, he found that prophecies were often conveyed to the experiencer as divine revelation, that is, occurring "in association with an encounter with guides or a being of light." Reminiscent of many historical examples, some NDErs even believed that they had been chosen by their god to deliver his message to people on Earth.

Ring (1982: 54, 6) found that the prophecies in the thirteen cases he analyzed bore remarkable consistencies, including that Earth will suffer devastation on a global scale due to a nuclear event and/or widespread natural disasters, and that this will occur sometime in the late 1980s, with 1988 being the most frequently specified year. A few years later, British psychologist Margot Grey (1985) independently replicated these findings, collecting a number of prophetic NDE visions that were astonishingly consistent with Ring's. Obviously, the prophesied events did not come to pass, demonstrating that the alleged divine revelations were false.

It is interesting to note that another common feature of these prophecies was that following the global devastation, Earth would experience an era of renewal and a Golden Age of "peace and human brotherhood." This dynamic is familiar from apocalyptic and millenarian prophecies throughout history, as Ring (1988: 4, 12) later highlighted. Revisiting the theme after a number of years, he wrote that prophetic visions during NDEs are best seen as "manifestations of a collective prophetic impulse that historically tends to arise during periods of cultural crisis," and as "expressions of the felt need for cultural renewal." In support of this, Ring noted a prophetic NDE account from 1892 that had all the typical features of his contemporary examples.

Mormon NDE scholar Craig Lundahl (1999: 201-02) demonstrated remarkable consistency between prophetic NDEs and Biblical prophecies. Perhaps unsurprisingly for a religion rooted in the Bible, canonical Mormon prophecies are similarly consistent, though they indicate that the end of the world would come at the beginning of the 21st century. While Lundahl interpreted the similarities as possible evidence for the veracity of these prophecies of global catastrophe followed by a Golden Age, their failure to materialize appears to rather support Ring's social-psychological explanation.

Such an explanation also recalls the relationship between NDEs and the indigenous religious revitalization movements discussed above. In both cases, the theme of death and return is reflected on cultural levels – regarding existential threats to the planet in Ring's accounts, and to a society's beliefs, way of life, resources, and economic sustainability in Native American and other indigenous societies. Likewise, in both cases renewal and regeneration – or *rebirth* – are the ultimate states to be attained following cultural or social "death." Just as in an NDE when a person's temporary death culminates in a rebirth with a new spiritual focus and other positive transformations, "prophets arise during times of cultural crisis," with "a messianic message of the need for cultural renewal" (Ring 1988: 12). In other words, prophecies about the future obtained during NDEs might be nothing more than human symbolic manifestations of anxieties about survival on Earth and a desire for a Golden Age.

Some NDE prophecies are vague as to the timing or other details, and are therefore not subject to verification. One late-20th century account, for example, predicted the Second Coming of Christ at some unspecified date, while another stated that an increasingly thick, dark, evil haze is slowly enveloping the Earth and will lead to upheaval (Lundahl 2001: 235-6).

Although long-term vivid recollection is a hallmark of the phenomenon, some who have revelatory experiences during NDEs are unable to remember certain details about them upon return. Zaleski (1987: 132-33) has noted that this kind of forgetting is known from both Medieval and modern Western NDEs, writing that experiencers "are permitted to keep their memories of the lesser sights of the other world, in order to bring a message to humanity; but they find it nearly impossible to retain a clear impression of that instant of direct, unmediated absorption in all of reality." This dynamic, too, has cultural and literary dimensions reminiscent of the nostalgia for a lost Golden Age, for it reflects cross-cultural notions of having forgotten some kind of essential, universal truths, and "speaks of the need to re-awaken and recover lost self-knowledge."

On a wider level, cross-cultural variations between revelatory content in NDEs raises some difficult philosophical and metaphysical questions. If we are to accept that NDEs are genuine experiences of an afterlife, what are we to make of their diversity? Are all manifestations of deities and beings of light, for example, genuine divine figures with identities that correspond to the experiencer's claims? Or are they perhaps the same divine figure, which manifests according to local cultural and individual preconceptions? These questions – which will be returned to in Chapter 7 – are further complicated by the fact that NDEs often conflict with the expectations of the experiencer. Furthermore, NDEs that do not feature an encounter with a divinity are also interpreted in spiritual or religions terms by those who have them.

By their very nature of "revealing" to the individual the experience of dualism and the phenomenon of surviving the death of the body, alongside knowledge of life after death in other worlds, NDEs can by definition be seen as revelatory experiences. This reflects the fact that beliefs in gods or adherence to any particular religious doctrines are not preconditions for belief in an afterlife.

Revelatory Symbolism and Apocalyptic Literature

As British theologian Paul Badham (1997: 10, 12) has argued, NDEs can be seen as a democratization of religious and revelatory experiences – particularly when we consider that modern medical advances enable more people to be resuscitated. Such advances have "made available to thousands an experience which has from the beginning lain at the heart of much of the world's religious perceiving and formed an important experiential basis for the future hope," that is, belief in a positive life after death. The NDE is not only a "profound and life-changing experience which people never forget," it also "shares many of the characteristics of the deepest religious experiences known to humanity."

Indeed, as a spontaneous experience rather than one sought within a particular religious or spiritual practice, revelations in NDEs are "not dependent on faith or adherence to a particular creed or religious tradition" (Fox 2003: 4). In a 20th century British example, a cancer patient had an NDE after wondering "what God really looks like." She found herself suddenly out of her body and "was carried, until with a shattering light I entered another world and found myself face-to-face with God" encircled by "a shimmering circle of light." "God," however, had the face of her "beloved therapist," which made her realize "that God is love. His face reflects that face which the individual loves" (ibid. 253).

This recalls an account by Carl Jung (1961: 289-97), the founder of analytical psychology, who encountered his living doctor during an NDE which he had in a Swiss hospital in 1944. He described a highly individualistic experience in extraordinarily vivid detail, in which he found himself in space with Earth visible below, the Indian subcontinent and the Middle East facing him. He then saw "a tremendous dark block of stone, like a meteorite … floating in space, and I myself was floating in space." It had been hollowed out to form a temple, as Jung had seen in South and Southeast Asia. Inside the temple "a black Hindu sat silently in lotus posture upon a stone bench. He wore a white gown, and I knew that he expected me." Candle flames burned everywhere and wreathed the doorway, as Jung had seen in Sri Lanka. As he approached, he felt that

everything was being sloughed away; everything I aimed at or wished for or thought, the whole phantasmagoria of earthly existence, fell away or was stripped from me – an extremely painful process. Nevertheless something remained; it was as if I now carried along with me everything I had ever experienced or done, everything that had happened around me. … I consisted of my own history and I felt with great certainty: this is what I am. "I am this bundle of what has been and what has been accomplished."

This experience gave me a feeling of extreme poverty, but at the same time of great fullness. There was no longer anything I wanted or desired. I existed in an objective form; I was what I had been and lived. At first the sense of annihilation predominated, of having been stripped or pillaged; but suddenly that became of no consequence. Everything seemed to be past; what remained was a *fait accompli*, without any reference back to what had been. There was no longer any regret that something had dropped away or been taken away. On the contrary: I had everything that I was, and that was everything.

Suddenly overwhelmed with questions about his life and his identity, he believed he would find the answers inside the temple. He then saw a figure arise "from the direction of Europe" below. It turned out to be his doctor, though "in his primal form" as an ancient Greek prince from Kos, a city associated with healing and medicine. They communicated telepathically, and the doctor explained to Jung that he "had been delegated by the earth to deliver a message to me, to tell me that there was a protest against my going away. I had no right to leave the earth and must return. The moment I heard that, the vision ceased."

It is perhaps unsurprising that a person who devoted so much of his life and thought to theorizing about dreams, myths, religions, symbols, and archetypes would have an NDE that reflects these preoccupations. Nevertheless, Jung did not interpret the experience as a product of his own learned and fertile imagination, and in fact it seemed to have had a profound influence on his thinking about consciousness and the possibility of life after death. A few months after the experience he wrote in a letter, "What happens after death is so unspeakably glorious that our imagination and our feelings do not suffice to form even an approximate conception of it." In addition to revelations about the nature of the afterlife, Jung also revived with a premonition of his doctor's death, which soon came true.

As Potthoff (2017: 10) wrote, apocalyptic literature such as the Revelation of John and the Apocalypse of Peter

> bases its authority on, and centers around, visions of and journeys to the other world during which the visionary receives heavenly knowledge, often revealed by an angel or other intermediary, about God's plan for history, the end of the world, what happens after death, and the geography of the postmortem realm. All these have been demonstrated in the various NDE accounts discussed here.

Another definition of *apocalypse* is equally fitting to NDEs. As defined by the Hebrew Bible (Old Testament) scholar J. J. Collins:

> *Apocalypse* is a genre of revelatory literature with a narrative framework, in which a revelation is mediated by an otherworldly being to a human recipient, disclosing a transcendent reality which is both temporal, insofar as it envisages eschatological salvation, and spatial insofar as it involves another, supernatural world (in Couliano 1991: 54).

Nor are NDEs the sole extraordinary experience type by which these kinds of revelations occur. Generally speaking, "Such heavenly revelations typically are associated with non-ordinary states of consciousness" which do not only occur spontaneously but can also be brought about via "ascetic practices like fasting, as well as singing and incantation, prayer, meditation on scripture, and the ingestion of hallucinogenic substances" (Potthoff 2017: 10). Though Potthoff was writing in the context of the ancient Mediterranean, similar shamanic-type practices are also known from around the world. In some Native American and Pacific Island cultures (see Chapter 4) in particular, certain shamanic practices were actually intended to replicate NDEs, so that practitioners and their communities could obtain revelatory information in the other world without actually dying, and use that information in ways that benefit the community (Shushan 2018: 211-13).

3

NEAR-DEATH EXPERIENCES IN EARLY

CIVILIZATIONS

~

Though spanning a period of over 4,500 years, the societies discussed in this chapter are all examples of early civilizations, meaning "the earliest form of class-based society that developed in the course of human history" (Trigger 1993: 6). I selected them for comparison according to two essential criteria: they emerged largely in a state of cultural independence, and they produced texts that contain afterlife descriptions prior to periods of significant external cultural influence (Shushan 2009: 29ff). In contrast to Greco-Roman, Abrahamic, Buddhist, and later Hindu texts, the beliefs and ideas summarized here *have no known forebears or previous textual models upon which they could have been based, and thus contain* the world's earliest recorded conceptions of the afterlife. This means that any cross-cultural similarities between them cannot be explained by transmission from one civilization to the next. We must therefore look elsewhere for an explanation of their shared ideas.

It is important to understand that in these early periods, the uses to which writing was put was very much limited to bureaucracy and religious texts. Personal narratives are largely non-existent, meaning that aside from China, there was simply no context for the recording of factual occurrences of NDEs. Nevertheless, texts from each of these civilizations reveal knowledge of individuals apparently dying, returning to life, and reporting experiences highly reminiscent of NDEs.

This chapter will review the more direct evidence for NDEs in each civilization, as well as providing summaries of their afterlife beliefs. This will reveal firstly that they all shared a number of basic thematic similarities in their afterlife beliefs, which happen to correspond to NDEs. This suggests that knowledge of NDEs is embedded in the accounts, meaning that the beliefs were grounded in such experiences to one degree or another. Secondly, it will demonstrate that each of these civilizations had highly distinctive conceptions of the other world and the journey there, and that overgeneralizations must be avoided: their beliefs should certainly not be regarded as being the same. Careful readers will, however, be able to identify NDE themes embedded in the descriptions.

Understanding both similarities and differences of afterlife beliefs will help to illuminate their relationships to NDEs. A comparative summary and analysis of parallels with NDEs will be found at the end of the chapter.

There is much that remains obscure in their texts, and examples of any kind of ancient exegesis are rare. Our understanding of ancient religious beliefs is thus incomplete, and in some cases our interpretations are likely to be at least partially inaccurate. This is especially the case with material written in extinct languages by long-dead cultures such as Egypt and Sumer.

Old and Middle Kingdom Egypt

Egypt's Nile Valley was originally populated c. 10,000 BCE by immigrants from the Sahara and North-East Africa, and from the surrounding desert areas between 6000–5000 BCE. Despite these multicultural beginnings, there is archaeological evidence of cultural continuity from the Predynastic Badarian period (c.5500–4000 BCE) through subsequent Egyptian history. The relevant texts contain ritual formulae intended to ensure the survival of souls of the deceased in the realms beyond, providing them with the knowledge to successfully negotiate the afterlife perils and obstacles, and to join the gods in the divine realm.

For the early periods under discussion here, there is no direct evidence for NDEs. The myth of Osiris, who died, was resurrected, and became lord of the other world, is perhaps the closest. Though only allusions to the myth are found in the early texts, the association between Osiris and the soul of the dead was a prominent part of Egyptian afterlife beliefs from the earliest times. One of the most relevant and intriguing aspects of these beliefs in relation to NDEs is found in a section of the Middle Kingdom *Coffin Texts* known as *The Book of Two Ways* (c. 2160-1760 BCE). It specifically associates the soul of the dead with Osiris's decaying corpse. That corpse is hidden in a region of the otherworld called Rosetau, "in darkness, with fire about it." Rosetau is characterized as a goal for the deceased, for "He who sees the dead Osiris will never die." Indeed, encountering his corpse actually enables the deceased to proceed on the afterlife journey. Souls become gods through knowledge of the paths of Rosetau; otherwise, they face annihilation (Shushan 2009: 64-5; Faulkner 1973-78).

Most importantly, Rosetau is also a place of rebirth, where the deceased will make the corpse of Osiris "raise itself." Because The deceased then becomes Osiris in death, the encounter with the corpse of Osiris is also an encounter with one's own corpse. Enlightenment is brought about by souls witnessing their own decomposition, leading to the realization that they are physically dead, yet spiritually still alive. This realization actually enables immortality. It also reflects many NDE testimonies in which individuals did not know they were dead until seeing their own corpse from a vantage point outside it.

A text known as *The Teaching for King Merikare* (c. 2025–1700 BCE) (Simpson 2003: 158–9) contains references to what may be a life review. A "tribunal which judges sinners" does so based upon their earthly lives. These judges "regard a lifetime as but an hour," examining the soul's deeds which are placed before them like a treasure, playing "as though it were a biographical film" (Assmann 2001: 74). Those who have "done no wrong" become god-like for eternity. Life reviews and moral accountability are also evident in the numerous Old and Middle Kingdom autobiographical funerary texts which affirm the deceased's positive actions and behaviors and deny their negative ones. These accounts were intended to be recited by the deceased at judgement in the afterlife (Robinson 2003: 148).

On a more thematic, general level, even the earliest source for Egyptian afterlife beliefs, the *Pyramid Texts* (c. 2350 BCE), contain descriptions that evoke NDEs. In general terms, they describe how souls of the dead undergo multiple experiences, including leaving the body in spiritual form, journeying to afterlife realms associated with creation and rebirth, and entering darkness and emerging into light through descent into and ascent from the Duat, or "undersky" (Assmann 2001; Allen 2005). The experience also includes encounters with – and transformations into – various divine beings including a "being of light" sun-god and the resurrected god of death. It also features barriers and water crossings, meeting deceased ancestors, judgement based on a review of one's earthly conduct, dangers and perils.

More specifically, the texts detail how after being released from the body, the *ba* soul – the unique self, or personality, as opposed to the *ka*, or life force – ascends with the sun-god Re and is bathed in the "cool waters of the stars" before boarding Re's celestial boat. On a journey of cyclical renewal, the soul sails on the cosmic waters of the heavens, then under the earth through the Duat. Raised by the Imperishable Stars – divinized individuals who have become the circumpolar stars (more beings of light) – the deceased ascends to the Earth-god, Geb, who is also father of Osiris (and thus now father of the deceased).

Upon entering the horizon, or Akhet, the deceased is transformed into an *akh*, a transfigured, divinized, radiant spirit. Each body part is identified with the creator god Atum, as well as various other deities. Despite these divine associations, souls are assured that their "identity will not perish" and that they will not die.

The goddess Sothis (the star Sirius) and the constellation of Orion (associated with Osiris) accompany the deceased on the Nightboat to the Duat. There they are greeted by two groups of nine gods known as the Dual Ennead. As in the *Book of Two Ways*, the decaying corpse of Osiris is equated with that of the deceased, and with the inundation of the Nile, linking death, decay, and rebirth through life-giving waters. The deceased is commanded: "Raise yourself like Osiris!" and becomes a composite deity version of the god with jackal's face, falcon's arms, wingtips of Thoth, and lion's tail. The deceased becomes judge and governor of both the living and the dead and is worshipped by other *akhs*. Souls are ferried by the Ennead to the Marsh of Rest which provides spring water, and where the Imperishable Stars give them the plant of life. The *ba* and *ka* are spiritually purified and renewed, and the *akh* is clothed.

Though life is pleasant and happy in the Duat, the deceased continues with Atum-Re (a composite of both deities) on the solar circuit back up through the Akhet and the celestial realms. The soul ascends on a ladder made by Re, with Horus (falcon-headed god of kingship) and Seth (chaos-god and brother of Osiris) acting as psychopomps, or afterlife guides. The deceased's emergence from the Duat is seen as rebirth into a divine state.

The sky-goddess reassembles the bones, limbs, and head of the deceased – just as Isis (maternal goddess) reassembled her husband and brother Osiris when he was dismembered by Seth, thus enabling his resurrection. She then leads the deceased across the Winding Canal (the sun's path) in a ferryboat to the eastern side of the sky. After entering the Akhet, the deceased "eats people and lives on gods," absorbing their power, wisdom, hearts, and *akhs*, thereby becoming integrated into the divine realm (Assmann 2001). The deceased now becomes Nefertem, the deification of the blue lotus from which the sun was born; and Sia, the deification of intelligence and wisdom.

Souls of the deceased cross the Akhet by ascending their own funerary ritual incense smoke, and in the form of various kinds of birds. Along a path cleared by Isis and Nephthys (a protector deity, and sister of Isis), the deceased is now ferried by Re himself. At Stork Mountain souls are nursed by their two vulture mothers, purified in the Jackal Lake by Horus, then bathed and anointed by various other gods.

Grasping on to two sycamores (associated with mother- and sky-goddess Hathor), souls are then taken again to the eastern sky. They climb sunshine to the Marsh of Offerings (which are provided to the deceased through rituals on Earth), and are given a plot of land by Tefnut (lion goddess associated with the sun, moon, and water) in the Marsh of Reeds. This is where souls dwell with the Imperishable Stars, and where other *akhs* work the land to provide sustenance for them.

On the cosmic circuit, Re and the deceased are joined by sky-gods as they rise, and netherworld-gods as they set. The journey is fraught with perils, such as a "canal that leads to the dead," the "dangerous, painful" *ba*-house, snakes with fiery venom, monstrous female donkeys and hippopotamuses, and "apes who sever heads." The deceased is protected, however, by such entities as Grasper of Forelocks, Gory All Over, Serpent with Sweeping Head, and Thoth, the ibis-headed god of knowledge and scribal assistant during judgement of the dead. These beings will lasso, imprison, knife, disembowel, cook, decapitate, or remove the hearts of opponents. Knowledge was power over demons and other dangers, and was a prerequisite for becoming a divine spirit in the other world (Assmann 1984).

Gates of Horus and Osiris are guarded by gatekeepers and souls can pass through only by revealing their identity. Spells affirm that the deceased will eat with his mouth and defecate with his anus, breathe through his nose and ejaculate through his penis, and subsist on dates and offerings rather than urine and excrement, indicating that a reversal of the earthly order was also a danger.

Despite becoming a divine judge, the deceased is not beyond judgement. Souls must appear before the Dual Maat (gods who stand with the deceased during judgement) while their records are read aloud. If innocence is proclaimed, souls are interrogated regarding their purity and divinity while standing between two ladders made for Osiris, one by Re and one by Horus.

The focus in the texts is more on the journey than on destinations. It is possible that one never reaches a final realm, but instead spends eternity on the sun's circuit, journeying through netherworld realms of darkness and danger, and back through celestial realms of light and abundance. It is, however, difficult to imagine the point of being repeatedly judged on each cycle, and locales such as the Marsh of Reeds appear to be final goals and are referred to as dwelling places. It may be that the deceased completed the cycle only once, and depending on the outcome of the judgement (and ability to overcome dangers) was either annihilated or became divine in the Marsh of Reeds (Shushan 2009: 54-61).

The multiple states, realms, transformations, and divinizations also suggest the omnipresence of the deceased, and a state of universal totality of the self with the "Absolute," or "Ultimate Reality." The deceased ascends in multiple forms to perhaps *simultaneously* dwell in the Marsh of Reeds, in the Duat with/as Osiris, travel with/as Re on his eternal cycle of rebirth, become a star, and so on. Egyptian religious thought in general is typified by single concepts having multiple aspects. For example Re, Khepri, Horus, Atum, Aten, Amun-Re, Osiris-Re, Re-Harakhty as well as the deceased are all aspects of the sun. The *ba* and *ka* are microcosms of (and indeed, one and the same with) the complementary opposites of Re and Osiris, with the *akh* being analogous to the Osiris-Re union (Allen 2005). The dichotomy between the deceased both achieving divine unification and retaining individuality signifies the reconciliation of dualities characteristic of Egyptian thought (Allen 1988).

The accessibility and popularization of Egyptian afterlife texts gradually increased over time. The *Pyramid Texts* are believed to have been initially exclusive to the king, then later to the queen. The *Coffin Texts* were accessible to a wider segment of society, though still predominantly for the elite who could afford elaborately painted coffins

(Shushan 2009: 61-66). The New Kingdom texts such as the *Book of Going Forth by Day* (*Book of the Dead*) and the *Amduat* made the texts available to all who could afford a scrap of papyrus or even a potsherd on which to write the spells. While there is a great deal of continuity between these texts over time, with even the latest being firmly grounded in the *Pyramid Texts*, there was a marked intensification of focus on perils, guarded gateways, judgement, threats, and negotiating dangerous entities. This suggests an increased use of the texts by the elite as tools of control, coinciding with their rise in accessibility.

Although no explicit NDE references are known from the early texts, there are at least three relevant narratives from later periods: a 6th or 7th century BCE tale of a magician named Meryre, a brief 5th century BCE summary by Herodotus involving a king named Rhampsinitus, and a tale of Setne Khamwas from the 4th century BCE. All involve their protagonists journeying to the other world and having various experiences there before returning. It is unknown if the Meryre in the first tale was a known historical figure. Setne Khamwas, better known as Khaemweset, however, was a son of Rameses II, while Rhampsinitus is believed to be a Hellenized name for Rameses II. In any case, the accounts may reflect knowledge of NDEs, or are perhaps even mythologized versions of actual accounts. Egyptian afterlife conceptions were fully developed long before these tales were written, however.

Sumer

The Mesopotamian region of Sumer was settled around 5000 BCE, by people of unknown origin and whose language was a linguistic isolate, meaning that it is not related to any other language group. The main sources for the Sumerian afterlife are literary-religious texts written in cuneiform script on clay tablets. Much of their content dates at least as far back as 2000 BCE.

Despite claims in most popular and scholarly works on Mesopotamian religions, the Sumerian afterlife conception was one of transformation rather than eternal gloom. Though some souls are punished and perhaps annihilated, others are divinized, made judges, brought back to life, or otherwise transformed. Other general features include traveling through darkness, trials, obstacles and perils, deities radiating light who assist in the process of judgement, encounters with deceased relatives, an ultimate fate based upon one's earthly experience, and becoming a god or godlike.

Knowledge of NDEs is suggested not only by such themes, but also by a number of references scattered in the texts. For example, the underworld deity Nergal was said to have the power "to carry off and to bring back," that is, to cause death but also bring about revival from death. An Akkadian term *muballit miti* referred to "the one who makes the dead to live" (Heidel 1949: 208). The living can sometimes visit the underworld, though if they call attention to themselves they may be captured by deities such as Namtar, the footless and handless plague god. A king named Etana had a visionary dream in which he traveled to a heavenly realm and obtained the "plant of birth," then fell back from heaven, perhaps suggesting the NDE return (Shushan 2009: 81).

The text known as "The Death of Bilgames" (George 2003: 198-99) however, is another contender for the world's earliest documented NDE. Bilgames was a hero-king – widely believed to have been an actual historical figure – who is better known by the Babylonian version of his name in the eponymous *Epic of Gilgamesh*. The Sumerian text tells of how Bilgames traveled to the underworld while his body was lying on his deathbed. Instructed not to enter with an angry heart, he underwent a life review assisted by deities that radiated brilliant light. In determining his fate, this group of seven deities known as the Anuna reviewed his heroic career, his perpetuation of religious customs, foundation of temples, and the journey he undertook to the paradisiacal realm of Dilum to obtain the secret of immortality from Ziusudra (hero of the Sumerian flood myth).

The experience was transformative, and his heart was "undone" by a being of light, Utu the sun-god. At a funerary banquet in the otherworldly Great City where the souls of priests and priestesses dwell, Bilgames was greeted by his deceased relatives along with kings, governors, and military commanders known to him in life. He was then made a demi-god and a ruler and judge of the netherworld. Finally, he returned to his body and awakened. The narrative stresses that Bilgames's case was exceptional, perhaps reflecting the relatively rare occurrence of NDEs – especially in societies with pre-modern medical technology (Shushan 2009: 70-75).

The fact that Bilgames was probably a historical person sets his narrative apart from other Sumerian myths involving descents to the other world. The others feature deities, though they are also relevant. Of special note is a ritual lament to the healing god Damu, "the dead anointed one." The text describes how his disembodied spirit was taken to the underworld by demons. Unaware that he is dead, Damu met other spirits on the road to the netherworld. He asked them to take a message to his mother, hoping that she would rescue him by bribing the netherworld ranger. The ghosts could not make the living hear them, though Damu somehow managed to communicate to his mother. He told her to dig up his congealed blood, chop it into pieces, and take them to his sister, a leech named Amashilama who will make beer from it. Damu will then drink the beer, incorporating his own body within himself in order to be restored to life. Somehow Damu only realized he was dead when told that his mother and sister are looking for him and preparing the beer in order to revive him. His transcendence or omnipresence is suggested by descriptions of his spirit "lying in" the winds, "lightnings and in tornadoes," and "toward the foundations" of both heaven and earth (Jacobsen 1987: 51ff). As in the Egyptian texts, the realization of one's physical remains being separate from the self brings about the realization of having survived death (Shushan 2009: 78-79).

The other Sumerian afterlife journey myths are those of the goddesses Inana (associated with love and war), her sister Geshtinana, and the gods Enki, Enkidu, Dumuzid, and Ningishzida (Shushan 2009: 75-80). From these texts we learn that Ganzer, the underworld, can be reached by ferry on a river that devours people, or on a desolate journey by donkey and chariot. The entrance is guarded by gates and a gatekeeper. Souls of the dead are interrogated about their identity and purpose before being allowed to pass. Other perils include the *galla* – netherworld demons who inflict torments and humiliations such as blindfolding, securing in stocks, depriving of sleep, stripping naked, and menacing with nails, pokers and axes.

Namtar is minister to the queen of the underworld, Ereshkigala, who decrees the fates of the deceased. Ninazu is another underworld deity, associated with spring rain and ritual bathing, who sings sweetly and plays a musical instrument. The sun-god Utu is the father and judge of the netherworld, and was conceived of as ascending on a chariot into the heavens, then descending into the horizon and the netherworld. Ningishzida is the underworld's throne-bearer, and his wife Ninazimua (associated with Geshtinana) is a scribe who keeps records on the lives and deaths of every human being.

The newly arrived dead may be beaten with a stick by Nergal, the scimitar-wielding underworld warrior-deity described as "a dragon covered with gore, drinking the blood of living creatures," with the power to "create life," "determine destinies," and "render judgements." His "terrifying anger smites the wicked" and "tortures the disobedient."

As seen with Bilgames, one's afterlife fate is determined by earthly circumstances. In contrast to his fate, however, Inana was found guilty following her judgement, for she descended to the underworld with "an angry heart" in order to conquer it and depose Ereshkigala from her throne. Though she was killed, with the help of Enki and a life-giving plant and water, she was restored to life.

The fate of men who die without an heir is to eat bread that is like bricks. The number of a man's sons lead to similar judgements, so that those who had only one son will be mournful, and those with more sons will be given bread, water, and will be joyful. Those with five sons will attain the status of a scribe and live in the otherworld palace, while at the highest level those with seven sons will sit on a throne with the gods and hear judgements. Eunuchs sit uselessly in a corner, and childless women are considered as worthless as a broken or defective pot. Husbands and wives who never undressed each other will weep. Lepers subsist on grass and roots, are eaten by worms, and ostracized from the underworld city. Those without funerary offerings eat only crumbs and table scraps. Those who were eaten by lions lament the loss of their hands and feet, and those who drowned or suffered from pellagra are eaten by maggots. Those who blaspheme, cheat gods, and disrespect parents are denied water. If a man is cursed by his parents, his ghost will roam and his heirs will die.

The underworld river has no water, the fields have no grain, the sheep have no wool, and therefore inhabitants cannot drink, eat, or be clothed. Things simultaneously *are* and *are not*, with "cattle pens that are no cattle pens" and food and water that are not food and water. An underworld messenger "has eyes but he cannot see. He has a mouth but he cannot converse" (Jacobsen 1976; Katz 2003: 203; Black et. al. 2004).

Some souls, however, are given banquets, and men who died in battle are cared for by their parents. The stillborn play at a table of precious metals, eating honey and ghee. Those who died an early death lie "on the bed of the gods," and those who were burned to death ascend to the sky on their own smoke. A "prayer for a dead person pleading to be admitted to the netherworld" mentions an underworld palace with clear water in a forest full of birds, with Inana and the radiant protector deity Lama acting as guides. There are also prayers for peace and contentment in the underworld, "the most honored place."

Especially fortunate spirits travel ahead of the rising sun and reach Dilmun, a pristine land of light, peace, fresh water, and abundant grain, with no disease, old age, or dangerous animals. Other individuals, such as Inana and Etana (who himself became an afterlife deity) ascended to a heavenly realm but also went to the underworld.

In summary, the Sumerian texts describe a multiplicity of possible fates determined by one's earthly status, conduct, or mode of death. The numerous underworld deity-judges, and a bureaucratic infrastructure of accountants, sheriffs, gatekeepers, porters, scribes, and ferrymen indicate that individuals were judged and processed upon arrival after death. The netherworld darkness is illuminated by a succession of beings of light: Utu, the dream-god Sissig, and Enki, god of wisdom and water who radiates light, beauty and joy. In a hymn to Nergal the underworld is described as having an "awesome radiance" (Jacobsen 1987: 122–3). Lugalera – a shepherd aspect of the fertility and vegetation god Dumuzid who travelled to the netherworld and returned – emits "a bright light" to the underworld princes as they bow before him. There is a clear connection between "the judging of a dead individual with the bringing of light to the netherworld" (Katz 2003: 148-9).

The texts also make numerous correspondences between the death, underworld journey, and return of deities such as Dumuzid, and the cycles of plants in nature, indicating an afterlife of gestation, renewal and rebirth. Such conceptions reveal a theme of the reconciliation of life and death. Afterlife deities such as Ningishzida and Ninshubura are characterized as both heavenly and underworldly, as are Etana and Bilgames. The cosmic waters of Ea which border paradise is also the underworld man-eating river. The death-and-rebirth of the deceased in the afterlife was associated with the descent and return from the otherworld of the goddess Inana who was associated with Venus, and with Utu/sun, and Nanna/moon (Shushan 2009: 83-89).

Vedic India

The origins of Vedic civilization are somewhat obscure. Some scholars argue that it resulted from migrations of Indo-Aryan people from Central Asia in the 2nd millennium BCE, though others argue that it developed indigenously.

The ancient Vedic texts – the foundations of Hinduism – reveal beliefs in multiple possible afterlife fates. Some may be experienced in succession, some perhaps simultaneously, and some only to particular aspects of the soul. General features include existence in a non-physical form such as light or simply consciousness, ascent and descent to celestial and subterranean realms, encounters with deities and ancestors, fates determined by earthly behavior, barriers, obstacles, demons, and other perils, and identification of the deceased with various deities, celestial bodies, seasons, and natural phenomena indicating a transcendent, omnipresent state.

Evidence for knowledge of NDEs can be found in various texts. The *Jaiminiya Brahmana* (c. 900-700 BCE; Bodewitz 1973, I.167) contains a reference to individuals who visited Yamaloka – the realm of the afterlife deity Yama – and returned from death. The *Atharva Veda* (Witney 1905, VIII.1-2) from c. 900 BCE includes soul-retrieval texts called "charms to recover a dying man." They describe the soul as ascending from the underworld and returning to the body in terms similar to those used to describe heavenly ascent (Bodewitz 2002). A magical formula was intended to retrieve the breath and life from the underworld and restore them to the body. The departure from the body during shamanic-type journeys of the *asu* soul – a "free-soul" which enables consciousness – would cause a state of apparent death (Bodewitz 1991: 40).

Equally compelling is the continuous stream of NDE-like afterlife journey narratives that are prominent throughout the Vedic texts. They describe how a particular individual left the body, traveled to afterlife realms, and sometimes returned to the body. The primary function of these narratives was to provide religious or spiritual guidance through knowledge of what to expect after death, suggesting that the accounts were believed to be true and factual, despite their claims of direct involvement from deities.

The earliest, from c. 1700-1200 BCE, is found in a hymn in the *Rig Veda* (X.135; O'Flaherty 1981), a collection of ritual texts for recitation during sacrifices. It describes how a boy went to Yamaloka in order to find his father, who went there out of a longing to be with his ancestors. The journey was undertaken in a "chariot" constructed by the boy's mind (that is, by leaving his body) which can "travel in all directions." He encountered Yama sitting beneath a tree in his realm, drinking with other gods, and playing on a reed flute. We are not told if the boy returned to life, however.

The *Shatapatha Brahmana* (Eggeling: 1882-1900, XI) from c. 900-700 BCE relates an afterlife journey which includes a description of the hellish realm of Naraka. The deity Varuna (god of *Rta*, moral and cosmic order) sends his son Bhrgu on a journey to "all directions" in order to gain knowledge. In each direction, Bhrgu sees men dismembering and devouring each other, "sitting in silence" or crying loudly. In the northeast, the direction of the heavenly realm of Svargaloka, lies Yamaloka. Yama himself is described as a black man with yellow eyes and a stick, symbolizing wrath. He stands between an ugly woman and a beautiful woman, who symbolize faith and lack of faith.

The *Jaiminiya Brahmana* (I.42-44) contains a more elaborate version of this narrative, involving the same protagonists. Here, Varuna takes away Bhrgu's "lifebreaths" – that is, he kills him – which causes his journey to the beyond. The boy is incredulous as he travels to each of the directions, and asks repeatedly, "Has this really happened? What is the meaning of this?" He is answered (presumably by the inhabitants of each respective realm), "Ask your father Varuna. He will explain it to you." In the first three realms, those who carry out the Agnihotra (fire ritual) in ignorance are dismembered and devoured by men who used to be trees, animals, rice, and barley which were not used according to proper ritual strictures. This is a reversal of the earthly order, in which sacrificers are now eaten by sacrifices. In the fourth realm, Yama, Faith and Nonfaith are encountered as in the *Shatapatha Brahmana*. In the fifth realm are "two streams flowing on an even level." One is filled with the blood of those who have harmed Brahmins (the priestly and intellectual caste), and is guarded by Yama. The other is filled with ghee from which golden men fill their golden cups with "all desires." Only the exceptionally worthy gain the sixth realm – a place of beautiful fragrances, music, dancing and singing Apsaras (female spirits), where there are "five rivers with blue and white lotuses, flowing with honey like water."

The *Katha Upanishad* (Olivelle 1999, I-VI) contains the culmination of this type of narrative in the form of a dialogue between Yama and a young Brahmin called Naciketas, who is sent by his father to Yamaloka. The boy arrives while Yama is away and is left unattended without food for three days. When Yama returns, to compensate for his lapse in hospitality he grants Naciketas three wishes. The boy wishes for his father's kindness, for the secrets of the fire-altar, and of immortality. Yama explains that the altar's fire "leads to heaven, to the attainment of an endless world," a place of merriment where fear, hunger, thirst, sorrow and old age do not exist. Yama is reluctant to answer Naciketas' questions concerning whether or not one "exists" in death, and "what happens at that great transit"; though he does explain the concept of *atman* in relation to the afterlife. The *atman* is the inner unchanging self, and *brahman* is the Absolute, or ultimate reality. A key Upanishadic teaching is the realization of the individual's essential oneness with the divine: that *atman* is actually one and the same as *brahman*. The realization of this equivalency is a path to enlightenment and merging with the divine (Butzenberger 1996).

Yama tells Naciketas that the *atman* continues even in death and is immortal, and that understanding this leads to "that final step, from which he is not reborn again" (meaning *moksha*, or liberation from continual reincarnations). "A certain wise man in search of immortality," Yama tells the boy, "turned his sight inward and saw the self within." In the form of a swan, the enlightened deceased "dwells in the light" as a god in the sky. The unenlightened, who view reality as "diverse," will experience death after death. Some are reincarnated, while "Others pass into a stationary thing." On the various states of being the text explains: "As in a mirror, so in the body; As in a dream, so in the Father's world; As in water a thing becomes somewhat visible, so in the Gandharva [celestial beings] world; Somewhat as in shadows and light, so in brahman's world."

While these may not be "typical" NDEs as known from the contemporary west, it is important to stress that the accounts of the experiences of Bhrgu and Naciketas were brought about by their fathers murdering them. The narratives may be grounded in actual NDEs, though clearly have been elaborated and theologized to promote religious teachings.

Aside from the otherworld journey narratives, afterlife descriptions can be found elsewhere in the *Rig Veda* (Shushan 2009: 90-94; O'Flaherty 1981), despite its primary concern with life on Earth, and gods granting health, wealth, longevity and children. It states that the realm of the dead is located in the "spheres above which firmly support the heavens" and in the "third heaven of heaven." It is a place of "inextinguishable light," joy, freedom and fulfilled desires. It is an idealized mirror-image of earth, flowing with cosmic waters, with horses and pastures, grass and trees, and cycles of days and nights. The deceased are "fed and satisfied," and cared for by Yama.

The journey to Yamaloka takes three days, and upon arrival the deceased encounters Yama as well as Varuna, Soma (a deity and an intoxicating, life-giving ritual drink associated with him), the Fathers (*pitr*, ancestors), and "families of ancient poets, priests, and singers." The deceased joins them in feasting and drinking Soma, and is instructed to "unite with the Fathers, with Yama, with the rewards of your sacrifices and good deeds, in the highest heaven. Leaving behind all imperfections, go back home again; merge with a glorious body." Whether the "glorious body" indicates rebirth on Earth or a spiritual body in Yamaloka is unclear. Yama will remove "all impurities," possibly indicating that Yamaloka was (or could sometimes be) a purifying intermediate realm.

Those who are generous gain immortality "on the high ridge of heaven" where there are rivers of ghee. Whatever the deceased gives in this world results in abundant return in Svargaloka, a place of "splendors" and a shining sun. Souls are escorted there by Pushan ("the nourisher"), Agni (god of fire and light), and Savitir (dispeller of darkness) – all of whom are sun-gods.

Mirroring the concept of *atman* and *brahman,* the soul is a microcosm of the sun, an inner light hidden in the heart just as the sun hides under the Earth. Yamaloka is also the realm of the sun, revealing an association between death, light, and cyclical rebirth, drawing a parallel with the sun's eternal cycle of rising and setting. Drinking Soma makes one immortal, reveals the gods and the light of heaven, and enables the deceased to find the sun by sailing on a boat on the primeval ocean. The celestial and subterranean worlds and their deities are associated with each other; and the Fathers, Yama, and Varuna are all associated with both the upper and lower realms indicating a theme of the reconciliation of opposites.

Offering rituals assisted the deceased in moving beyond the limbo-like condition of being in an intermediary disembodied state at risk of "redeath" or annihilation, and joining the ancestors in a positive afterlife state. Yama has made each person their own path to the realm of the Fathers (Pitaraloka), leading either "downward" or "forward into the horizon." The deceased travels there on water and through straits, on a journey fraught with dangers. To avoid demons, the deceased must take the correct path, running past Yama's pair of four-eyed dogs which thirst "for the breath of life." Yama entrusts the dogs to "watch over" the deceased on the remainder of the journey, indicating that they functioned as both guards and guides.

The realm of Vishnu ("The Preserver," a major deity) was another positive afterlife destination, "where men who love the gods rejoice," and where "the fountain of honey" is to be found in the god's "highest footstep" (a reference to the three strides Vishnu took to cross the universe). The deceased might also travel to the sky, the earth, the ocean, the sun, the dawn, "the flowing streams of light," plants, mountains, "the whole moving universe," "distances beyond the beyond," the past and the future. Becoming gods (or godlike), they share a chariot with Indra, king of the gods, and partake of ritual offerings made to them by the living.

Those who are evil "without order or truth" go to an abyss located "below the three earths." Those who do not perform sacrifices or fail to prepare Soma are hurled into the pit by Indra. Torments for demons in the pit correspond to specific human-type sins, suggesting warnings of potential punishments the deceased may face (as in later texts such as the *Mahabharata*). For example, one is boiled in a pot for eating meat, hating priests and possessing the evil eye; "evil-doers" are pierced and thrown into an abyss for eternity; liars "become nothing" because they "talk about nothing"; and seducers and corrupters are devoured by a serpent or annihilated. There are also prayers against "falling into the pit," for protection from "the devouring wolf," and for the flames of Agni to burn evil-doers "to nothingness."

There is some uncertainty regarding the distinctions between Yamaloka, Svargaloka, Pitaraloka, and the abyss. Each may be particular regions of Yamaloka, or they may reflect changing conceptions over time (Bodewitz 2002). In the *Brahmanas* and *Upanishads*, Yamaloka became a negative intermediate state for the unenlightened or immoral prior to a low reincarnation; and Svargaloka became a temporary reward for meritorious behavior prior to a high reincarnation. The later texts also show a greater stress on wisdom, the realization of the nature of *atman*, and the knowledge of immortality (Shushan 2009: 91ff; 2011).

Pre-Buddhist China

Chinese civilization emerged from the interaction of diverse indigenous cultural groups of various regions, as far back as 8500 BCE. The earliest references to the afterlife appear on Shang dynasty oracle bones (animal bones used for divination) around 1766–1046 BCE. They describe souls of kings ascending to a heavenly realm and joining the "Lord-on-High" (Ching 1993: 19). The world of the ancestors appears to be the same as that of the gods. Shang documents also refer to feeding the ancestors with offerings (Yü 1987: 378).

There is no lack of evidence for NDEs in ancient Chinese sources, and one text contains perhaps the world's earliest documentary NDE account (if we do not accept the Sumerian "Death of Bilgames" as such). It describes how in 7th century BCE, a provincial ruler recovered from an illness and reported an enjoyable journey to the home of the Emperor of Heaven, who gave him precognitive information which was later verified. A similar case dates from 498 BCE (de Groot 1892: IV,

113–14) as seen in the previous chapter, and numerous further Chinese return-from-death accounts are known from the third century BCE onwards (Campany 1990: 91–2). Around the turn of the millennium, a document relates how a woman was revived from death after six days and reported having seen her deceased father-in-law who told her that it was not yet her time to die (Arbuckle 1997: 109). De Groot (1892: 123) cited a single source (*Taiping Kwang chi*) which gives 127 Chinese accounts up to the 10th century CE.

There is also evidence for knowledge of NDEs in literary texts. The 3rd century BCE poem "Zhao hun" (Hawkes 1985: 233) is intended to call the soul back to the body from dangerous afterlife realms. In a 2nd century BCE poem called 'Ai shi ming,' a spirit reluctantly returns to the body when his path is blocked by a river (ibid. 337).

Although there were changes over time and variations between regions, certain ideas about the afterlife persisted throughout Chinese history: ascent to a heavenly realm, meeting deceased relatives, and dwelling with the gods in a divine-like state. Judgement and punishment are not particularly stressed in the early texts, and there appears to be no moral division between the different realms. How fates are determined is unclear, as are obvious distinctions between heavenly states and universal oneness. The notion of divine omnipresence may hold the answer, for if souls become gods they are capable of multiple experiences, separately or at once. Indeed, the afterlife is characterized as eternal cosmic wandering, and heavens and underworlds are associated with each other.

Texts with more detailed afterlife conceptions began to appear during the Zhou dynasty (1046–256 BCE). Although the Confucian Classics (some of which actually predate Confucius) are concerned primarily with proper ritual and behavior, afterlife descriptions are found scattered among them (Legge 1879; 1885). They describe how individuals have two souls, which after death become brighter and more ethereal as they grow stronger, until they are fully spiritualized, disembodied intelligence. The *hun* is the intelligent, spiritual soul which ascends to Shangdi, the Lord of Heaven in the sky-realm of creation. *Hun* souls of the "greatly virtuous" are "displayed on high in a condition of glorious brightness." The *po* is "the animal soul" which returns to the underworld with the body. It possesses "abundant and rich" powers, is silent and invisible, and enters into all things. Both souls attain a state of divine transcendence.

The heavenly realm, Tien, is ruled by the ancestors, such as King Wen who shines in "glittering light." In a divine state, he "ascends and descends; on God's left hand, on His right." Spirits of the dead are "very bright, very glorious." Tien is the realm of creation, and of joy, "where we shall have our place ... where no sad songs are sung," and where the Milky Way is a flowing river. "Tien" is synonymous with Shangdi, and is also the unifying force of order in the universe and the collectivity of ancestors. It is sometimes said to be located in the west, and sometimes in the sea to the east.

Afterlife fates could also be dependent upon earthly conduct, for Tien is "that happy kingdom where we shall get our due," though slanderers are thrown to the afterlife deity Yo Pei. If he refuses them, they are thrown to Shangdi. The latter acted as an afterlife judge who "pacified the good and humane ones in death," and "suppressed the inhuman ones."

The underworld, Yellow Springs, was located in the north, and described with the word *you*, which can mean hidden, deep, moon, night, dark, far away, blood, and so on (Thompson 1992). Though this may suggest a shadowy Sheol-like place, it may instead indicate the realm's mysteriousness, underground location, and inaccessibility to the living. It is also described as a place where "joy and concord will be found," and springs are associated with life, regeneration, and immortality. The cycle of life and death is compared to those of nature, and "the characteristics and conditions of spiritual beings are similar to those of Heaven and Earth" (Chan 1963: 265).

The duality of souls reflects "the Yin-Yang antithesis of two fundamental forces in the universe" (Needham 1974: 86), and their return to their original realm reconciles these forces. The word *po* is related to the word for "bright light" and the moon's cycle of death and rebirth (waxing and waning). These radiant souls going to "the dark region" also indicates the reconciliation of dualities, as does the dual nature of afterlife-related deities: Yo Pei was both ruler of the realm of the dead and an astral god, and in earlier times Shangdi was a chthonic fertility deity (Erkes 1940).

Early mystical-philosophical Daoist texts such as the *Zhuangzi* (c.319 BCE; Watson 1963, Paper 1995) contain still more elaborate afterlife conceptions. After leaving the body, souls "wander free and easy in the service of inaction," "turning and revolving, ending and beginning again, unaware of where they start or finish." Some will join the Creator in a positive realm, "to wander in the single breath of heaven and earth," "roam the infinite," and forget about earthly life. The Perfect Man becomes "godlike," riding clouds over the sun, moon and seas, through the elements and beyond the infinite, experiencing a loss of selfhood to "become identical with the Great Universality" (Paper 1995: 133–4). Other advanced spirits "enter into the mother of breath," ascend to the "cloudy heavens," dwell in the Dark Palace, or become stars in the Milky Way. The spirit of The Nameless Man rides on a bird "beyond the six directions, wandering in the village of Not-even-Anything and living in the Broad-and-Borderless field." Earthly or earth-like landscapes are also visited, such as mountains and subterranean waters. Dying is compared to awakening from a dream.

Even more colorful are the poems in *Chu ci* (*Songs of the South*, Hawkes 1985), which more intensely focus on metaphysical concepts such as transcending the self and merging with deities, quasi-earthly locales, mythical beings, river crossings and other obstacles/barriers, and more explicit solar, lunar, and celestial associations. "Li Sao" ("On Encountering Trouble," after 343 BCE), for example, describes a spiritual ascent on a phoenix-shaped chariot pulled by jade dragons to the "fairy precincts" of the "Hanging Gardens" on Mt. Kunlun. Dragons which carry souls to the other world drink there from the Pool of Heaven. They are tethered to a heavenly tree which the sun ascends, and in which ten suns roost at night. The tree connects heaven, Earth, and Yellow Springs, and is associated with the underworld deity Queen Mother of the West, who maintains cosmic order and ensures the continuance of immortality and rebirth.

The soul stops the sun from setting, and accompanied by the charioteers of the sun and moon, the Wind God, the Bird of Heaven, and the Thunder God, he is welcomed by whirlwinds, clouds, and rainbows. A porter allows him through the gate of heaven and he crosses White Water to the House of Spring, a celestial locale presided over by the Green Dragon. After visiting other places, he reaches Mt. Kunlun via a long, winding road which passes through the Ford of Heaven and beyond the western horizon. He is accompanied by phoenixes to the Desert of Moving Sands and the Banks of the Red Water where water-dragons make a bridge for him so that he may cross. The God of the West assists his crossing, though the journey becomes long and difficult. He is accompanied by a thousand chariots of jade drawn by dragons with "cloud-embroidered banners," past the celestial Mt. Buzhou in the west of Mt. Kunlun and is finally welcomed with music and dancing.

Obviously, there was not a single, all-pervasive Chinese conception of the afterlife, but rather differing ones held by different people (Poo 1998: 211). Nevertheless, a core of thematic similarities can be discerned across them all, including such typical NDE elements as ascent to another realm seen as the true home, deceased relatives, beings of light, evaluation of earthly life, joy, universal oneness, and divine omnipresence.

Pre-Columbian Mesoamerica

Mexico was settled at least 13,000 years ago by descendants of peoples who had earlier crossed a land bridge from Siberia, and eventually migrated southward. The pre-literate Olmec civilization developed c.1200 BCE, and it is believed that their religious system was the root of subsequent Mesoamerican traditions.

A Spanish missionary and early ethnographer, Bernardino de Sahagun (1997: 179), related the NDE of Quetzalpetlatl, the daughter-in-law of Moquihuix, a Mexica ruler from 1467 to 1473. Though the narrative is obviously deeply culturally embedded (and the text incomplete), it nevertheless includes the thematic elements of out-of-body journeys to other realms, a guide, a sense of joy (singing, gifts given to the NDEr), other spirits and deceased relatives, idealized mirror-image of Earth, encountering a divine presence (the rain-deity Tlaloc), and a return characterized by a positive transformation (healing the sick on Earth). The fact that the account immediately follows a description of beliefs about the underworld demonstrates a clear link between NDEs and afterlife conceptions. Sahagun also referred to the return-from-death experiences of Aztec noblewomen in the context of prophecies they delivered upon their return, demonstrating further that the NDE was familiar in pre-conquest Mesoamerica.

An Aztec book that combines myth and history, the *Annals of Cuauhtitlan* (1570), contains an interesting narrative of the death and divine transformation of the tenth-century Toltec ruler, Topiltzin Quetzalcoatl. When he refused to perform human sacrifices, a sorcerer-deity went to him and said, "I've come to show you your flesh." Quetzalcoatl replied, "What is this flesh of mine? Let me see it." The sorcerer held up a mirror and said, "Know yourself, see yourself." What Quetzalcoatl saw was his own reflection as a corpse, with sunken eyes and a swollen, "monstrous" face. He was then placed in a stone sarcophagus for four days, before traveling to the celestial ocean to cremate himself. His ashes ascended in the form of "precious birds," and his heart as a colorful bird known as a quetzal. He then entered the sky, became the Morning Star, and after eight days was deified as Lord of the Dawn (Bierhorst 1992: 5.53 ff).

The meaning of this narrative seems to be that without realizing it, Quetzalcoatl was already dead when the sorcerer-deity went to him with the intention of revealing to him his true state. The realization, brought on by the encounter with his own corpse in the mirror, enabled Quetzalcoatl to proceed and to be reborn into a transformed, divinized state of being.

Because Topiltzin Quetzalcoatl was a historical figure, this text could conceivably have been grounded in an NDE – though he does not seem to return from death following his divinization. The ruler was often conflated with the feathered serpent sky god Quetzalcoatl, presumably due in part to other myths involving that deity's journey to otherworlds (Shushan 2009: 130-31, 135).

Sahagun's (1973-78; Shushan 2009: 132-36) sources described the afterlife as "our ultimate home," "where reside the wind people, the flower people"; and they explained how one's status and achievements determined otherworld fates. As if they had "awakened from a dream in which they had lived," members of the royalty become immortal, divine, celestial bodies. Those who are sacrificed or killed in battle are taken by the goddess Teoyaominqui to the House of the Sun, a large open space with an abundance of mesquite groves, cacti, and maguey (a plant used to make the intoxicating drink, *pulque*). They live a life of wealth, pleasure, happiness, and rejoicing at the daily appearance of the sun – though only those whose shields were pierced in battle may look upon its radiance. Babies and young children live in happiness, peace, and contentment in the House of the Sun. They are cared for by "the older sister of the gods," Chicomecoatl. Women who die in childbirth enter this realm through the horizon, escorting the sun in a litter made of quetzal feathers to the dwellers of the afterlife realm, Mictlan. They then carry the sun into the underworld, and the dead arise. After four years in the House of the Sun, the deceased become birds or butterflies and live off the nectar of flowers. In an apparent reference to reincarnation, the deceased will "once again blossom on earth." It is also said that souls go to nourish the sun.

Those who drown, are struck by lightning, or die of particular illnesses go to Tlalocan, the realm of Tlaloc, who is described as being "bluish green," spotted with soot, and wearing a feathered crown and jade necklace. He is assisted by *tlaloques*, priests who have long, disheveled hair. Tlalocan is a place of riches and abundance, with plentiful maize, squash, chilies, amaranth, and other local produce. It is "eternal spring, never is there withering, forever there is sprouting," and the deceased lives in Tlaloc's "house of the quetzal plumes." Despite it being in the sky, souls are "submerged" into Tlalocan.

The morally good and the prematurely dead become "as precious green stones and dwell in the realm of Tonacatecutli, Lord of Our Flesh." It is a realm of gardens, and flowers full of nectar to feed upon beneath a sacred tree.

Everyone else goes north to Mictlan, sometimes referred to as Ximoayan, "Place of the Fleshless" (an epithet also used for Tlalocan). The journey takes four years through the "nine places" of the underworld, which are simultaneously also one place. A small yellow dog leads souls across nine rivers – dogs of any other color will refuse. Trees, sand, and cacti are blown about by strong winds. A person's diet is determined by what they ate on Earth: those who ate tamales must eat foul-smelling underworld equivalents stuffed with beetles; those who ate black bean stew must eat hearts. In a reversal of the earthly order, whatever is not eaten on Earth is eaten in Mictlan, including "poisonous herbs" and "prickly poppies." Those who wasted grain on Earth will have their eyes torn out. The Lord of Mictlan, Mictlantecuhtli, is described as "unsatiated, thirsting there for us, panting..."; though he is also referred to as "our mother, our father" who gives souls all their funerary offerings: pipes, incense, wooden figurines, clothes, and so on. After four years, the deceased proceeds "to the nine places of the dead, where lay a broad river."

The earliest Mesoamerican text with afterlife descriptions also features a journey to the otherworld. It is a Maya mythological-historical work called the *Popol Vuh* (*Book of the Community*) (Tedlock 1996). Though not fully recorded until c. 1701-03 by Spanish missionary Francísco Ximénez, the text originates as far back as 300 BCE. It describes how the Hero Twins 1-Hunahpu (a fertility god) and 7-Hunahpu are led by owl messengers to the underworld realm of Xibalba. It lies "beyond the visible sky" and is reached by descending a path over the intersection of Rustling Canyon and Gurgling Canyon, across Blood River, Pus River, and rapids filled with scorpions (the constellation Scorpius). At a crossroads of four different colored paths (red, white, yellow, and black), the black one leads to the "council place" of Xibalba.

The Lords of Xibalba are eager for conflict, "not really divine," "ancient evil . . . makers of enemies," "inciters to wrongs and violence," and "masters of stupidity" and confusion. They repeatedly trick the Twins in a series of tests, and different perils are described, including being sent to the Dark House, Jaguar House, Bat House, and Razor House. Other dangerous underworld entities include Scab Stripper, Blood Gatherer, the staff bearers Bone Sceptre and Skull Sceptre, and the demons of Pus, Jaundice, Filth, and Woe.

The underworld is a place of transformation and renewal, as demonstrated by the Twins becoming one person and merging into a melon tree. As they tell Blood Moon, the virgin daughter of Blood Gatherer, in death "one does not disappear, but goes on being fulfilled . . . you will not die." When Blood Moon relays this message to the Twins' mother on Earth, she says the Twins are not dead but "have merely made a way for the light to show itself."

Made pregnant by the tree's saliva, Blood Moon gives birth to another set of divine twins, Hunahpu and Xblanque, who repeat the underworld journey of their forebears. They, however, outwit the Lords of Xibalba, indicating attainment of knowledge and wisdom in the underworld. After being burned to death in an oven, they return to life with divine and transformative powers, and the ability to work miracles including their own repeated death-and-rebirth. Their feats are accomplished "only through wonders, only through self-transformation." Though they kill the Lords of Xibalba, the Twins show mercy on the other gods, on the condition that they no longer live on human sacrifices – with the exception of "worthless" beings, such as "the guilty, the violent," and "the wretched, the afflicted." Afterlife fates thus became determined by conditions and behavior on Earth. The Twins ultimately ascended into the heavens and became stars.

The Twins were protectors of the sun, which is associated with rebirth in the afterlife through underworld descent and celestial ascent. There are also references in the text to the cycle of Venus, which was seen as the "sun-carrier" and a symbol of rebirth. As a fertility god, 1-Hunahpu's death and resurrection also reflects the agricultural cycle (Coe 1989). The afterlife journey is thus one of transformation, rebirth, and renewal, paralleled by the cycles of nature and the cosmos. The Twins state of stellar divinity is brought about by their afterlife journey, death, spiritual transcendence, and rebirth.

The association of heavenly realms and deities with their underworld counterparts, and of creation and rebirth with death, reveals a theme of the reconciliation of opposites. Xibalba and Mictlan are realms of both positive and negative experiences (though the latter is less desirable than Tlalocan or Tamoanchan). Maya judgement is indicated by the Council of Xibalba, and the various obstacles and perils. Aztec judgement was largely pre-mortem, with one's fate determined by social position or mode of death. The latter is decided by the gods based upon one's moral behavior, purity, and valor – thus ensuring that everyone gets the afterlife they deserve (López Austin 1988).

Common thematic afterlife features that persisted over time and across the Mesoamerican cultures include the association of the circuit of the sun and Venus with the ascent and descent of the soul, fertility and agricultural parallels in rebirth themes, life emerging from realms of the dead, meeting ancestors and divinities, interrogation and perils, a reliance on knowledge or wisdom to negotiate the otherworld, and multiple transformational and divinizing experiences.

Understanding Afterlife Conceptions Across Cultures

Despite innumerable differences, on a thematic level all traditions reviewed here include descriptions of leaving the body and existing in non-physical or quasi-physical form, journeys to other realms seen as a return to the origin-point or "home," experiences of both darkness and light, meeting deceased relatives, judgement or evaluation of one's earthly conduct, an afterlife fate determined by the outcome, encounters with deities and other beings associated with light, obstacles or barriers, divinization or the association/union of the self with the divine or Ultimate Reality, and a preoccupation with the reconciliation of opposites suggesting transcendence. The notion of an encounter with one's own corpse leading to the realization of survival after death was also common.

These are also some of the most commonly reported elements of NDE reports. This suggests that people across cultures may have been familiar with the phenomenon and that it influenced their afterlife beliefs – filtered, of course, through layers of culture, language, and individuality. The very existence of the cross-cultural similarities indicates that the experience preceded conception. To argue the reverse does not explain how a set of thematically similar ideas could be independently invented, or how it could influence/create spontaneous, unsought NDEs.

Nevertheless, the myriad cross-cultural differences show that NDEs cannot have been solely responsible for the afterlife beliefs in any of these civilizations. When seeking to explain afterlife beliefs in general within any tradition, they are best understood through a consideration of multiple culture-specific and cross-culturally relevant interdisciplinary factors, including social and political, environmental, ritual, psychological, neurophysiological, individual, and, crucially, experiential.

This chapter can only scratch the surface of my detailed comparisons and analyses of afterlife beliefs in these diverse ancient civilizations. Despite focusing on NDEs as a likely common denominator, I have sought to give a taste of how these beliefs differ as well as how they correspond to each other. Readers interested in exploring the details in greater depth, along with learning more about alternative hypotheses and the attempts to integrate them in a single over-arching theory, are directed to my book *Conceptions of the Afterlife in Early Civilizations*.

4

SHAMANISM AND NEAR-DEATH EXPERIENCES IN THE INDIGENOUS TRADITIONS OF OCEANIA

~

In this chapter, I explore the place of NDEs in the indigenous societies of Polynesia, Micronesia, Melanesia, and Australia. Rather than culture, ancestry, or history, the divisions between these four regions are based on geography. Only Australia and Polynesia can be considered actual cultural or ethnic categories. In Melanesia there are hundreds of ethnicities, and in Micronesia at least half a dozen (Oliver 2002: 2).

While the previous chapter was somewhat constrained by the scant evidence for NDEs, and therefore partly speculative, a comparative wealth of NDEs from Oceania allows for a very different approach. Rather than looking at evidence for NDEs across those ancient civilizations, we are here looking at the various ways that NDEs were received in different societies. It should be noted that prior to my research, only a very few NDEs from these regions had been documented in near-death studies, and most were from the late 20th century.

Despite cultural and ethnic variation across the Pacific regions, there are some pan-regional similarities of afterlife beliefs, including that the soul could temporarily leave the body during illness or through shamanic practices. It was also understood that apparently dead individuals might be in a trance from which they could awaken. It was commonly accepted that at death souls left the body, remained for a time near the corpse, then traveled to another place via the rising or setting sun or through caves, holes, or volcanoes. They encountered various guardians, gatekeepers, interrogators, and judges on the journey, and underwent ordeals or tests. The next world was situated on a distant island or mountain, in the sky, or under a lake or the ocean. Admission was determined by rank, wealth, virtue, mode of death, or proper funerary rites. Social status was maintained in the otherworld, though in some cases the unworthy went to less favorable realms or were annihilated (Moss 1925: 9, 112, 118-31).

Spirits could continue to influence the living in both helpful and harmful ways, either from the other world or as ghosts on Earth. The notion of ultimately merging "into an undifferentiated company of 'ancestors' or some even more inclusive category of spirit beings" (Oliver 1989: 771) was also widely attested. Less common were beliefs in reincarnation and that the soul died with the body, and in many cases there was simply little interest in afterlife speculations (Oliver 1989: 132-133, 153).

While concerns in the previous chapter about cultural contact and independent development are less relevant here, we must still consider whether the accounts genuinely reflect purely indigenous beliefs, or if they were significantly influenced by foreign religions through missionary activity. While the primary conversion religion of Oceania is Christianity, it was relatively slow to take root, beginning as late as the mid-20th century in some regions (Ernst & Anisi 2016: 591). In undertaking this exploration, I conducted an exhaustive search of the relevant primary sources: accounts of early missionaries, explorers, and ethnographers from the mid-19th to mid-20th centuries. While I focused on those written prior to wide-scale conversion, some clearly show Christian influence as will be seen. Indeed, the role of NDEs in response to colonial and religious threats is itself a fascinating dimension of these accounts.

Given the religious and political contexts of the missionary and explorer accounts, they are sometimes marred by attendant agendas and ethnocentricities. Such biases do not, however, always indicate inadequate reporting, and indeed many of the descriptions found in these sources were later confirmed by qualified anthropologists. The fact that these accounts attest to knowledge of NDEs well over a century before the phenomenon was popularized in the West also indicates a degree of reliability.

Many of the NDEs I found in my search are presented below in summary overviews, and placed in the context of the societies' afterlife beliefs and shamanic activity. They are organized by region, then followed by a comparison of how NDEs were received across the different cultures.

Polynesia

Polynesian "song and myth delight in recounting the adventures of those who have visited spirit-world" (Gill 1877: 3). Such visits were said to bring new knowledge and transformation, from the restoration of sight in the blind to the discovery of fire (Williamson 1933: II, 190-195, 200, 205).

In Hawaii, information about the afterlife originated with people "who have been brought back to life from the dead" (Keauokalini 1860: 48). Accounts of their NDEs were elaborated upon over time and accepted as divine teachings (Jarves 1843: 42-43). NDEs could occur when helpful ancestor spirits "bring back the spirit and restore life to the body":

> Many people who had died and come to life again ... even some people of this age, who have swooned or perhaps lain dead for a few hours or half a day, have related their [afterlife] experiences. ... The reason they were believed in was because so many had died and come to life again and had told innumerable stories about these places (Kamakau 1866-71: 47-49)

The last king of the Kingdom of Hawai'i, David Kalakaua (1888: 39), wrote that Po, the underworld, "could be visited by favored mortals, and the dead were sometimes brought back from it to earth."

American missionaries noted that "various accounts have appeared in print ... of the adventures of spirits, who after a protracted stay among the spirits of the dead, have been forced back into their bodies to resume active life among the living" (Emerson 1902: 13-14). Missionaries also cited beliefs that souls could be "driven back into the body by other ghosts, or persuaded to come back through offerings or incantations given by living friends, so that a dead person could become alive again"

(Westervelt 1915: 248). In his exhaustive survey, James Frazer (1922: 428-429) confirmed that "when persons recovered from a death-like swoon, it was supposed that their souls had gone to the underworld and been sent back to earth by Milu" the god of the underworld, or by a family's guardian deity. Food was often left near bodies in case the soul returned, and graves were not prepared until it was certain that it would not (Green & Beckwith 1926: 181).

In an account from Kuala (Hawai'i) reported by German ethnologist Adolf Bastian in 1833, a man died but revived after eight days. He told his family that he had been to a pleasant realm of light and abundance, ruled by Milu who chose the souls of the most beautiful women for his wives. Souls of the dead retained the bodily conditions they had at death, even the old and the sick (Frazer 1922: 428-429).

A more detailed 19th century NDE is that of a Kona woman named Kalima (Haley 1892: 83-85). As her family and friends mourned at her funeral, near her "rigid form and ashen face," Kalima suddenly breathed and opened her eyes. After recovering, she recounted her experience:

> I died, as you know. I seemed to leave my body and stand beside it, looking down on what was me. The me that was standing there looked like the form I was looking at, only, I was alive and the other was dead. I gazed at my body for a few minutes, then turned and walked away. I left the house and village, and walked on and on to the next village, and there I found crowds of people ...

Though this was apparently an earthly village, it was much larger than the one she knew, with many houses and people of all ages.

> Some of them I knew and they spoke to me, – although that seemed strange, for I knew they were dead,—but nearly all were strangers. They were all so happy! They seemed not to have a care; nothing to trouble them. Joy was in every face, and happy laughter and bright, loving words were on every tongue.

Kalima passed through more villages, meeting people she had known in life. She "felt so full of joy, too, that my heart sang within me, and I was glad to be dead." Feeling "happier every minute," she proceeded to a large village near Pele's volcano – a barren area in earthly reality. She was greeted cheerfully but told, "You must go back to your body. You are not to die yet."

> I did not want to go back. I begged and prayed to be allowed to stay with them, but they said, "No, you must go back; and if you do not go willingly, we will make you go."

Kalima wept and resisted but was ultimately forced to return the way she had come. The people in the villages turned against her and drove her back to her lifeless body.

> I looked at it and hated it. Was that my body? What a horrid, loathsome thing it was to me now, since I had seen so many beautiful, happy creatures! Must I go and live in that thing again?

She refused to re-enter the body, so the spirits pushed her "head foremost into the big toe." Her "body came to life again, and I opened my eyes." According to Mrs. E. N. Haley (1892: 83-85; Kellehear 2001) who reported the NDE, Kalima never varied her account "and never ceased to regret coming back to her body" and being forced to leave the joy she had experienced in the otherworld. According to beliefs on Oahu, when a body grows cold during a near-death state, "it becomes difficult to force the reluctant spirit to reenter," and a shaman would coax it under the nail of the big toe (Emerson 1902: 13-14).

In a narrative from Maui (Westervelt 1915: 100-107), a man named Ka-ilio-hae died from an illness but revived and "told his family all about his wonderful journey to the land of ghosts." His soul left his body through his left eye, and looking back, the body appeared like a great mountain with eyes like dark caves. Suddenly afraid, Ka-ilio-hae went to the rooftop but was disturbed by the sound of people mourning him, so he flew away towards the spirit world. His deceased sister met him at the entrance and took him to her house, but warned him not to enter or eat anything if he hoped to return to Earth. They proceeded to "the place of whirlwinds" – a hill where spirits danced and played – then to Walia, "the high chief of ghosts." After successfully clearing obstacles intended to test one's religious knowledge and devotion, they finally met Walia. Ka-ilio-hae recounted to Walia the history of his people and was then told that he must "go back and enter his body and tell his people about troubles near at hand," or else be thrown to Milu. A beautiful woman gave Ka-ilio-hae directions home, and although he was reluctant to leave, his sister forced him, for she had "the power of sometimes turning a ghost back to its body again." When he saw his body he felt "very much afraid" and was repulsed by the smell. He tried to escape, but his sister pushed him in through the foot.

In a 19th century legend from Oahu (Rice 1923: 126-132), a farmer named Makua was swallowed by a fish and taken to the land of the deity, Kane. Two deities explained to him that if he successfully completed a series of trials, he could remain in that beautiful realm of joy and abundance and become a god himself. If he failed, he would return to Earth as "a messenger and will tell to men the beauties of this land." After meeting his deceased family members, he ultimately failed a test by weeping when he thought his spirit wife had drowned.

> Suddenly a very dazzling light shone. ... Makua saw that the heavens were open and he beheld two bodies clothed in light and accompanied by many spirits arrayed in glorious raiment, but with sorrowful countenances. The spirits spoke, saying, "Dust to dust," and then the doors of the heavens closed.

Makua wandered through the woods to the seashore where the giant fish took him home, and he told his people what had happened to him.

Legends such as those of Ka-ilio-hae and Makua seem to be midway between actual NDEs and myths, suggesting a stage in the mythologizing process. Such accounts involved culture-heroes from the distant past rather than recent individuals. In contrast, the historicity of Kalima is not in doubt, and her narrative is more consistent with NDEs from other parts of the world.

Hawaiian afterlife beliefs sometimes had shamanic origins. People of Ka'awaloa village, for example, knew about the otherworld from the dreams and visions of shamans. Echoing NDEs, these beliefs included meeting deceased relatives and a being of light, and traveling to a heavenly realm before returning to Earth to watch over their people (Ellis 1823: 107).

There are also numerous examples of "Orpheus"-type myths. In the midst of intense mourning, the protagonist travels to the other world in order to retrieve a recently deceased loved one and bring them back to Earth – and thus back to life (e.g., Emerson 1902: 66-68, 712-714; Fornander 1918-19: 188; Kamakau 1866–71: 51-52). These myths recall the shamanic practice of soul-retrieval– traveling to the otherworld to rescue a soul in danger of death. Some have overt shamanic contexts, involving shamans assisting the mourning individuals on their mission. In one example, a shaman told Hiku how to retrieve his deceased wife

Kawelu. Hiku descended to the underworld on a vine, but when he found Kawelu she was reluctant to return with him because of his bad smell. Though she eventually agreed, when they returned to Earth she refused to enter her body because it had begun to decay. Hiku eventually succeeded in coaxing her back in and restoring her to life (Fornander 1918-19: 186ff).

In the Society Islands, people who were believed to be dead sometimes revived, "and after returning to consciousness confirmed the statements about the Po, which they believed they had seen." In one example, a man named Pupu-te-tipa "was once taken bodily by the gods down into the Po and kept several days, but at last for the sake of his family was released and returned home" (Henry & Orsmond 1928: 202).

In a mid-19th century NDE from Raiatea, a woman named Terematai revived after days of unconsciousness, claiming that she had "been to heaven" where she saw both Raiateans and Europeans she recognized. She concluded, "I wished to remain but God sent me back to exhort my family that they may be saved." She was described as being "in a very happy state of mind and appeared wholly absorbed in spiritual subjects" (Gunson 1962: 218).

Another mid-19th century NDE, from the island of Huahine, involved an elderly queen who "visited the other world" while in a cataleptic trance. When she revived, "she told her friends that, when there, she glided about among numerous people whom she had formerly known." They communicated with her telepathically and could pass through each other in a "bodiless state." The queen returned to Earth, for "by order of a spirit she had to enter again into her body, though it was in a state of corruption" (Williamson 1933: I, 373).

Robert Louis Stevenson (1891: 215-216) recounted the legend of a princess who died and went to Raiatea, where a spirit forced her to climb trees and collect coconuts for him. She was discovered by a spirit-relative who took her back to Tahiti "where she found her body still waked, but already swollen with the approaches of corruption." When she saw the horrifying sight, she prayed to remain dead, though the spirit compelled her to enter via "the least dignified of entrances, and her startled family beheld the body move."

Towards the end of the 19th century, "the last queen of Tahiti" returned to her body "many days" after her death. Upon revival, she described "the departure of her soul through the air to Paradise and ... its subsequent unwilling return to its putrefying body in obedience to the command of a chief who appeared to reign in the world of happy souls that she had gone to." The chief forced her to return in order to facilitate his own forthcoming reincarnation, by becoming her lover. He instructed her not to convert to Christianity, and when she was forced to do so by some authority, the chief was unable to complete his reincarnation (Handy 1927: 85-86).

Tahitian afterlife beliefs also incorporated knowledge of NDEs. Three days after leaving the body some souls would land on the Stone of Life, and the deity Tu-ta-horoa "would under certain conditions tell it to return to its body to remain a while longer in this life." Those who landed on the Stone of Death proceeded to a spirit realm, and the body on Earth died. NDEs are also evident in Tahitian Orpheus myths, such as that of the deceased moon goddess, Hina. Her husband, Tafa'i, attempted to catch her at "the last place whence spirits could be recalled to this world." Though Hina was reluctant to return, Tafa'i succeeded in bringing her back to Earth where she "re-entered her body, which was still well-preserved, and opened her mortal eyes," to the joy of her people (Henry & Orsmond 1928: 63-564).

On the Cook Islands it was believed that souls of the dead sometimes met friendly spirits who told them, "Go back and live" and sent them back to "re-inhabit the once-forsaken body" (Gill 1876: 160-161, 221-224). A number of myths and legends also had NDE contexts and themes. In a Rarotonga example, a woman named Akimano had such an intense sexual experience "that her spirit departed from her body and went up to the god Tiki." When Tiki learned of her cause of death, he refused her entrance to his realm, telling her, "There is no place here for those who have died that death." He made her return to Earth, and "the spirit of the woman returned again to its body and so came to life again." An Aitutaki myth told of a man named Tekauae who traveled to the underworld while near death. After avoiding eating a bowl of live centipedes, he was sent back to Earth by the goddess Miru. Though she instructed Tekauae never to speak of what he had experienced, when he reentered his body and returned to life he told his friends what to expect in the other world (Savage 1916: 145-146, 173-175).

According to a report from 1874, on Tuamotu island (Fangatau) it was believed that souls could leave the body during illness and travel to the otherworld. At the entrance they met the deity Tama "who tried to send them back to their bodies. If they persisted in going on, they found themselves definitely separated from their bodies" and had to remain in the otherworld (Williamson 1933: II, 81).

A Marquesan myth from Fatuhiva also parallels NDEs. When two deities took Taa-po as their wife, she died and her soul traveled to the spirit-world. The deities decided to send her back to Earth where she "entered into her body," revived, and told her joyful relatives of her experiences in the spirit world. When a chief questioned her story, Taa-po insisted that she had died but clarified that she was taken only "to the threshold" of the otherworld. In another narrative, a deified shaman took Tiki-tu-ao to the sky-realm where he saw his brother-in-law who was undergoing an out-of-body journey while chanting in a ceremony on Earth. The encounter was premonitory, for the brother-in-law was killed soon after Tiki-tu-ao returned to Earth (Handy 1930: 82-84, 133-134, 137).

Samoans believed that if the soul of a recently dead person struck a certain tree in the underworld, it "went back at once to its body" (Turner, 1884, pp. 258-259). Samoan afterlife beliefs were "confirmed by ... accounts of men going to the other world and returning again to this one." The soul was conceived as an immaterial duplicate of the body which could temporarily separate from it during unconsciousness (Brown, 1910, pp. 219-224, 364-365). In a brief narrative from 1902, a princess died, but her soul returned to her body after a visit to "the ninefold heaven" (Beckwith 1940: 150).

Narratives of individuals visiting the underworld realm of Pulotu were "fairly common" in Tonga. In one myth, Tui Hattala instructed his people not to bury his body. He then traveled in spirit form to Pulotu and met the deity Hikuleo, who told him that he must return to Earth because he had visited Pulotu before his death. When Tui Hattala did so, however, he discovered that, against his instructions, his body had been buried, and he thus had to remain in spirit form (Gifford 1924: 153-155).

In New Zealand, the Maori believed that souls of the dead crossed the underworld river on a plank. A deity either assisted them or drove them back to their bodies "in order that he may take care of the family he has left behind" (Taylor 1855: 104-105). The writer and politician Edward Tregear cited beliefs that "in illness the soul journeys away and is sometimes on the brink of crossing to Hades, but returns" (1890: 118-119). He concluded that narratives about the otherworld originated in "the dreams of people in trance through illness." Similarly, the ethnographer Elsdon Best (1905: 231-232) wrote that Maori afterlife beliefs were "the result of persons dreaming of having descended to the underworld ... A person recovering from a trance would be said by the Maori to have returned from the spirit-world."

The Maori also believed that the living could travel temporarily to the spirit world of Reigna by leaping off a precipice called Te Rerenga Wairua (Dieffenbach 1843: 66-67). It "often" happened "that persons who have died, and actually descended this precipice, have returned again to earth to relate what they had seen below, and lived for many years afterwards" (Shortland 1856: 150). There were "many stories of persons who have descended into the Reigna and returned" (Taylor 1855: 105-106). According to shamans, when souls arrived at Te Rerenga Wairua they were questioned about their identity and occupation on Earth. The soul "replied by giving a history of its life" (a life review) before proceeding to a river crossing. Some were refused passage, however, and were "sent back to life." Such beliefs explained recoveries "from insensibility caused by a blow, or fit, or trance" (White 1891: 145-146). A recently deceased person could also return to life when his or her soul was sent back from the netherworld "by its relatives, for the purpose of caring for its children" (Goldie 1904: 20).

One Maori man recounted the NDE of his aunt, who revived a day or two after her death and told of her out-of-body journey to Te Rerenga Wairua. She descended on a vine, and an old man ferried her across a river, then led her to her family. Her father instructed her to "go back to earth, for there is no one now to take care of my grandchild." He warned her not to eat anything in Reigna, ferried her back across the river, and told her to hurry. As she struggled up the precipice "two infant spirits" tried to drag her back, but when she threw sweet potatoes they leapt after them. She then "flew back to the place where she had left her body," revived, and realized "that she had really died, and had returned to life." "Those who listened to her tale believed firmly the truth of her adventures" (Shortland 1856: 150-155).

The NDE of Te Atarahi was reported by various scholars and missionaries (Shortland 1882: 45; Taylor 1855: 104–105; Tregear 1890: 118–119), demonstrating consistency and lasting importance over time. Te Atarahi died and travelled to Reigna where he met deceased relatives who told him not to eat anything. They sent him back to Earth five days later, and when he returned to his body he described his visit to the wonderful otherworld.

In a rare shared-death experience (see Moody 2010), two men died, revived, and told of how their souls had descended a cliff then climbed over a wall to the spirit land – "a very good sort of place" similar to Earth. They found their people, including their parents who sent them back to their bodies (Best 1905: 231). In a brief account, a woman was "carried off by spirits ... and she saw the spirits of all the dead-and-gone people" then returned to life (Best 1900: 232).

An early 1960s Maori NDE should also be noted. A woman named Nga revived as her body was being taken for burial. She described an OBE in which she hovered above her head before exiting the room and proceeding to Te Rerenga Wairua. After bathing in a spring, she prepared to slide down to the underworld on a root of a tree, but a voice stopped her, asking her identity and her purpose there. She replied that she sought her "old people," but the voice told her, "They don't want you yet. Eat nothing and go back where you came from until they are ready. Then I shall send for you." She obeyed and returned to her body (King 1985: 87-88; cf. Kellehear, 2001; Tassell-Matamua 2013: 113).

Maori afterlife myths also featured NDE and shamanic journey elements. One told of how the deity Tane followed his daughter to the underworld hoping to bring her back, though she told him to return to Earth in order to raise their children. In another version, the woman was sent back from the underworld after being questioned by the "daughter of the light" (Taylor 1855: 131-132, 146).

Micronesia

Evidence for knowledge of NDEs in Micronesia is scant. While this could be due in part to the fact that the islands saw far less extensive fieldwork than did other parts of Oceania (Dobbin & Hezel 2011: 13), the pattern is far too evident for this to be a full explanation. Indeed, the less I was able to find relevant material, the more intensely I searched.

On Waqab (Yap) in the Caroline Islands it was believed that during illness the soul was trying to escape and that it "may or may not be enticed to return." Epileptic seizures were thought to result when a returning soul collided with the body after wandering on the winds (Furness 1910: 147-151).

Though there were occasional myths involving otherworld journeys (see Frazer 1924: 196-197, 201-202), they lack near-death or even OBE contexts and share little with NDE phenomenology. A Palau Islands myth concerns the goddess Milad returning from the dead, though it lacks details of any otherworld experience (Parmentier 1987: 159).

Notable exceptions are the late 20th century NDEs of three Chamorra women in Guam. Though the Chamorro are primarily Catholic and have had long-term influence from Spain, the Philippines, and Mexico (Dobbin & Hezel 2011: 12), the NDEs feature some elements typical of small-scale societies, such as walking along a road and spirit journeys to Earthly locales. Rather than islands or volcanoes, however, the NDErs visited family members in the United States. Additional elements include a paradisiacal realm, deceased relatives, encountering a spiritual entity, being told to return (one on the grounds of mistaken identity, another being "not ready to enter"), and reluctance to return (Green 1984).

Melanesia

Various Melanesian religious movements had foundations in NDE-like accounts. In a New Guinea legend recorded in 1854, Manarmakeri followed a pig to a beautiful otherworld village where people sang and danced in the prime of youth. Manarmakeri wanted to stay, but a voice told him that his "time has not come yet" because he was "still in the husk." After returning to Earth he fell into a listless depression, though he ultimately became a religious leader, preaching resurrection, immortality, non-violence, and a return to a golden age state called Koreri. The narrative was considered historical fact and became the basis for further religious movements.

In 1932, a Wandamen man was found alive three days after drowning. He described his visit to the underworld where he met the dead, then became a medium, a prophet, and the founder of the Sade Koreri movement (Kamma 1954: 23-26, 40, 65, 76-77, 278-279). Likewise, a man who was killed by a snake returned to life with new "magico-medical curative techniques" and founded the Baigona movement (Worsley 1968: 54).

In 1919 at Orokolo Bay, a man named Ua Halai was dying from an illness. He instructed his people not to dig his grave and not to approach his body too closely but, rather, to "wait and see what they would see." Though the people claimed that "Ua Halai was so 'dead' that the rats had gnawed his ears," he revived after three days and claimed that he had been to the other world where he was given moral strictures against theft and adultery. He became a leader of the so-called "Vailala Madness" religious movement and built temples for spirit mediumship (Williams 1934: 374-375).

In 1935 in the Markham Valley, a man named Marafi founded an apocalyptic, anti-mission movement after claiming that Satan "had taken him into the bowels of the earth, where he had seen the spirits of the dead who dwelt there." Marafi taught that Satan would allow spirits to return to Earth if the people accepted him as "the Supreme Being."

On Karkar Island in 1949, a local cult was reinvigorated following the NDE of the prophet Kaum. He claimed that he had been killed and had gone to Heaven where he met God, saw deceased ancestors "making Cargo," and was given a new ritual symbol. On Buka Island around 1932, a prophet named Pako returned from the dead after being hanged. Another prophet of his cult was "said to have gone to Heaven where Saint Peter told him that people were to go to church regularly, to abandon their old dances and rituals, and to levy tolls and demand higher wages from the Whites." The Fijian Tuka cult was founded by a man named Kelevi who "claimed to have visited Heaven and to have supernatural powers" (Worsley 1968: 30, 101-102, 115, 118, 215).

NDEs were also known from other areas. On Biak island, a dying man "dreamt of a golden ladder which took him up to the heavenly house" (Codrington 1891: 102). Biak myths of "the resuscitation of dead persons through the love of their relatives" were intended as explanations of local afterlife beliefs (Kamma 1954: 73-75).

On the Tami Islands, information about the afterlife was obtained by women who could "go down alive into the netherworld and prosecute their enquiries at first hand among the ghosts" (Frazer 1913: 291-292). On Misima Island, it was "not uncommon" for the souls of "living men and women to journey to Hiyoyoa [the otherworld] and return to this world." Most people "fully believed in the truthfulness of those who asserted that they had."

A man named Tokeri visited Hiyoyoa and obtained prophetic information about an impending tsunami. Another man, Wakuri, traveled there many times through the use of a certain "medicine." He even claimed to have a wife and child there, though he never ate anything, for doing so would make him unable to return to Earth. In contrast, on the island of Tubetube, a man named Maritaiyedi claimed that despite having dined with the spirits he was able to return from his numerous visits to the Earthly otherworld of Beswebo.

In northern Massim, various people claimed to have visited an idealized Earth-like afterlife realm beneath the island of Tuma. During an illness, the soul of a man named Marogus went there and met the deity Topileta "who ultimately sent him back to the upper world." In a legend of the Koita people of Port Moresby, a man died and returned to his body, though it had already begun to decay. His wife refused to wash him, and had she done so, other souls would be able to return to their bodies after death (Seligman 1910: 189-191, 654-657, 733-734).

Many Kiwai narratives concern people who visited the otherworld of Adiri and returned (Landtman 1912: 71–2). A woman named Amara died from an illness "and subsequently returned to life." She described having traveled on a road and through clashing iron bars to a realm of abundance. She met other spirits, including her deceased husband who asked the "big man" of Adiri if Amara could stay. She was allowed one day of dancing and festivities before being told that her time on Earth was not yet finished and that she must return. Her husband warned her not to eat anything, then gave her a shove which propelled her back into her body. She surprised the mourners when she revived, for she had been dead a long time. She told them about life in Adiri and "kept on telling" them.

A man named Asai likewise "died, returned to life and told his fellow villagers about Adiri." He traveled there by canoe and was greeted by his father and friends, who were dancing, singing, and drumming. Asai enjoyed it so much that he decided he wanted to stay. Sido, the first man to die, offered him a wife, but Asai was so taken with his surroundings that he ignored her, and Sido kicked him back into his body. When Asai awoke, his mourners told him that he had been dead since the previous day. In a related narrative, Asai died and his spirit traveled westward, but he decided to return to his body when he thought of his wife and child. Before doing so, he made a mark on a tree so he could later prove his story. He told his people that he had not seen any other spirits and that he did not know what happens when someone dies. They concluded that Asai had only traveled on the path towards Adiri and not to the realm itself. Because Asai now knew the road, he was no longer afraid of death.

When a man named Duobe was injured in an accident, his spirit went to the otherworld where he met "dead people who were making a garden." Seeing that he was not dead, they asked him why he was there, and Duobe replied that he only wanted to look at them. His NDE then assumed distressing features: A half-human/half-pig asked if he wanted to look like him, and when Duobe replied that he did not, the man's pig nose fell off exposing a bare skull beneath. Duobe fled home in a canoe before the man could kill him. "Just as his spirit was entering his body he woke up shrieking," terrifying his wife. He said he had been to "devil-place" (Landtmann 1917: 170–171).

In another Kiwai legend, a man named Ânai fell through a hole at his brother's grave. After four days they reappeared together and told of how they had been to the land of the dead, which was similar to Earth but more populous. They brought back new medicines, a yam, and various agricultural techniques. One of the brothers said that as a result of his experience, "he would not be afraid when he was going to die." From such narratives, "some people concluded that the place of the dead was underneath the ground." In addition, there are many examples of Kiwai afterlife dreams that bear similarities to NDE accounts, as well as return-from-death narratives without descriptions of afterlife journeys, which serve to explain new rituals, beliefs, or abilities (Landtman 1912: 71-77, 187-188, 264, 343-344, 442, 569). Numerous Kiwai accounts of contact with spirits of the dead described them as radiating light (Landtman 1917: 110, 167-168, 170-172, 181-191, 306, 313, 588).

The Trobriand Islanders believed that the spirit world could be visited by the souls of "those who were almost dead, but returned to life again." These NDErs revived with new information, songs, or precognitive knowledge of the death of a family member (Malinowksi 1916: 154, 162).

The Orokaiva believed that people could "die and come to life again." When souls saw friends and relatives in mourning, they were "so affected by compassion as to return; whereupon the corpse is reanimated" (Williams 1930: 269). In the Wedau and Wamira areas it was also believed that those who died before their time were sent back to Earth (Newton 1914: 219-220).

In the Tanga Islands, people who revived from prolonged unconsciousness were "regarded as having been dead and refused admittance to the underworld." In one example, a man revived by his wife described "what he believed to be his *post mortem* emotions and experiences." He was taken by a whirlwind (implying tunnel-like sensations) to the land of the dead where he met his deceased grandmother. She told him that he was too young to remain there and "to go back to his family and his garden." Afterlife beliefs reportedly derived from such experiences (Bell 1937: 317-318, 337-338).

In a report from the Nggela Islands (Solomon Islands), a man "appeared to die, but revived to tell the story of how he had passed with others along the path of ghosts, and had come to take his place in the canoe which came for them at night." A spirit he recognized "forbad him to come aboard, and sent him back into the world again" (Codrington 1891: 256).

On Alu Island, it was believed that those who revived from illnesses had been sent back to the body following assessment in the otherworld. Shamans could undertake OBE journeys, and afterlife myths contained NDE features (Wheeler 1914: 87, 98ff, 111). On Makira, shamanic healers undertook trance-journeys to the otherworld to retrieve souls, including those who were unwilling to return (Beckwith 1940: 150).

On the Banks Islands of Vanuatu it was accepted that

at times a departed soul has come back from the *sura* [entrance to the other world] to his body; and the man has revived to tell how he was hustled out of the *sura* by the ghosts, who said there was no room for him, and he must go back.

Reports of such journeys were "by no means uncommon." Afterlife conceptions were said to have derived from them and were sometimes validated through shamanic experiences (Codrington 1881: 283). Upon arrival at *sura*, souls were asked if they were there to stay, and those who were merely unconscious were sent back to their bodies. Deceased friends or relatives would explain that "his time has not yet come; so he relates when he returns." Likewise, on Pentecost Island, when a person lost consciousness then revived "he says he was not allowed to enter" the spirit world.

On Maewo it was believed that the soul encountered "the stone of thought" on the journey to the other world. If a man "remembers there his child or his wife or anything that belongs to him, he will run back and come to life again." He will also return if he fails to clear a certain ravine. The belief that shamans could visit the otherworld in order to rescue souls was common (Codrington 1891: 208-209, 266-267, 274-275, 287; cf. Beckwith 1940: 172).

On Malekula it was believed that "the sacred men have often been on a visit [to the otherworld], and consequently know all about it" (Somerville 1894: 10). Afterlife myths in these islands often paralleled NDEs (see, for example, Codrington 1881: 283; Codrington 1891: 278, 286; Humphreys 1926: 97-98).

Soul-retrieval beliefs were also common on Fiji, as were narratives of OBE visits to the underworld (Williams 1860: 190-194). A deity named Taleya ("the Dismisser") "sifted out the real dead from the trance-smitten" and sent the latter back to life. Those who died naturally, as opposed to in battle or by drowning, were told, "go back and re-enter your body." Some refused, however, for "so gloomy and joyless is the prospect of a return to life that the Shades who are offered the privilege by Taleya do not all obey" (Thomson 1908: 125, 132).

From the Lau Islands comes a narrative that was considered "a true story of what actually happened," despite its obvious mythological character. In one relevant section, upon returning from one of his four journeys to the otherworld, a man named Tui Liku was horrified to find that a bird had been pecking at his corpse and had removed one of his eyes. "I refuse to get into that," he cried, but the deity Ligadua gave him no choice (St. Johnston 1918: 19, 44-45).

In New Britain it was believed that "when a man dies his soul goes to the spirit-land and meets his friends there, but if they do not want him at that time, they all drive him away, and so he returns to life again." In one brief reference, a man named Warulung "returned from the dead and brought messages to the people from departed spirits." Related practices included shamanic soul-retrieval as well as having dreams of accompanying souls on their afterlife journey and returning with descriptions of the spirit world. "This suggests that such practices were responsible for "certain conceptions of the afterlife" (Brown 1910: 190, 194, 398; Moss 1925: 120-21)."

Three early 1980s Kaliai NDEs should also be mentioned. Though converted to Catholicism in 1949, the Kaliai have retained many indigenous traditions—particularly funerary beliefs. In the first NDE, a man named Frank died of an illness and met deceased ancestors who directed him to a road. On the road he encountered a bearded, robed, white-skinned being of light who motioned him to turn back.

A Kaliai man named Andrew also died of an illness and returned. He described having entered darkness and then emerging into a "field of flowers" and a realm of clarity. On a road he met "a woman whose death had occurred shortly after his and about which he could have had no knowledge." Arriving at a village, he climbed a ladder up to a house. A voice told him it was not his time to die and that he should wait for someone to take him back to Earth. As children assisted him down the ladder, he realized that the house was floating and rotating in the air. Inside, people were building cars and ships—reflecting "cargo cult" beliefs associating whites and their technology with the spirit realm. Again he was told it was not his time and to wait for a return guide, but he continued along a beam of light and down a flight of steps to a forest. He was then informed that if his people had begun mourning him, he would have to stay in the other world. The beam of light led him down a path, and he found himself back in his body. He was reluctant to return for he had felt happy in the other realm.

The third Kaliai NDE similarly had common NDE elements alongside idiosyncratic features. A man named Luke described undergoing judgment on a pair of magnetic scales and then shamans meeting deceased relatives who told him to return to Earth. When a woman with bloody eyes and lolling tongue tried to stab him, he ran away and found himself back in his body (Counts 1983: 115-116, 118, 119-121).

Australia

There are a few brief Aboriginal accounts of "living people who have been to the Land of the Dead, voluntarily or otherwise." A Lower River Murray man revived on his funeral pyre, claiming to have visited the home of the culture-hero Ngurunderi. This hero was himself associated with an afterlife journey. He made a path for spirits to follow in order to join him in the Sky-world, and provided the "dazed newcomer" with a place to live and new wives (Berndt & Berndt 1964: 204, 412, 417).

A dying Gunaikurnai woman claimed "that she had gone up to the [sky-realm] in sleep, but returned because she could not get through." In a Gunaikurnai legend, a man traveled to the spirit land with the soul of his friend's gravely ill son and saw deceased relatives and friends (Howitt 1904: 434-437).

The Gunwinggu believed that when souls traveled to the spirit world, a "powerful being" knocked out their middle teeth. "If the person is really dead, there is no blood," but if the gums bled, the spirit was sent back to the body, which then revived (Berndt & Berndt 1964: 414-415).

Most Aboriginal otherworld journey accounts have shamanic rather than NDE contexts, however. In a Barkindji legend, a shaman named Barpoo visited the other world by eating a piece of the thigh of his recently deceased teacher. His "spirit flew away beyond the sky" and encountered a beautiful goddess who "showed him all the abundance of the joys prepared for his people" after death. Barpoo became a religious leader, and his people "believed he had actually visited their heaven" (Newland 1887-88: 31).

The Gunwinggu believed that shamans "can heal a sick person by following his spirit in a dream, catching it and returning it to his body" (Berndt & Berndt 1964: 258). Such experiences resulted in "a conception of the individual apart from the body, not only during life but also after death, as an immaterial, invisible being" (Howitt 1887: 52).

Interestingly, despite a general lack of NDE narratives, shamanic initiation practices were often linked conceptually with NDEs, involving "symbolic death followed by resurrection." This demonstrates a clear link between the two experience types. Initiates in trance states were mourned as if recently dead, and during "ecstatic experiences" would undertake "ascents to heaven and descents to the subterranean world." They returned transformed and "reborn," with new knowledge or abilities received from the "supernatural beings" they encountered (Eliade 1973: 130, 144-145).

At Port Stephens, shamanic initiates were "killed" in a fire, then emerged as "a new personality" who could travel to the sky-world in dreams, retrieve souls, and practice sorcery. At Ooldea, initiates were mourned while in trance, and their bones were broken. After conversing with spirits, they were reborn with supernatural powers. Initiates of the Djerag and Djaru peoples were "killed" by the rainbow-serpent, causing an illness and madness that enabled them to ascend to the sky and visit the dead (Elkin 1945: 91-92, 112-114, 138). Aranda initiates traveled to the other world by being "killed" in a sacred cave by spirits, who replaced their internal organs and inserted healing stones into their bodies. When the initiate "comes to life again" he "dwells upon his experiences" for a year while learning the shamanic craft (Howitt 1904: 391-392).

Comparing Cultural Dynamics in the Reception of NDEs

Claims that afterlife beliefs originated in NDEs are found in many accounts from both Polynesia and Melanesia. Further beliefs that attest to knowledge of NDEs were widespread, especially that individuals who returned from apparent death had been sent back by beings in the otherworld. It can therefore be no coincidence that afterlife beliefs in these regions largely correspond to NDEs on general, thematic levels. The interaction of beliefs with experiences, alongside widespread knowledge of NDEs, also correlates with a greater number of afterlife journey myths.

Beliefs in OBE visits to the otherworld in non-death contexts, such as dreams, trance, and shamanic soul-retrieval were also found in both areas. Although detailed examples of shamanic experiences were scarce, quite a few narratives have shamanic themes or contexts, demonstrating a clear association of shamanic and near-death experiences. All of these data indicate among Polynesian and Melanesian peoples a general receptivity to NDEs together with a high level of interest in afterlife-related phenomena. Indeed, possession, trance mediumship, and deathbed visions are also known from both regions. Yet, whereas

Polynesian societies focused more acutely on otherworld journey experiences and myths, Melanesian societies seemed more open to all forms of spiritual experiences and had an intense interest in the afterlife overall.

There is only a single marginal example of a relevant Polynesian new religious movement, and it is of a more shamanic character. It was founded after a Hawaiian woman named Kahapuu – who was "subject to visions and trances" – visited a heavenly realm during a trance state and returned with Christian teachings. A greater number are found in Melanesia, including the Vailala, Tuka, Koreri, and Baigona. Such movements were legitimized, promoted, and sustained through their leaders' additional visits to the otherworld, as well as through other kinds of visions, dreams, and prophecies (Worsley 1968: 20ff, 69ff, 103-104).

As will become clear when we compare these regions with Micronesia and Australia, funerary rituals are an important factor in understanding the relationships between NDEs and afterlife beliefs. In both Polynesia and Melanesia, they explicitly allowed for the possibility of the soul returning to the body. In other words, the eventuality of NDEs occurring was built into the ritual and belief system surrounding death and the afterlife. In Hawaii especially, great care was taken to avoid premature burial, with bodies being checked periodically for a heartbeat for a number of days prior to interment (Green & Beckwith 1926: 177). Practices were similar on Tahiti, and much effort was expended in keeping alive those in danger of death (Oliver 1974: 488, 496). Maori burial was performed a minimum of three days after death (Frazer 1922: 20), and efforts were made to restore souls of the recently dead to their bodies (Best 1901: 10; Goldie, 1904: 20). This was also the case on Mota Lava in Melanesia (Codrington 1891: 266-267). On Kiwai and in the Tanga Islands, bodies were not buried until decomposition (Landtman 1917: 12; Bell 1937: 321-322). The Dobu of the D'Entrecasteaux Islands believed that otherworld spirits ensured that souls were truly dead by admitting only those whose bodies had begun to decay (Fortune 1963: 181–182).

Such practices and beliefs likely facilitated the occurrence of NDEs, though it is important not to overgeneralize. In New Guinea and on Fiji, individuals were buried alive if it was believed that they would not recover or if there was danger of witchcraft. It was also customary for the sick and elderly on Fiji and Mota to request that they be killed (Brown 1910: 391-392; Williams 1860: 144). On Mota, they were sometimes buried alive (Codrington 1880: 125). On the Banks Islands, a lack of both

NDEs and detailed afterlife beliefs correlates with a fear of ghosts and graveyards, hasty burial practices, and attendees fleeing the gravesite as soon as the individual stopped breathing. If the dying process was prolonged, the person might request live burial (Humphreys 1926: 166).

The diversity of Melanesian attitudes toward the afterlife is reflected in varying methods of corpse disposal, interest in both possession and otherworld journey experiences, and concern with both benevolent and malevolent spirits of the dead. There is also variation in Polynesia, including a report that the Maori rarely attempted to revive the dead and that the sick were often left alone to die (Tregear 1890: 119-120). In general, however, Polynesian attitudes appear to have been more homogeneous than Melanesian. This finding is unsurprising given Polynesia's greater overall cultural homogeneity in comparison to Melanesia's "hundreds" of ethnic groups (Oliver 2002: 2).

Micronesia and Australia had an almost total lack of NDE reports, not a single indigenous statement that beliefs originated in NDEs, and few afterlife journey myths. The reasons for these shared dynamics, however, are due to rather different cultural peculiarities.

Micronesian shamanism was focused on possession and trance mediumship rather than on soul travel or retrieval (Dobbin & Hezel 2011: 213-214; Frazer 1924: 265). These practices effectively brought the dead to the living for purposes of divination, so there was little need for the living to visit the dead. Even in the rare examples of NDE-like narratives, the deceased does not reenter the body upon returning to Earth but remains in spirit form (Goodenough 2002: 150), reflecting a "Micronesia-wide" concern that the dead do *not* return except as benevolent spirits (Dobbin & Hezel 2011: 215).

This concern is reflected in Micronesian funerary practices in which corpses were quickly disposed of to prevent their souls from returning to them, and large stones were placed on bodies to prevent them from rising (Dobbin & Hezel 2011: 79, 155). In the Gilbert Islands, burial practices were designed to drive away the soul. In the Mortlock Islands, bodies were bound prior to burial; and in the Marshall Islands they were eviscerated immediately after death (Frazer 1924: 43-44, 90, 116-117, 171-172, 234-235, 265). Nor did Micronesian religious revitalization movements have NDE foundations. Rather than NDEs generating afterlife beliefs, it was dreams and visions of spirits of the dead that reinforced *established* beliefs.

Although afterlife journey narratives were almost entirely absent from Micronesia, Yap Island is the exception that proves the rule.

Much effort was expended on reviving the dying, the dead were buried only after a number of days (Furness 1910: 163-164), and hasty burials were believed to carry a risk of misfortune (Frazer 1924: 171-172). These practices—which encouraged revival both before and after apparent death—correspond to a greater number of afterlife journey narratives as well as soul travel and soul retrieval practices and beliefs, and a greater interest in the afterlife in general.

Though descriptions of shamanic and near-death experiences are often similar, and share transformative powers (see Shushan 2018), Australian accounts of otherworld journeys had primarily shamanic contexts. Although it is possible that such practices were attempts to reproduce NDEs, it may be that they were developed independent of knowledge of NDEs and naturally became the focus of afterlife beliefs. Rather than seeking details about the otherworld or the fate of the soul (Berndt & Berndt 1964: 278), the "fruits" of the experiences – the positive transformations – were the primary reasons for undertaking them. A pragmatic, this-worldly orientation gave Australian shamanism a focus on charms, healing, and divination. Indeed, the marked diversity of Aboriginal afterlife beliefs may be due to their being grounded in more culturally constructed shamanic experiences rather than in spontaneous, evidently universal NDEs. These varied beliefs included reincarnation (Spencer & Gillen 1927: 421-423, 453), traveling west "to a large pit" (Eyre 1845: 356), ascending to a sky-world, a continual process of cyclical birth and rebirth, and component souls that could simultaneously become a spirit on Earth, go to the realm of the dead, merge "with the great ancestral and creative beings, and so on" (Berndt & Berndt 1964: 204, 409, 419). The Murngin even had a myth explaining why people "stay dead and never come back to life." Unsurprisingly, their afterlife beliefs little resembled NDEs. Though one soul component went to the spirit world, the true self became a fish-like creature living in sacred emblems underwater. Even a rare otherworld journey myth is notably unlike an NDE: the protagonist traveled there bodily and was killed by ghosts upon his return (Warner 1937: 445-446, 523-528).

As in Micronesia, the elderly in Australia who had become a burden were put to death. Corpses were regarded with fear (Berndt & Berndt 1964: 391) and were bound immediately after death, then buried or cremated the next day. The arm and leg bones of chiefs were removed immediately for distribution to relatives (Dawson 1881: 62). The Dieri took pains "to prevent the body from rising" by tying together the thumbs and the toes (Howitt 1904: 449).

As one of the world's oldest continuous cultures, it would be surprising if NDEs were unknown to Aboriginal Australians. It may be that they were typically interpreted *as* shamanic phenomena— and reported as such—and that individuals were considered shamans by virtue of having had the experience, as in some Native American societies (Shushan, 2016, 2018). However, the almost total lack of return-from-death contexts in the shamanic narratives makes this conjecture perhaps overly speculative. The dearth of Australian and Micronesian NDEs is more likely related to the combination of preemptory funerary practices, a comparative lack of interest in the afterlife, and shamanic practices that had similar benefits to those resulting from NDEs.

It should be noted that a lack of common ancestry (Friedlander et al. 2008) means that cultural diffusion cannot explain the greater similarities between Polynesia and Melanesia on the one hand, and Australia and Micronesia on the other. Polynesia actually shared greater ancestral links with Micronesia, whereas Melanesia had marginally greater links with Australia, despite the fact that these pairs of regions had fewer religious and cultural similarities. The greater incidence of NDEs in Polynesia and Melanesia must therefore be due to coincidentally similar cultural patterns, including a greater receptivity to NDEs and funerary practices that facilitated their occurrence.

In my book *Near-Death Experiences in Indigenous Religions* I examined how NDEs are incorporated into the belief systems of different indigenous societies around the world. I found that many cultures valorized NDEs, and even based their afterlife beliefs upon them. This was most often the case with Native American peoples across the continent. In contrast, while other cultures also incorporated knowledge of NDEs into their belief systems, they did so in very different ways. In many African societies, NDEs were regarded with fear, as something aberrant, dangerous, and perhaps even due to witchcraft and sorcery.

The indigenous societies of Oceania can be seen as almost a microcosm of the findings of that book. As with the Native American model, some cultures exemplify the experiential source hypothesis – that NDEs gave rise to afterlife beliefs. Others, however, are more aligned to the African model – that NDEs are viewed as a possible threat to the natural order.

5

NEXT WORLDS IN VICTORIAN AND
EDWARDIAN MEDIUMSHIP

In this chapter we will explore alleged descriptions of the afterlife by spirits who dwell there, as communicated through trance mediums. There is a stark division in the ways that scholars of different disciplines treat these descriptions. Generally speaking, psychical researchers focus only on assessing the evidential value of information reportedly received by mediums from spirits in the other world. They largely ignore untestable statements about the nature of the afterlife. Such descriptions are left to historians and social scientists seeking to understand the social and cultural background of Spiritualism and psychical research, unconcerned with questions of evidential or philosophical worth.

Understandably, scholars are simply concerned with the questions of their own disciplines. However, examining only particular aspects of the narratives in isolation can only result in partial understandings of them. The present chapter will explore the implications of each approach in light of the other, while also examining the mediumship accounts in light of NDEs. The aim is to move towards a deeper understanding of the narratives, beyond disciplinary boundaries, and taking seriously both scholarly concerns and experiencer testimony. The texts will therefore be considered in terms of their cultural meanings, their implications for claims that they represent an actual afterlife, and their relationship to NDE accounts.

Discussion is limited to descriptions reported by mediums who have been the subjects of what investigators have regarded as evidential cases. This means that the alleged spirit communicated "knowledge of facts about the past lives of dead persons and about the present actions and thoughts and emotions of living ones, which is too extensive and detailed to be reasonably ascribed to chance-coincidence, and is quite inexplicable by reference to any normal sources of information open to the medium" (Broad 1962: 259). While some such cases have been compelling, one concern for our purposes is that the afterlife descriptions almost invariably do not occur *during* evidential sittings.

There is even more scientific and philosophical skepticism about mediumship than about NDEs. Some refuse to engage with the material at all. The philosopher Paul Edwards (1996: 140) has "no doubt that if one were to investigate" mediumistic communications they would prove to be false for the very "fact" that they are impossible. Critics of the survival hypothesis who actually have considered the evidence argue that there has been no indisputably water-tight case in which telepathy can be completely ruled out. They typically postulate a theory of "super-psi": that evidential cases can be explained by a hypothetical "universal telepathy" between the medium and *living* people (Gauld 1982: 53). However, when applied to some of the more persuasive cases, the theory must be stretched to such elaborately complex and convoluted lengths that it arguably strains credulity more than the survival hypothesis it is attempting to discredit.

While telepathy would also be involved in the communication between a discarnate spirit and a medium, the spirit would be communicating information that was consistent with their identity and history, but not previously known to the sitters or mediums. In contrast, the "universal telepathy" required by the super-psi hypothesis involves the mediums having such advanced telepathic powers that they can obtain accurate information unknown to them, and sometimes even to the sitter. The claim is not that the mediums are simply *receiving* information through interaction with some other living person, but that they have the ability to actively seek out, pinpoint, and access from disparate sources specific information that will be meaningful and relevant to the sitter.

In certain cases when fraud and coincidence have been ruled out, super-psi seems to be the only conceivable alternative explanation to genuine mediumistic communications from spirits in another world. For example, there have been numerous experiments involving proxy-sitters – individuals who sit for a reading on behalf of a person who is unknown to the medium. Information unknown to all three parties is then "communicated" through the medium, and later proves to be correct. In some cases, the information could not have come from a single living person. The super-psi hypothesis would thus demand that we accept that the medium is able to telepathically determine and locate the appropriate living individuals, retrieve from their minds the data relevant to the anonymous sitter, and coherently present the results, often in language displaying the personal characteristics of the alleged spirit who was unknown to the medium in life. According to psychologist Alan Gauld (1982: 46, 56), the evidence from Gladys Osborne Leonard's mediumship (see below) would require that she had "extrasensory access to any identifying detail whatsoever relating to any living or recently dead person in the whole of the Western world" – a scenario which he finds "grotesquely implausible."

It is also significant that such a high degree of telepathy allegedly occurs only in mediumship contexts – it is otherwise unknown, even in successful laboratory ESP experiments (Moore 1981: 95-6; see also Gauld 1982). This is notwithstanding the experiments in remote viewing conducted for the CIA by the Stanford Research Institute, wherein individuals demonstrated the ability to perceive and accurately describe a distant location or scene unknown to them (Braude 2003: 10 ff; 80). While impressive, this is not the same thing as choosing specific pieces of information from a variety of living individual minds and combining them in meaningful and accurate ways as required by the super-psi hypothesis. The philosopher Stephen E. Braude (2003: 86ff) ultimately calls the hypothesis "self-defeating," arguing that it cannot accommodate the most evidential communications.

The merits and otherwise of such cases have been analyzed in depth elsewhere, and therefore only brief contextual summaries of each will be provided in the sections below. Interested readers may find that the most lucid and balanced summary of the earlier cases is Gauld (1982), though also see Becker (1993b) and Braude (2003). All three summarize the detailed and complex arguments for and against a survival hypothesis in relation to the evidence from mediumship, a thorough assessment of which is beyond our scope here.

Although serious scientific research into mediumship was at its peak in the late 19th and early 20th centuries, there has been a resurgence in recent years. The earlier accounts are especially significant here, for they cannot have been influenced by the popular conception of NDEs as popularized by Moody in 1975. While they will be the focus of this chapter, we will also consider selected cases after that date for comparative purposes. They help to illuminate some of the cultural and social dynamics at play over time. The later material is also of interest in that it derives from serious research with claims of high scientific standards, yielding exceptionally positive results and published in peer-reviewed journals.

Cases Before 1975

The descriptions in this section derive from some of the most highly regarded mediums in psychical research. Other important mediums, such as Eileen Garrett and Winifred "Mrs. Willett" Coombe-Tennant, cannot be considered due to space considerations, though the descriptions of the afterlife "communicated" through them were broadly consistent with those discussed here. Even with the restrictions to the more evidential mediums and cases, the material is voluminous, and much detail and repetition is omitted. The summaries provided, however, are representative.

The "cross-correspondences" case (1901-1932) is still considered by many to be the best mediumistic evidence for survival. The experiment was allegedly devised by the spirits of three of the founders of the Society for Psychical Research (SPR): classicist and philologist Frederic Myers, psychologist Edmund Gurney, and philosopher Henry Sidgwick. Their intention was to prove their own postmortem survival. They purportedly communicated various different elements of a single message through more than one medium at different times and places, which only made sense when put together. The content of the messages related largely to specialist and erudite points of classical scholarship, allegedly far outside the range of the mediums' personal knowledge and experience. As Badham (1982: 97) has summed up, if "two uneducated people write half of an obscure Greek poem which after much research is tracked down to a very obscure book, and if it is later discovered that one of the alleged correspondents had lectured on this book, then the case begins to be evidential." Gauld (1982: 77-8) concluded that "no ordinary explanation will suffice."

The main criticism of the cross-correspondences is that with literally thousands of scripts, the connections could be all in the minds of the investigators, though "attempts to generate artificial cross-correspondences by collating pseudo-scripts" have been "largely unsuccessful' (Gauld 1982: 80; Moore 1981 105-6; see also Moreman 2003 for one debunking attempt, countered by Keen & Roy 2004). Psychical researcher H.F. Saltmarsh (1938: 126) argued that the specificity of the cross-correspondences virtually rules out the suggestion that they are random; and the fact that they occur in the context of statements of intent to communicate them adds to their evidential value.

Three important mediums involved in the cross-correspondences also reported descriptions of the afterlife communicated to them by spirits: Leonora Piper, Gladys Osborne Leonard, and Geraldine Cummins.

Leonora Piper

In numerous SPR tests, the American professional medium Leonora Piper produced an enormous mass of reportedly evidential material. There are aspects to her mediumship that raise alarms, however, including "fishing" for facts, covering up mistakes, and a string of unconvincing spirit communicators, including a Native American girl with the absurdly unlikely name of "Chlorine." Piper's main control – the spirit who works through a medium to facilitate communication with other spirits – was a fictitious French doctor called "Phinuit," who knew neither French nor medical terminology. Nevertheless, Piper was cleared of fraud by lawyer and philosopher Richard Hodgson of the SPR, whose *raison d'être* was exposing fraudulent mediums (Sage 1903: 3).

The important Harvard psychologist and SPR president William James was another prominent investigator. He was so convinced of Piper's abilities that the case prompted him to write his famous dictum: "If you wish to upset the law that all crows are black, you musn't seek to show that no crows are; it is enough if you prove one single crow to be white" (James 1896: 884)." The part of that statement that is usually omitted is: "My own white crow is Mrs. Piper." To be clear, while James was convinced that Piper was "in possession of a power as yet unexplained," he was unsure if that "power" was genuine spirit communication or telepathy.

According to Piper's scripts, there is a period of darkness after death, followed by a gradual return to consciousness which is accompanied by feelings of joy. One spirit spoke of "many faces beckoning me on and trying to comfort me." The soul and consciousness are one in the afterlife, with an astral body which no longer has "passions and animal appetites," for "evil thoughts die with the body." The other realm is described as a place of "peace and plenty," with "music, flowers, walks, drives, pleasures of all kinds, books and everything." Time may be spent in occupations such as helping others to "advance" (Sage 1903: 101-2, 104, 106, 108).

Leonora Piper appears to be the only Victorian medium to have recorded her own near-death experience. It is provided in full as an appendix at the end of this book.

Gladys Osborne Leonard

One of the most highly regarded mediums in the history of psychical research, Leonard was the subject of intense critical investigations conducted by the physicist Sir Oliver Lodge, Cambridge principal Eleanor Sidgwick, and psychical researcher and Spiritualist Rev. C. Drayton Thomas – a man "loyal to the scientific method." The latter had over five-hundred sittings with Leonard over a period of twenty years (Hodges 2004: 24). Some investigations also involved the skeptic Professor E. R. Dodds who was sufficiently impressed to write that neither fraud, telepathy, coincidence, nor prior knowledge could account for the positive results of the experiment he had instigated (Gauld 1982: 51; although also see Dodds 1934, which reveals the great intellectual lengths to which he went to avoid a survival hypothesis).

As well as numerous successful proxy sittings, Leonard gave many "book-tests" in which specific page and line numbers of a particular book – unknown to the medium and usually the sitter – provided an evidential message, such as a response to a question, or personal information. The location of the book was often specified – which was also information unknown to the medium – including where it was housed and the shelf on which it would be found (Thomas 1928). Leonard had more consistently evidential sittings than perhaps any other medium. Nevertheless, as with Piper, there are problems with the fictitious nature of her communicators (Gauld 1982: ch. 4), and she gave the same stock descriptions for different deceased relatives in at least fourteen different séances (Badham 1982: 94).

The afterlife descriptions in Leonard's scripts are far more extensive and detailed than those in Piper's, and correspondingly more problematic.

It is difficult to accept the descriptions at face value when so much of the content seems calculated to reassure a hopeful, middle-class Edwardian reverend that the afterlife preserves the earthly status quo.

One spirit described the afterlife journey as travelling "upward" through a cave-like opening to meet "our Lord." Another described a sense of "swaying about in the dark" accompanied by feelings of giddiness, followed by the atmosphere becoming suffused with an expanding light, feelings of content, meeting deceased relatives, an intense clarity, and a burst of light. A spirit "enters the judgement immediately" upon arrival, though it is a self-judgement. There is no eternal punishment or devil, though there is a "merciful" god who "will not be mocked" as evidenced by those in the lower realms, "living in chains of their own making." Even those who were good on Earth will end up in that realm if "they mocked God by insincerity and humbug" (Thomas 1936: 41, 130, 192-3, 227). How this arrangement co-exists with self-judgement is unclear.

The afterlife state is compared to the dream-state, but more real and apparently solid. "The spirit world has been created in such a fashion [through a dream-like process] through all time" (Thomas 1936: 5). The realm is thus mind-dependent according to Thomas's own father in the spirit world, though only in part for "material" exists with which to work (Thomas 1928: 152). However, according to the spirit of "Raymond" – ostensibly Lodge's son – although it appears to be a "thought-world," it is not. Souls have the ability to create matter "from certain unstable atoms" with a large wheel beneath which sparks accumulate. Souls also gravitate to other like-minded souls. We will return to the subject of a mind-dependent afterlife in the last chapter, and the notion is also better developed in the Cummins scripts as will be seen below. It should be noted that Lodge admitted that "Raymond's" information regarding the afterlife did not come from evidential sittings, and some of the content he deleted from the published account (Lodge 1916: 230, 268-9). It's not clear why he allowed certain descriptions to remain and not others.

The spiritual body seems "real" and at the prime of life. In children, it corresponds to mental and spiritual age rather than physical earthly age. What the earthly body did affects the spiritual body and results in various "limitations." Some are "entirely ugly." There is no sleep because there is no unconsciousness, though some have a long rest or even a deep sleep when they first arrive (Thomas 1928: 27-8, 107-8, 109, 110).

Spirits live on one of seven spiritual spheres but can visit others. To reach the lower spheres, they travel over a "dark-coloured carpet ...

neither grass nor flowers...passing into greater density" as they progress (Thomas 1936: 115). On the lower spheres are slums, though buildings there are less permanent and easier to dissolve than on the third sphere. The lowest is for the "definitely evil," while the next is for the merely "weak and selfish." They dwell in a grey, drab, depressed state, visited on occasion by higher beings – "like sending missions to the heathen."

Below the lowest sphere (sic) is yet another, for animals that survive not as individuals but as "soul-force." Pets are an exception, and they are allowed to remain with their owners while they adjust. Only "natural pets" are eligible, however, which includes not only dogs and cats, but horses, "a few monkeys," and birds.

Those who are worthy proceed to the third sphere, described as "a picture of fairyland" despite being a replica of one's home, including identical furniture and grounds (Thomas 1936: 8, 12, 15). This sphere is also known as Summerland, or Homeland. People normally have homes out of habit, but some have outgrown such needs and instead live outdoors in trees, on hillsides, or in valleys. Anyone can go anywhere freely. Nothing is dirty or muddy, there are no clouds, no overcrowding, or large cities. There are small cities, however, which are heavenly reproductions of earthly counterparts, even retaining their original names. The notion of the afterlife being an idealized mirror-image of Earth is taken to its logical extreme: the counterparts are literally layered one on top of the other, so that the earthly England is just below that of the lowest spiritual sphere, and the higher spiritual Englands are stacked above (Lodge 1916: 26, 128-32, 229-30). It is unclear why the most spiritually enlightened individuals in the highest spheres would still require the familiar material comforts of these rarefied Englands.

Only the lower spheres have government, though all individuals are responsible to the levels above them (Thomas 1928: 167, 171; Thomas 1936: 80, 102). There is no "judge and jury," but there is a "reformatory." Ancient cities are also reproduced, and ancient peoples are "available to students" (Lodge 1916: 205, 229-30). There are also colleges and classes on afterlife "rules and regulations." One young boy studies chemistry and goes ice-skating in the summer. Any earthly career might be followed, including going to sea. Music, which is listened to with the mind as well as the "etheric ears" is the highest art, followed by painting. Some individuals work by helping the newly deceased to adjust, or by helping people on Earth (Thomas 1936: 9, 18, 33, 37, 74).

Races self-segregate, "choosing to live among their own people." Some spirits retain the servants they had on Earth, "but they are old servants who are attached to them, and who are not spiritually and mentally ready to emancipate themselves for other work." Buddhists, Muslims, "and others" do not immediately accept Christ upon passing into the spirit realm, though they eventually do. Such individuals "are unlikely to qualify for such high place as those who sincerely follow Christ; because their lives are generally influenced by practices which are neither good nor moral." Such statements are presumably a reflection of the claim that one can carry earthly difficulties with them, such as disliking certain people – and indeed ignorance, racism, classism, and religious intolerance. This is despite the fact that one supposedly gains a passion for intellectual and spiritual development in the afterlife (Thomas 1936: 4, 17, 154).

Interestingly, Thomas (1945: 63) later reported on another case of Mrs. Leonard's that contradicted claims of afterlife segregation. It concerned an anonymous elderly woman, whom Thomas called Agnes, who wished to contact her deceased nephew Edgar and her sister Helen. She asked Oliver Lodge to recommend a medium, and with the help of the SPR, Agnes was introduced to Leonard. In 1922, "Helen" communicated through Leonard that the purpose of idealized duplicates of earthly places was to make newly arrived spirits feel more comfortable. As with England, there is also a spiritual Japan, for example, so that Japanese people will be more at ease when surrounded by a familiar environment. The soul will later "mingle with other races and so progress," as spirit-Helen explained. "When one reaches a certain stage the racial differences are less noticed, because the highest in each becomes paramount. We have no hatred and no jealousy between different races, but tolerance and sympathetic understanding." The problem of racial, religious, and social divisions in the afterlife will be returned to in greater depth later in this chapter.

There is a curious lack of comment on the fourth sphere, though the fifth, sixth, and seventh are described as heavenly realms, with fewer houses, people who "rest outside," wear clothing "of a lighter texture," and have progressively fairer complexions the higher one goes. Thomas's spirit father visited one of these higher realms with St. Francis. To reach it, they crossed "a wide river or sea" made of a "more solidified, opaque air." Its banks were golden, and there was a rocky sapphire and amethyst coast. A winding road separated different states of being manifested as different scenery. They reached a plinth where St. Francis addressed a crowd of followers. The ground was sand, but grass, flowers, and trees grew from it (Thomas 1936: 91-2, 215).

On the fifth sphere, flowers renew their spirit bodies and much is made of alabaster. There is a white temple building with church pews and colored lights inside, and matching stained-glass windows. When spirits stand in the lights, they obtain qualities they may have lacked while on Earth – blue for spiritual healing, red for love, and orange for intellect. On "Raymond's" visit, seven teachers from the seventh realm arrived, and placed their hands on the foreheads of the congregation causing the three lights to combine, resulting in complete understanding (Lodge 1916: 264-5, 269).

There is no further description of the sixth sphere for it is indescribable, though the seventh is still solid and a yet more idealized mirror-image of earth, though with more colors. Thomas's father encountered "our Lord" on the top step of a white alabaster pillared building, surrounded by followers. "He is a little different from some of the pictures of Him," Thomas's father remarked (ibid. 127, 216).

The spirit of Agnes's brother William also communicated through Leonard, affirming that there are seven spheres in the other world. According to "Edgar," souls who dwell in the upper spheres can time travel into the past with their minds: "Suppose for my enlightenment it were desirable to learn what happened in ancient Egypt three thousand years ago; I should be taken to one of the higher realms and conducted to one of its observation temples where the scene would be re-enacted." "William" elaborated on this idea, referring to "Halls of Vision, places where one can see enacted the events of long ago; say in Egypt, Rome, or later in France or England .... These visions are projected memories given by those who actually took part in the events." He also remarked that the dead can put ideas into the heads of the living, expressing hopes that he would one day convey to a composer on Earth an opera he was writing in the otherworld (Thomas 1945: 56, 73-4, 87).

Geraldine Cummins

William James was also impressed with Geraldine Cummins's mediumistic abilities, as were Professor of Logic and Ethics at Columbia University James H. Hyslop, the skeptic Frank Podmore, and more recently, Stanford philosopher Dr. Robert Almeder (1992: 223). The anthropologist Eric Dingwall (1985: 171), however, found her scripts to contain erroneous information. Cummins also credited her communicators with some frankly ludicrous statements, such as that there are monkeys in the sun, according to the spirit of Sir Walter Scott.

In another example of a cross-correspondence, "Frederic Myers" allegedly confirmed through Leonard information he had given through Geraldine Cummins – though the two mediums had never met (nor had Cummins known Myers). Much of "Myers's" descriptions of the afterlife are similar to those in Leonard, though generally they seem more coherent, consistent, and sophisticated in their conception – despite some logical inconsistencies and dubious statements. In fact, Leonard's descriptions read like a more confused version of Cummins's. Whether this is due to Myers being a better communicator than Raymond Lodge and Drayton Thomas's father, or to Cummins's subconscious having more detailed ideas about the afterlife than Leonard's, it is impossible to determine.

There are also significant differences between the Leonard and Cummins afterlives. For example, while "Myers" also speaks of seven levels of existence, the first is the Plane of Matter which includes earth and celestial regions. Following physical death, spirits hover above the body, then enter an intermediate realm which "Myers" called Hades. Here one undergoes a life review (an element missing from Leonard's scripts) and self-judgement, assisted by the "Light from Above." The nature of Hades depends on the individual. For "Myers" it was "a place of half-lights and drowsy peace." Some wander there aimlessly, meeting "strange beings" who cause sorrow. The realm is returned to each time one considers progressing to a higher level, and additional life reviews assisted by the being of light help in the decision-making process. Some choose to return to Earth or go to another planet (Cummins 1932: 38-9, 81-83).

As with Leonard's scripts, the third level is Summerland, here also called The Plane of Illusion, where souls unconsciously create an illusory mirror-image of Earth as a source of comfort to aid adjustment. Contradictorily, Summerland is also said to be created by advanced spirits from the deceased's memories. New arrivals are often greeted by these spirits and by deceased loved ones.

Punishment can occur in this realm, though "Myers" seemed to be concerned only with what he regarded as sexual transgressions. Sexual sadists will be miserable at their inability to cause pain, though eventually they will realize the suffering they have caused and will be purified. Sexual masochists are not mentioned. Others who have a "sex history of a reprehensible kind" will be drawn to similar spirits and create an illusory sex paradise which leads to a "horrible satiety." They will come to loathe sex, but "find it extraordinarily difficult to escape" from the clutches of their fellow orgiasts (ibid. 36-7, 40, 44, 46-7). Incidentally, a similar dynamic can be found in the case of the medium Minnie "Mrs. Chenoweth" Meserve Soule channeling "Cagliostro." Although investigator James Hyslop expressed disapproval at Cagliostro's immorality, Hyslop himself "repeatedly encountered nonspiritual, immoral, and 'sensuous' characters in sittings he conducted" (Braude 2003: 41). This may be an example of the so-called experimenter effect, in which the investigator psychically (and subconsciously) influences the proceedings. In "Myers's" case it could have been Lodge or fellow psychical researcher E. B. Gibbes , if not Cummins herself.

Summerland fades with increased "spiritual knowledge" and spirits decide when to move on to the next level, usually because of boredom. It is not explained why or how one would come to feel ennui in a mind-dependent world, in which boredom itself might be banished with a thought, and spiritual enlightenment created with another.

The fourth level is the Plane of Colour (Cummins 1932: 77). One must journey from there to Hades or Summerland to contact the living through mediums, but all memory of the higher realms vanishes. This is contradicted, however, by the fact that "Myers" himself was communicating from the fourth level. Like the third level, it is a mind-dependent world, so it can be ugly, beautiful, or bizarre, depending upon the individual. In contradiction to this, it is also the "luminiferous ... original of earth," the present Earth being but "an ugly smudged copy." There are radiant flowers, colors, and lights beyond the earthly spectrum, and memory of Earth is temporarily lost.

Communication is telepathic and one learns how to control matter, as well as to "send out protective rays" in case a former earthly enemy is encountered. Sensations, emotions, and intelligence are heightened. Like-minded souls are drawn together to form "group souls" which are "bound together by one spirit" on which they depend for "nourishment." In yet another contradiction, despite comments regarding the superiority of Christianity, souls must be free of any religious dogma before progressing to the fifth plane (Cummins 1932: 55-8, 60-1, 65-6).

On the fifth level, the Plane of Pure Flame, "the soul becomes aware of the pattern his spirit is weaving in the tapestry of eternity and realises all the emotional life of the souls fed by the same spirit." All experiences on all previous planes are perceived, yet there is no form, color, appearance, or feeling. The deceased merges with the group soul, though retains a sense of self, existing in "an outline of emotional thought" shaped by the group. There is further spiritual and intellectual development, but also "severe discipline" and limitations. Spirits glimpse "infinite horizons" and experience "all the passionate existence of [their] comrade souls" while becoming closer with the "unifying spirit." It is "glorious ... despite sinister aspects," and is like a continual flash of genius. A realization of oneness with all living things occurs (ibid. 34, 67-70).

The sixth level is the Plane of Pure Light, where the soul gains "an intellectual conception of all the previous existences within the group-soul" and "realises all the emotional life within the body of the world or earth soul." In contradiction, it is also a realm of pure reason, without emotion or passion. In it is achieved "the assimilation of the many-in-one," and "the spirit which contains this strange individualised life passes out Yonder and enters into the Mystery, thereby fulfilling the final purpose, the evolution of the Supreme Mind" (ibid. 34, 71).

On the seventh level, "the spirit and its various souls are now fused and pass into the Supreme Mind," though still one retains individuality, like "a wave in the sea." Beyond time and space, yet pervading everything like the rays of the sun, the spirit has become "wholly aware of the imagination of God" in which everything is contained. Few reach this state: some go no further than the sixth level, and others reincarnate on Earth. The ultimate goal is to overcome being "individualized" – to achieve unification, first with the group soul, then with the Supreme Mind (ibid. 34, 51-2, 72-3). The influence of the Hindu concepts of *atman* and *brahman* are clear, as is reincarnation, likely having been filtered through the Theosophical writings of Helena Blavatsky.

Yet another inconsistency arises from "Myers's" statements that there is a male creator god who controls individuals and designs their futures, yet also that "each soul makes its own bed ... there is always free will" (ibid. 31, 98). How these competing statements can be reconciled with the above mixture of mind-dependence, self-judgement, life-reviews, and personal choice of spiritual progression is a mystery.

In addition to the many contradictions, the Cummins material contains numerous absurdities and obscurities. For example, according to certain "higher beings," "at one time, there was, or will be" people on Venus composed of vapor and water. Extraterrestrial beings are also included in group-souls for we are all of one spiritual race – we are just incarnated differently. One may choose to be reborn as a "star within the Milky Way" composed of "radiant atoms." There is more solar life than "so-called human life," and salamander-flame beings live on the stars (Cummins 1935: 111, 114, 119, 179-80). Nevertheless, in their main points the descriptions are largely consistent with those from other mediums.

Leslie Flint

Leslie Flint claimed to be the UK's "most tested medium" (1971: 10, 159, 168-69). In a series of SPR experiments, he demonstrated the apparent ability to manifest clearly spoken discarnate voices (a phenomenon known as direct voice communication) – sometimes seemingly more than one simultaneously – while his mouth was sealed and his arms restrained. The voices were often recognized by the sitters as belonging to the persons they claimed to be, though the individuals were unknown to Flint. Hundreds of Flint's sittings were recorded on audio tape from 1945-1965 by SPR member and fellow medium George Woods. The fact that Woods was a paying client who was told by "communicators" that "much depends" on his regular sittings does nothing to inspire confidence in Flint's authenticity, however. Flint also faced a number of allegations of fraud, and his roster of celebrity communicators is suspect, including Oscar Wilde, Rudolph Valentino, Queen Victoria, Mae West, and others.

Nevertheless, the picture of the afterlife that emerges from the recordings is broadly consistent with the earlier descriptions: travelling out of the body, bright light, deceased friends and relatives (and pets), life review, self-judgement, an idealized mirror-image of Earth described in nearly identical terms to Cummins's "Myers" scripts, a mutual attraction between like-minded souls which gather in groups, and spiritual evolution. In one case, a spirit recalled leaving his body when he died, and hearing living people discuss his death (Randall 1975: 14-15, 17, 25, 32, 41, 54, 81, 95, 145).

Some differences and absurdities should not be ignored, however. The spirit of the poet Rupert Brooke did not have an OBE, but suddenly found himself in a new body which "did not feel anything" and had no reflection. Animals work in mine-pits and gather on plains. They communicate telepathically on a human level, but need to be cared for. Cats become more like dogs in behavior. There are no frogs, gnats, flies or other "crawly, creepy things" which exist on a lower vibration, though there are butterflies. People are vegetarians, living on fruit and nuts. "Incompatibility is recognized in Heaven as grounds for divorce"

– despite the fact that there is no marriage or sex. The music is neither "highbrow" nor "jazz muck" nor "religious," but simply "pleasant." Lionel Barrymore performs morality plays for unfortunate individuals in the lower realms, and Shakespeare is writing even better plays than he did in life. Oscar Wilde lives a life of "delicious sin" which in Heaven is "natural" (ibid. 34, 82, 91-3, 102, 108-10, 112).

Although such acceptance of homosexuality is as surprising as it is admirable, once again we encounter racism. There are no "coloured people" in evidence, because they "wouldn't be happy … in a white man's sort of atmosphere." Therefore, they self-segregate. Nevertheless, no matter how "lowly" they are, all are equal after death (ibid. 137).

Cases After 1975

The Scole Experiments

The Scole experiments are regarded by some researchers as among the most significant in the history of parapsychology. They were investigated by SPR researchers Montague Keen, psychologist David Fontana, and Arthur Ellison who stated that it was the worthiest mediumship case since the 1930s (Keen et. al. 1999: 157). While not under laboratory conditions, the experiments were subject to intense scrutiny and numerous restrictions imposed by the investigators. The results deeply impressed not only the investigators themselves, but also a series of guests which included SPR Council members, members of the Scientific and Medical Network, representatives from NASA, an electrical engineer, a biologist, a physicist, a chemist and so on – none of whom found any evidence of fraud. James Webster, a retired professional stage magician and psychical researcher who "does not tolerate fake mediums at all" (as Guy Lyon Playfair told me in 2004), concluded that the phenomena he witnessed could not have been created by conjuring tricks or any other normal means. Indeed, most observers were wholly convinced of the authenticity of what they witnessed. That included a great deal of physical phenomena, such as sentient lights, apports of objects apparently out of thin air, images appearing on factory-sealed film in locked boxes, and intriguing links with the cross-correspondences.

However, there were some dubious and unconvincing aspects to the experiments. For example, the sittings ended because of interference from a malevolent "personality from the future" who was "interfering with the interdimensional doorway [by] experimenting with a crystalline timeprobe" (Solomon and Solomon 1999: 193). When I asked David Fontana about this claim in 2003, he agreed that it sounded absurd. However, he added that whether the claims were true or not, as Broad pointed out there is no reason to believe that the afterlife is composed entirely of well-meaning spirits (contrary to Piper's assertion that one no longer has "evil thoughts" in the afterlife). Fontana found it feasible that an ill-intentioned spirit individual was in fact interfering with the experiments. He also stressed emphatically that he cannot doubt what he personally experienced during the sittings – phenomena such as a three-dimensional luminous flower blooming under a glass bowl inches from his face, and an apparently sentient point of light which he could not only see, but hear and feel as it passed through solid objects, including the table and even his own hand.

Nevertheless, claims that the ancient Egyptians used "sound vibrations" to build their monuments (ibid. 180) are not encouraging. But most damaging is the fact that the "spirits" had to approve the investigators' scientific protocols, including the use of equipment and lighting. Braude (2003: 98) has noted that, as with the cross-correspondences, the communications are overly complex and obscure to the point that their meanings are debatable, weakening their evidential value. He calls the Scole material "transparently questionable" (ibid. 100, n.7). Gauld is not entirely convinced it was not all a hoax, though the investigators vehemently deny this (Keen et. al.: 422).

Because the experiments focused on physical mediumship, there are unfortunately few descriptions of the afterlife. According to Fontana, the investigators did not ask the spirits about it because they were more concerned with phenomena and communications of an evidential nature. The descriptions that do exist are published not in the official SPR report, but in the popular book by Solomon and Solomon (1999).

The alleged communicators were part of a "Council of Communion" made up of "thirteen evolved souls." They described how, after a period of adjustment and confusion, new souls are comforted by familiar surroundings and loved ones. According to the main communicator, Manu "from what you now call South America," souls have no "physical body or physical senses," but "mind and soul, blended as one" (ibid. 2, 38, 54, 174-6).

There are "many other realms of existence." The afterlife is "much more real" than the earthly realm – despite the fact that it is a "mental world." "Our spirit selves are really travelers and the point at which you are now is the place to which you have decided to travel"; "the overall aim is for every soul to obtain spiritual knowledge and to move towards the light itself." The only mention of a morally-determined fate is that it is decided by the life led on Earth.

The afterlife is comparable to a dream-state, and is "the true state ... the real home of consciousness." The realm contains "flowers and fields," but it is beyond description. "It is a world of beauty in which you can live for many, many earth years." There are contradictory statements regarding time, however: "time is not a reality, so there is no hurry," though the spirits don't "have a great deal of time on [their] hands." Everyone is engaged in some sort of activity or exploration, often with the assistance of more spiritually evolved guides and teachers. Without practice or "mental turmoil," souls can instantly express themselves musically with "joy and depth." There are councils of healing and of "physical phenomena" (ibid. 38, 174-6, 193). The spirits "go on 'retreats' sometimes," and "they live in each other's consciousness," as Fontana explained to me.

Interestingly, there is also a video which purports to show images of the other realm. The video experiments were conducted with lawyer and SPR member Dr. Hans Schaer, though they were not part of the main SPR experiments, nor were they subject to the same rigorous conditions. Some were shot in darkness with the camera pointing towards a mirror, and others in full light. One appears to show "grassy plains and crystal mountains in another world." Others show "beautiful leafy forests," "pyramids set in a great lake below orange red skies," and "a world composed of ice." Since it is a "world without limitations," according to Manu, and souls are "able to create beauty," it is unclear if these images depict mind-dependent thought projections or an objective "place" (ibid. 143-44).

The Afterlife Experiments

The psychologist Gary Schwartz (2002) has reported positive results from his experiments, in which the medium and the sitter had no apparent communication or contact whatsoever. For example, one experiment involved a medium in Arizona giving a reading for an anonymous sitter in California, prior to the scheduled time of the reading when the sitter did not know she was being "read." In a telephone experiment, the reading was conducted with the receiver muted so the medium had no input whatsoever from the sitter. Specific, accurate information was retrieved in both sittings. In a normal telephone reading in which dialogue between medium and sitter was allowed, accurate information previously unknown to the sitter was obtained, including the birth place of the spirit communicator, a description of a place the sitter had never been which was important to the communicator, and the illness of a relative (Schwartz & Russek 2001: 257, 265-6).

Although Schwartz claimed that chance, fraud, and cold-reading had all been ruled out, unsurprisingly others have not been convinced. Most notably, psychology professor Ray Hyman (2003: 22) dismissed the cases as typical cold reading, while also criticizing Schwartz's methodology, concluding that "Probably no other extended program in psychical research deviates so much from accepted norms of scientific methodology."

The published information regarding the afterlife from Schwartz's research is minimal. We are told only that amidst "beautiful golden light," the soul travels in spiritual form to a different dimension "where we continue to grow and unfold" (Schwartz 2002: 79; via medium Anne Gehman). One spirit "works with children" in the afterlife; while another apparently has a new body, though there are still "ups and downs" (ibid. 88, 96, 104; via medium George Anderson).

As with the earlier mediums, in the absence of relevant descriptions from his actual experiments, we must look to the writings of his best-performing mediums. Most prominent was John Edward of the television program *Crossing Over*. Edward (1998: xv, 152, 159-160) claims that spirits have given him "glimpses" of the afterlife, but that "the true nature of the spirit world remains elusive." Nevertheless, the following information can be gleaned from his books: Edward was shown by spirits a "Hall of Knowledge," though he considers such "visions" as symbols. In this case, the symbol was meant to convey that there is a spiritual evolution of souls which pass through different levels. Souls undergo self-judgement and choose when to proceed, or when to return to earth in order to learn further lessons. Some souls are still sorrowful or angry, but others – including murderers and those who committed suicide – have become "very loving and contented." Souls also act as guides or guardians for people still on Earth.

Edward was also shown an echoing place with "infinite feeling to it." He saw faces of old men and heard the phrase "Council of Elders," though again he interprets this symbolically, as conveying that there is a hierarchy of spirits. He also saw a scene of indescribable beauty: "a hill, with beautiful, lush trees and the most vibrant green meadows. There is something that looks like a fountain with water that seems to spray up, then evaporate." He is unsure if these visions are what the afterlife is really like, or if they, too, are symbolic (ibid. 153, 155-6).

George Anderson, who had also been tested by researchers before Schwartz, purportedly gave numerous evidential readings as detailed by Martin and Romanowski (1989). Based on his spirit communications, Anderson described the afterlife experience as comprising the familiar elements of tunnel, light, astral body, deceased friends and relatives, life review and self-judgement, mind-dependence, levels of spiritual ascent (including a negative, purgatorial realm) and progression, choice of whether or not to reincarnate, deciding or designing the circumstances of the rebirth, and universal knowledge/wisdom. Anderson added that the feeling of heavenly ascent is due to being spiritually uplifted. Individuals have occupations, such as working with spirit-children and animals, and helping the newly deceased to cross over. Those in higher realms can visit lower ones, and many wait for their less spiritually-advanced loved ones to catch up to them before progressing. Souls remain with those they felt close to in their earthly life, or they are reborn in groups. Anderson is unsure if animals "technically" have souls, but their "life force" can join their human loved ones (ibid. 240, 242-3, 249).

Anderson (1999: 24-5) also stated that for some, the experience of dying and the transition to the afterlife state is more subtle than typical NDE reports. One example is a man who drowned, had a sudden burst of energy, and swam to the surface where he was greeted by deceased relatives and realized he was in another world. Fear or confusion may cause familiar earthly people and places to appear in order to comfort the newly deceased. A child, for example, might be greeted by Santa Claus, or by animals.

Anderson also seemed to claim that the afterlife itself is sentient, for he wrote that it will do "whatever it takes to create an atmosphere of trust and comfort to ease the transition" and to attract the soul. He may have been writing figuratively, for the notion seriously contradicts that of a mind-dependent afterlife. His statement that it is also "a world of constancy, yet always building to suit the reality of the individual who inhabits it...[and] a fixed place with many levels of consciousness" (ibid. 26, 39, 96) does nothing to clarify matters.

Uniquely, Anderson wrote that the life review involves only our misdeeds, which we experience from the perspective of those we have harmed. Our good deeds, however, "have not been forgotten by the Infinite Light" which is our goal, our origin, and destination. "Salvation" is mentioned, but details are not provided, though "no sin is beyond the understanding of the Infinite Light" (ibid. 26, 35, 39). Such Christian concepts – along with "grace" and "intercession" are notably absent from the other mediumship narratives. It may be that Anderson was presenting his afterlife vision in a form palatable both to Christian and non-Christian (for example, the substitution of "Infinite Light" for "God"), or that this is simply how his mind filtered the concepts being conveyed to him.

Anderson defined the Infinite Light as the god of all religions, which are like facets of a diamond – culture-specific manifestations of a One Truth. On one of the happier levels, which is "like a perfect endless summer day ... everything is bathed in a beautiful light," the Infinite Light radiates love and peace, and energizes everything, including inanimate objects. There is no darkness, and no need for sleep. It is an idealized mirror-image of Earth, with communities, work, and relationships. There is no pain or illness, only loving selflessness and "a perfect, carefree, permanent vacation." Souls can satisfy any material desires and possess anything they wish until they outgrow such needs. Victims of terminal illnesses have a special "house of reflection" surrounded by "fields and meadows, flowers, birds, and small animals, all exuding peace and security" (ibid. 31, 33, 36, 38).

Souls in the hereafter do not like to discuss reincarnation, and Anderson does not know if it is a possibility or not. He does know that there are no accidents or coincidences – everything is carefully decided and planned (ibid. 45, 47).

Another of Schwartz's best-performing mediums, Suzane Northrup 1995: 122, 124-6, 133), described the afterlife in much the same terms, though with some elaboration and minor variations. She added that a person's mode of death will also influence their afterlife experience. Faith is also a factor, for believers in life after death "will move more quickly, as if in a dream state, into the light" while experiencing feelings of "love and guidance." Unbelievers may have to stay in a shadowy Hades-like realm until they are ready to see the light. There is a resting stage where souls realize that they are dead, meet deceased friends and relatives, and undergo a life review with self-judgement, along with a consultation with the "masters" regarding the individual's spiritual progress. The realm is tuned to a higher vibration than Earth, and souls have bodies that are identical to their former earthly ones, but "of a finer material."

There are five levels, or "astral places" which largely match Anderson's. The first is Earth, and the second is the equivalent of hell, filled with "negative energy" and "lost souls." Some of them are unaware they are dead, and could remain there for eternity. There is, however, no devil. Most souls bypass this realm and go straight to the third level, a realm of light, deceased loved ones, and an "awakening." Some attend "spiritual school" in order to recover and adjust before proceeding to the fourth level: a realm of love, populated by angels, where one's consciousness is expanded. The spirit is given the option of being reincarnated on earth or proceeding to the fifth level, where there is a final opportunity to return to Earth. The fifth level is the realm of creation, as well as the source of artistic and scientific inspiration on Earth (ibid. 131, 133-4, 163).

Finally, Gordon Smith (2003: 128-9) is one of the few mediums of modern times to give readings for the SPR, and has been endorsed by astronomer Archie Roy among others. His sittings have stood up to the scrutiny of the research group PRISM (Psychical Research Involving Selected Mediums) and the Scottish SPR at Glasgow University. According to the alleged spirits speaking through Smith, the afterlife is mind-dependent and thus subjective: "each mind will gravitate to a level of understanding most suited to its concept of Heaven."

Smith also claimed to have journeyed to "the other side" during shamanic-type trance. He described leaving his body, travelling "at high speed toward a light" followed by a lack of any physical sensation, meeting deceased loved ones and other spirits, telepathic communication, feelings of vitality and oneness, and a profound understanding of "life, love, and beauty" – though the overall experience is ineffable. His deceased cousin acted as a guide throughout the experience, and took him on an indescribable "journey through this realm of spiritual beauty" (ibid. 112-114).

Spiritual Enlightenment, Intolerance, and Historical Inaccuracies

Racism, classism, and religious intolerance are disturbing trends in the pre-1975 narratives. This has some important ramifications for those who wish to view the afterlife descriptions as genuine, for they indicate either that the next world is truly a systemized bigoted realm, or that the spirit communicators were portraying merely their personal intolerant mind-dependent afterlife. However, the latter possibility is inconsistent with the recurring claim by the spirits themselves that death brings about spiritual transformation. If the afterlife (particularly on the higher spheres) is a place of equality and enlightenment, surely our spirit communicators would have risen above their negative and harmful social conditioning. The other possibility is that the information conveyed by spirits was filtered through the mediums' minds and thus overlaid with the institutionalized bigotry of their times.

Such attitudes are common throughout 19th and 20th century mediumship literature, and can be traced to the earliest days of Western spiritualism. For example, according to alleged spirit communications via French medium Adèle Maginot, "The souls of Negroes are as white as ours; it is only in the skin they differ from us; but in heaven everyone is white." While perhaps a tone-deaf attempt at inclusivity, Maginot continued, "There are no negroes who like their color. When they compare it with that of the whites, they envy the white color. They prefer us in all. Black women seek after white men, and black men after white women. They have no affection for their color, had they any they would be deprived of it in heaven where all men are white" (Louis-Alphonse Cahagnet, *The Celestial Telegraph,* 1845; in Ferguson 2012: 119). It will be recalled that "Raymond" (via Leonard) similarly stated that the higher the spirit realm, the lighter the complexion of its inhabitants (Lodge 1916: 269).

Racial segregation was also a characteristic of the afterlife as described by alleged spirits through Andrew Jackson Davis, the so-called "American Swedenborg" and proponent of free love. In addition to an "exclusively African realm" ridiculously named Monazolappa, there were two Native American realms, Wallaveesta and Passaeta. Unlike Leonard's and Flint's scripts, however, this was not a system of self-segregation, for Davis explained that whites have "pre-eminence" in the other world, and represent "the higher race to come" (*Death and the After-Life,* 1865; in Ferguson 2012: 120-1). In other writings, Davis characterized black skin as a disability alongside "defective cranium" and "weak physiological structure" (*The Great Harmonia,* 1850; in ibid. 32-3).

In 1898, renowned naturalist and evolutionary theorist Alfred Russel Wallace wrote that according to spirits in the afterlife, there are "millions of undeveloped and degraded spirits" of uncivilized and "less advanced races" in the other world, whose "reclamation and education" "is a sore burden" to "more advanced spirits" (ibid. 12-13).

Racism also occurred in SPR experiments. In one notorious incident, "Hodgson" (via Mrs. Piper) claimed that before his death he told James

Hyslop that if he died first he would communicate to Hyslop through a medium in African-American "minstrel"-type dialect. The word Piper used, however, was a racist slur, and despite its common usage and acceptance in white society of the era, it was considered derogatory at least by the early 19th century. It is important to note that Hyslop had no recollection of ever having had such a conversation with Hodgson. When he said as much during the reading with Piper, spirit-Hodgson replied that it must have been William James. However, William James also had no recollection of such a conversation (Hyslop 1907: 97-98). This means either that spirit-Hodgson was making it up, or, more likely that Piper was. Indeed, even in comparison to her contemporaries, there is a notable preoccupation with race in Piper's scripts, and it can be no coincidence that she also attributed the same derogatory phrase to spirit-Myers.

Although there was very little non-white participation in spiritualism itself, one exception was the African-American medium Paschal Beverly Randolph, who was "routinely disgusted by the automatic attribution of his own statements under trance to the elevating influence of white spirits" (Ferguson 2012: 15). This situation contrasts sharply with the ubiquity of alleged Native American, African-American, and ancient "Oriental" spirit communicators during séances. Rather than being empowering forces for minority races, or modes of multiracial community bonding, historian Christine Ferguson (2012: 116-18) sees such characters more as fulfilments of white stereotyped fantasies and akin to "minstrelsy" entertainment. In a later example, according to Arthur Findlay, a converted Native American spirit-guide allegedly recommended particular Christian prayers to séance sitters (Hazlegrove 2000: 59).

Christian supremacy was also a common theme in the afterlife descriptions, featuring in both Leonard's and Cummins' scripts. For example, non-Christian religious practices were characterized as bad and immoral, and will prevent their devotees from reaching higher realms (Thomas 1928: 154). Similarly, Eileen Garrett communicated a statement from a spirit – said to have progressed as high as the third sphere – that "the Christian religion is above all others" which are simply "wrong"; and that it is the duty of Christians to enlighten "heathens" and "savages" (Thomas 1928: 131).

Historical inaccuracies in mediumship accounts not only reveal plain ignorance, they are also emblematic of fantasies that exoticize the Other while promoting notions of white Christian superiority. One of

Garrett's ostensible communicators, for example, conflated religious figures of different eras, claiming to be "Tahoteh" – presumably a mistransliteration of "Thoth." Although Thoth was a legitimate ancient Egyptian deity, in Garret's account he is anachronistically described as a Muslim, as well as "the Devil" Lucifer (Thomas 1928: 69, 169).

In 1931, a medium named Rosemary claimed while in trance to have been an ancient Syrian woman who lived in Egypt and worked as a temple dancer. Rosemary was guided by "Telika-Ventiu, or Telika of the Fenkhu," or "the Lady Nona," the alleged spirit of a Babylonian princess and consort of the Egyptian pharaoh Amenhotep III. It was claimed that Rosemary manifested xenoglossy – spontaneous, paranormal knowledge of a previously unknown language – of ancient Egyptian, with a purportedly "infallible use of Egyptian grammar." This was, however, thoroughly discredited by Egyptologist Battiscombe Gunn in 1937. While some Egyptologists conceded that Rosemary did produce actual Egyptian words and phrases, her "morphology, syntax and idiom" were either wrong, idiosyncratic, or anachronistic (such as the use of the Arabic definite article *El* in an Egyptian place name). "Nona" also mentioned "people travelling in tents on camels' backs," though camels would not be common in Egypt until over a thousand years after the era she allegedly lived (Griffiths 1986: 149-53, 155-8).

This overall pattern of ignorance and bigotry is usefully seen in the context of Ferguson's (2012: 2, 70) analysis of afterlife descriptions in popular 19th century Spiritualist books, which promulgated "hard hereditarian thought, eugenic doctrines of sexual reproduction, and occult raciology." Ferguson cites the example of Sophia De Morgan, writing in 1863 that "spectral dogs were really the ghosts of human 'imbeciles' whose low mental organization had prevented them from acquiring a recognizably human spirit." Being only "nominally human," the afterlife state reveals these "imbeciles" to be the animals they really are. Likewise, Andrew Jackson Davis wrote that according to the spirits, "certain kinds of idiots" have no afterlife at all, and simply die (*Death and the Afterlife*, 1865; in Ferguson 2012: 71). In 1868, the celebrated medium D. D. Home conveyed an ostensible message from the spirit of "mesmeric-physician" John Elliotson, stating that it is "very wrong to allow persons to marry who are not properly fitted to perpetuate their race."

Ferguson (2012: 9) sees such sentiments as being rooted in Victorian and Edwardian Spiritualism's "abiding love-hate relationship with individualism, free will, materialist theories of mind, degenerationism and the eugenics ideology." This is supported by the references to afterlife self-segregation, evidently designed to maintain the oppressive status quo, while also alleviating the guilt of these self-styled free-thinkers. The practice of racial segregation in the afterlife evolved from being seen as systematic and presumably divinely ordained, to being a matter of choice. Alleged former slaves in the spirit world even testified to their *happiness* at their resumed slavery. In 1857 white medium J. H. Connant claimed that a former slave she had channeled told her that slaves were happy with their lot in the otherworld, that their master didn't make them work hard, and that when he went away they were happy when he returned (Ferguson 2012: 118). The notion of the guilt-free ownership of slaves in the otherworld recalls one of Leonard's communicators explaining that some servants lacked the mental or spiritual capacity to desire emancipation from their benevolent masters (Thomas 1928: 154).

While a sexist afterlife is not overt in the mediumistic descriptions, claims of evidentiality were bolstered with false assertions about female mediums which were rooted in misogynistic presuppositions. These women were routinely characterized as uneducated, "simple," and therefore unable to "invent" on their own the ostensibly spiritual messages they conveyed. However, Leonard was born into a wealthy family and was trained as an opera singer and in theatre. Cummins was a biographer, novelist, and playwright who worked for a time at the National Library at Dublin, and who had hoped to follow her father (a professor of medicine at National University of Ireland) into a medical profession. Garrett was also a novelist, as well as director of a publishing house, editor of a literary magazine, founder of the Parapsychology Foundation, and close friends with philosopher, socialist, early gay rights activist, and poet Edward Carpenter. The historian Alex Owen (1989: 242) emphasized that despite the liberal and liberating aspects of spiritualism in the women's rights movement, there was also an assumption that the power of women mediums rested in some "innate feminine characteristics" such as "receptivity and passivity," which could "bind women into a paradigm of weakness, instability, inferiority, and social powerlessness."

In this kind of social and philosophical climate, it is unsurprising that the afterlife as allegedly communicated through mediums would reflect such repressive, parochial attitudes. As historian Jenny Hazlegrove (2000: 27) writes, Spiritualism appealed "to those who recognized in the spirit plane of existence their own vision of heaven." In this case it is one characterized by racial, social, and religious intolerance aimed at maintaining 19th and early 20th century earthly class hierarchies, in a homogenized, segregated spiritual realm exclusive to white Anglo-American middle-class Christians.

However, the descriptions can also conflict with mainstream Christianity, reflecting the generally (comparatively) progressive beliefs of Spiritualism, and a dissatisfaction with certain orthodox teachings. The occurrence of sex and marriage in the afterlife, for example, is common in Spiritualism but expressly denied in the New Testament (22 Matthew 30; ibid. 86). Spiritualists found "Raymond's" Summerland appealing because it "matched expectations in heterodox pockets of Christianity," including that the other world is a mirror-image of England (Hazlegrove 2000: 25). It also favored reincarnation, self-determination, and divine union in opposition to traditional Christian beliefs. "Once one has dispensed with the constricting vision of heaven as a site of theocentric fixity," writes Ferguson (2012: 93), "the afterlife opens itself up to narration and aesthetic experimentation in hitherto unimaginable ways." Flint (Randall 1975: 137, 112) is a prime example of how this toxic combination of intolerance and progressiveness became entrenched in Spiritualist afterlife conceptions. There are no "coloured people" in Flint's heaven because they self-segregate, though Oscar Wilde's homosexual proclivities are accepted and validated as "natural."

Such dynamics are almost entirely absent from the afterlife descriptions associated with the more recent mediums, as seen above. While these accounts also share with the earlier literature typical NDE elements (darkness, light, subtle body, relatives, life review, being of light, universal consciousness, choice of fate) and other afterlife concepts (idealized mirror-image of earth, mind-dependence, levels of spiritual ascent), they are inclusive and non-judgmental. John Edward (2003: 26), for example, "communicated" that the afterlife is a realm of equality, where only the spiritually enlightened proceed to more "advanced levels" – specifically stating that this includes overcoming racism. While only one medium of those listed above (Anderson 1999: 35-9) reported specifically Christian themes (salvation, grace, intercession), he also described judgement by "the Infinite Light," defined as the deity of all religions which is manifested differently in different cultures. Mediumistic descriptions of the afterlife are infused with contemporary spiritualist attitudes to racial and religious diversity, while also following historical changes in social consciousness over time.

Navigating the Cultural and Experiential Contexts

The social history of Victorian and Edwardian spiritualism provides a backdrop to the mediumistic afterlife descriptions. At the same time, despite all their dubious and idiosyncratic claims, the descriptions feature some of the most common elements of NDEs, many decades before Moody. These factors raise two important questions: If, as argued by some psychical researchers, these mediums were relating genuine spirit communications, what are we to make of such obviously culturally situated perceptions of the afterlife? And how can we explain the general but undeniable similarities between the mediumship accounts and contemporary and historical reports of NDEs cross-culturally?

Philosophical Intelligibility

Due to their lack of evidential value and often dubious content, mediumistic afterlife descriptions were often dismissed as worthless by psychical researchers. Both Hodgson and Lodge actually edited them out of their publications (Sage 1903: 99, Lodge 1916: 230), while their apparently trivial nature contributed to William James's (1902: 105) doubts about the survival hypothesis. More recently, the psychiatrist and criminologist Donald West stated that some of the material from the Scole experiments was so "implausible if not nonsensical" that it throws doubt on the validity of the entire case (Keen et. al. 1999: 396). Philosopher C. D. Broad characterized mediumistic material as predominantly "twaddle, vagueness, irrelevance, ignorance, pretension, positive error, and occasional prevarication," and found the parochialism in Cummins' (1935: lii-liii) afterlife descriptions to be unconvincing. Despite this largely negative assessment, however, Broad (1962: 259) believed that Cummins's scripts also contained "gems of correct, detailed, and relevant information."

In attempts to uphold claims of evidentiality in the face of such dubious descriptive content, justifications were made on behalf of both spirits and mediums. The mediums were said to be "temporarily delirious; they do not know what they are saying," while the spirits themselves "constantly repeat" that being in the medium's atmosphere is, for them, a dream-state (Sage 1903: 172, Cummins 1932: 124). However, "Myers" reportedly stated that although Cummins's descriptions of the afterlife were not always exact, they were "fairly" representative of what he tried to put across, and "the truth as I perceive it" (Gibbes 1932: 29). Ellison (2002: 161) suggested that the material was genuinely from Myers, but distorted by the medium's subconscious activity.

Alternatively, the philosopher and physicist R. C. Johnson (1957: 238) suggested that the more suspect material came from souls in a lower realm, who not only find it difficult to communicate accurately, but also have a continued attachment to earthly life. This leads them to self-create implausible mirror-images of Earth, which would vary between souls – though would also be similar considering the fact that the "spirits" were mostly English or American. Spiritualist author Paul Beard (1980: 24-5) argued that the afterlife is ineffable and that difficulties arise when spirits try to describe a state of being which does not exist in our world, resulting in the use of earthly similes that appear suspiciously too familiar. According to geologist Robert Crookall (1961: 8, 208), the "poor quality" of communications is due to the fact that most people are of only average intelligence – or even "jokers" or "liars" – and they remain so in the afterlife. Similarly, Thomas (1936: 4, 17) stated that spirits carry earthly difficulties with them, such as disliking certain people. While the offensive and ignorant statements might thus be blamed simply on a particular spirit's personal views and lack of education, this would again conflict with the claim that one undergoes intellectual and spiritual evolution and enlightenment in the afterlife.

Gauld (1982: 219) stressed that even hypothetically genuine spirit communications would be filtered through the medium's psyche, with a deceased personality's communications "overshadowing" the medium's psychological processes, including memories, knowledge, and personality. This was also the conclusion reached in three separate cross-medium comparisons of afterlife descriptions: Hart (1959: 233, 236), Crookall (1961: xxiv), and Beard (1980: 7-8). Rather than seeing the overall consistency of the descriptions in terms of a common socio-cultural background, each favored the notion that the descriptions originated with spirits, though were compromised to some degree by mediumistic interference (see also Hart 1959: 201-2, Johnson 1957: 235, Becker 1993b: 9).

Mediums themselves stressed the great difficulties involved in spirit communication, characterizing it as a collaborative effort, in which the medium must interpret psychic impressions through his or her own cultural and educational limitations. The result can often be muddled or confused (Gibbes 1932: 23). The "Myers" spirit allegedly asked his medium to read particular books so that she would have the vocabulary to accurately convey his ideas (Cummins 1935: 15, 17). More recent mediums, such as John Edward (1998: chapter 1), continue to describe such communication as collaborative and interpretative. This may be relevant, for example, to the fact that while Piper characterized physical passion as evil, only in Cummins' scripts does the "sex history" of the deceased determine afterlife fates. Whether the notion originated with medium, spirit, or sitters, however, is impossible to say.

In any case, we are left with a somewhat obvious conundrum: communication difficulties cannot explain why statements about the afterlife and its denizens could not be clear, specific, accurate, and consistent while evidential information allegedly could. Gibbes (1932: 159) made much of the fact that the spirit "Myers" (via Cummins, who, it will be recalled, also reported salamander-flame beings living on stars) used neologisms coined by the "real" Myers, such as "metetheric" and "telaesthesia." However, spirit-"Myers" also stated that mediums do not receive thoughts from spirits in the form of words, and that their minds "cannot conceive or apprehend what [they] cannot translate." This would suggest the impossibility of Cummins receiving Myers's neologisms.

The notion of mind-dependent, self-created group afterlives allegedly put forth by some of the spirits could address some of the problematic aspects of these scripts. The notion allows for individual idiosyncrasies and cultural particularities, for a world created by the imagination in conjunction with those of other like-minded souls would probably retain much continuity with the individual and cultural conditions of people on Earth. This hypothesis will be explored in greater depth in Chapter 7.

In contrast to those researchers who found the afterlife descriptions problematic or even embarrassing, others had no such issues with them. Johnson (1957: 263) described the Cummins material as "reasonable, attractive, and sublime in its conception." He suggested that this was because the communicator, "Myers," was at a more elevated spiritual level than most. Lodge (1932: 10), who was a close friend of Myers, believed the descriptions to be genuine and found them consistent with Myers's views. Likewise, Thomas (1936: ii) accepted the afterlife descriptions in Leonard's scripts on the grounds that he accepted the identity of her spirit communicators, who were well known to him in life. He argued that if their identities are accepted, so should their information regarding the afterlife. Sociologist Hornell Hart (1959: 104, 233) found the descriptions to be meaningful and "worthy of serious study and critical examination."

In summary, if the spirit communications were genuine, it would seem reasonable to expect them to contain philosophically intelligible, plausible, and meaningful descriptions of the afterlife. Some aspects, such as the notions of a mind-dependent afterlife and groups souls, do seem to have those characteristics. Ultimately, however, if we are to accept the claims of evidentiality, we must also either (a) accept the offensive and absurd statements as coming from a mind-dependent context, and reject claims of spiritual progress; (b) understand them as being filtered through the medium's psyche and thus their culture and beliefs, thereby contaminating and misrepresenting the words of the spirits in the otherworld; (c) accept that the afterlife is genuinely racially and religiously oppressive, as well as a chaotic, nonsensical, yet highly bureaucratic realm; or (d) reject the claims altogether as meaningless and confused, even if they do actually originate with spirits.

The Problem of Differences and Similarities

It is interesting to look at how earlier researchers attempted to address the problem of differences and similarities between afterlife descriptions in these kinds of texts. C. D. Broad (1962: 337) compared the statements of Mrs. Leonard with those of "Mrs. Willett." He pointed out that Leonard stated that the subconscious is "the soul's mind" (Thomas 1936: 45) and that in the afterlife it "becomes fully conscious" and retains memory. Memory, in fact, "operates consciously" – it is not recalled, but rather functions in totality with the present. Willett, on the other hand, stated that one enters a "transcendental" state "over and above" ordinary consciousness or subconsciousness, and that a division between the latter two is retained. Broad (1962: 347-8) suggested that the differences can be accounted for by the communicators being in different stages of development, and to the subjective experiences of the recently deceased in a personal dream-like existence. Broad also compared these reports with the NDE-like visions of the 18th century Swedish mystic Emanuel Swedenborg, and found that they agree with and "supplement [them] in a reasonable way."

Two different SPR researchers have attempted to synthesize mediumistic descriptions into a single composite conception of the afterlife. The attempts, however, have grave methodological problems. The first are by psychologist and geologist Robert Crookall (1961, 1978), who rather bizarrely relied expressly on "books which are rejected by most psychical researchers as having no value," and often "not produced in connection with acknowledged psychics." In the 1978 volume he also used anecdotal and even literary material. He concluded that "the experiences described by communicators through first class mediums [including those considered above] are identical to those in the 'popular' books" – as are "spirit-communications" he cited from Europe, India, Hawaii, China, New Zealand (Maori), and Tibet (Crookall 1961: xxvi-v, 187-96). Crookall argued that the consistency between the accounts is only explicable if they actually originated with deceased spirit communicators. The consistencies he found were OBEs with sensations of rising, sinking, and/ or moving through a doorway or tunnel, "an expansion of consciousness," meeting deceased friends and relatives, a cord linking the soul with the body below, and a life review followed by judgement then "assignment" to one of seven spheres or planes (ibid. 12-18). All these features except the cord (a Theosophical belief which is also largely absent in NDEs and reincarnation intermission memories) are prominent recurring elements in the cases examined above. We should also add preternatural light, an idealized mirror-image of earth, mind-dependent existences, judgement and spiritual progression being determined by the individual, group-souls, and an ultimate goal of divine union.

Interestingly, Crookall (1961: 22) found differences between the reported experiences of those who died natural deaths, and those who died sudden or painful deaths. The latter had a "sleep period" while the former were immediately "awake." Instead of peace, happiness, and clarity the latter experienced confusion, mist and fog. They also lacked a cord connecting them with their bodies, and experienced greater delay in seeing deceased friends and relatives.

The second attempt at this kind of synthesis is by Paul Beard (1980: 7-8, 33), who rather than focusing on convincing cases or reputable mediums, instead relied on "post-mortem minds of good caliber," including "Myers," "Lodge," "T. E. Lawrence," "Henry David Thoreau", and others. He also incorporated some descriptions from NDEs, and the visions of Rudolf Steiner. Despite this apparently haphazard and uncritical approach, Beard's composite afterlife does not significantly contradict the information "communicated" through the mediums as described above. This is unsurprising considering that Beard used some of the same material.

In a comparison of sixty-three books which contain mediumistic afterlife descriptions together with what he believed to be evidential material, the sociologist and parapsychologist Hornell Hart (1959: 233,

236) found an overall consistency of the descriptions (also Johnson 1957: 235, and Lorimer 1984: chapter 11). It should also be mentioned that both Carl Jung (1935; coll. 1999: 29) and philosopher and theologian John Hick (1976: 407) noted the similarities with the afterlife as described in mediumship narratives and in Tibetan Buddhism (Hick also added the visions of Swedenborg).

All this consistency may add cumulative weight to the validity of the information, though one might also ask what sort of alternatives would there be to the Western mediumistic visions of the afterlife? It is an all-encompassing experience of many levels and states of being, some of which are mind-dependent, some of which are objective, some of which are a combination of the two, and some of which add reincarnation to the mix. Effectively, there is little it does not contain, and therefore it becomes similar or comparable to virtually any kind of afterlife conception.

Borrowing or Extraordinary Experience?

Similarities between mediumistic accounts suggest some degree of intertextuality: borrowing from and elaborating upon preexisting written sources, such as Spiritualist books or articles in psychical research journals. Whether subconsciously or otherwise, the mediums were almost certainly influenced by afterlife conceptions as found in Theosophical and Spiritualist literature. Such descriptions have been widely published "since the mid-19th century, and are not only part of the common currency of mediumship, but are deeply ingrained in the Western popular imagination. Thus, the similarities between the 19th century narratives and the more recent examples might be explained simply by cultural continuity, rather than the suggestion that they are all independently accessing spiritual truths. Indeed, Ferguson (2012: 92-3) describes spiritualist afterlife descriptions as "remarkable works of creativity" which synthesize "elements from [medieval] Christian cosmic tour literature, pagan underworld lore, classical mythology, contemporary ethnography, science fiction, and the utopian tradition."

However, this ignores the experiential context of the mediumistic material, implying that anomalous experiences did not occur, or that the mediums were either self-deluded or fraudulent. As Hazlegrove (2000: 23) acknowledged, spiritualism offered "a way of organizing supernatural experiences and assumptions in relation to existing cultural realities."

It is important to note that while the issues outlined here make it difficult to accept the descriptions at face value, the recurring similarities between the descriptions are on a broadly thematic level, while most of the main differences occur with more detailed descriptions. These general thematic similarities may in fact be the "gems" of afterlife descriptions we are looking for, to borrow Broad's term.

It is especially significant that they correspond to some of the most common elements found continually in other afterlife-related experiential phenomena, namely the NDE and (as will be seen in the next chapter) reincarnation memories of states between lives. Indeed, while widely considered to be "untestable," the descriptions in these scripts are, in fact, testable by comparison with these other experiential phenomena. What we make of the results of the comparison must remain subjective to some degree, but while similarities don't *necessarily* point to the survival hypothesis or to the narratives being true and accurate representations of the afterlife, nor do the differences deem them purely fictitious. Whether or not we accept them as genuine spirit communications, the consistent similarities with the other types of phenomena require explanation.

Furthermore, even if mediumistic descriptions of the afterlife derive entirely from the workings of the mediums' subconscious, they are still of potential value as visionary experiences. It is possible that mediums genuinely underwent some shamanic-like experience that bore some similarities to NDEs, or had some kind of intimations of such experiences. Some examples – such as the visions of John Edward and Gordon Smith – are comparable more to shamanic trance-journeys in small-scale societies than to NDEs. Even if none of the phenomena themselves are veridical experiences of an actual afterlife, this would not rule out the possibility that visions emanating from the subconscious reveal what an afterlife state – or indeed simply the dying process – is like. Indeed, Jung (1999: 314) suggested that the unconscious might provide hints about the nature of the afterlife.

In this context, NDEs may also be seen as being partly responsible for afterlife conceptions in the medieval Christian and "pagan" literature Ferguson mentions; and these conceptions (perhaps along with the occasional contemporary NDE account) were drawn upon by mediums and other Spiritualist writers for their own afterlife descriptions.

While any final "answer" is ultimately a matter of speculation or belief, this discussion demonstrates the complexities involved in analyzing such material, and the problems inherent in reducing it to either socio-cultural, parapsychological, philosophical, or experiential factors in isolation.

6

BETWEEN LIVES: REINCARNATION
INTERMISSION MEMORIES

~

This chapter explores descriptions of the other world, and the journey there, by people who claim to remember not only a past life but also experiences between lives. There are two types of accounts of such narratives: those related by people who have undergone deliberate past-life regression (PLR) through hypnosis or other psychological techniques; and cases in which a child begins spontaneously to report memories of a previous life.

Although the scientific evidence for PLR is extremely weak, some researchers who have written about the phenomenon have focused on intermediate states and journeys to afterlife realms, making them particularly relevant to our inquiry. The evidence for spontaneous cases is much stronger, and most of those discussed here come from non-Western and/or pre-modern societies.

In broadly thematic ways, accounts of intermission memories in both PLR and in spontaneous cases correspond largely to NDEs. That in itself requires explanation, while the claims of evidentiality in spontaneous cases make them especially worthy of our attention.

Spontaneous Cases

For over fifty years, researchers at the Division of Perceptual Studies (DOPS) in University of Virginia's School of Medicine have been investigating spontaneous cases of children who claim to remember past lives. DOPS was founded by the psychiatrist Ian Stevenson, who published fourteen books and hundreds of papers on what he termed "cases suggestive of reincarnation." Stevenson (1980: 350) believed his subjects were genuine in their testimonies in the sense that *they* believed what they were telling him, and he largely ruled out the possibility of fraud or hoax. Despite the various difficulties with these cases, Stevenson (1980: 369-70), Gauld (1982: 187), Tucker (2005, 2013) and many other researchers have concurred that while the evidence is not decisive, it is enough to permit "a rational belief in reincarnation."

The phenomenon occurs across cultures, spanning Thailand, Burma, Lebanon, India, Turkey, North America, and elsewhere. Two of the main recurring characteristics Stevenson (1980: 354) found were that the memories first manifest between the ages of two and five, and that a significantly large proportion claimed to have died violent deaths. It has also been found that more cases are reported in cultures in which reincarnation beliefs are prevalent (Gauld 1982: 176). Intermission memories are relatively uncommon, however, occurring in fewer than 300 cases out of the roughly 2,500 collected by DOPS (Sharma & Tucker 2004: 102). Reports of intermediate states were rare among Hindus in India, and among Buddhists in Sri Lanka (though some had memories of time on Earth before their new incarnation, such as their soul remaining in an earthly location) (Stevenson 1977: 12).

The main argument against a reincarnation hypothesis in explaining spontaneous cases is the possibility of cryptomnesia, in which the subject recalls information they already possessed but did not consciously remember. Such information would have been learned in normal ways, through books, television, films, newspapers, or overheard in early childhood, only to emerge from deep within the subconscious mind and then experienced as actual personal memories. Combined with a subconscious imaginative dramatization of the alleged past life individual (Badham 1982: 105), this could make for a convincing, internally consistent personality.

There is, however, no consensus about the existence of cryptomnesia outside of past-life memory contexts, and the evidence is unclear. Even if cryptomnesia were demonstrated conclusively, it does not automatically follow that all past-life memory cases can be explained in this way. Furthermore, cryptomnesia cannot explain why children with such memories often recognize people and places wholly unknown to their current personality (Gauld 1982: 167-8; Badham 1982: 106, 108). Significantly, they also display consistent behavioral and emotional reactions to particular individuals they knew in the previous life, and those reactions are appropriate to the past personality and relationship (Stevenson 1980: 362).

Stevenson (1980: 344, 347-8) objected to the cryptomnesia hypothesis on the grounds that the children in most of his cases were simply too young to possess the store of knowledge and memories they displayed. Their comprehension and powers of recall were also reportedly beyond normal childhood scope and ability. Gauld (1982: 187) argues that because of this, some of Stevenson's cases can only be explained by reincarnation, or by resorting to the super-psi hypothesis as discussed in the previous chapter. However, children hardly ever display ESP in any context, so an exceptional ability confined largely to past-life memories is highly unlikely (Stevenson 1980: 360-1, 364). Furthermore, the knowledge, behavior, and personality traits the children display are not explained by the super-psi hypothesis – though they *are* consistent with the alleged past life identity. What super-psi phenomenon could result in a toddler spontaneously manifesting an entirely different behavioral and personality repertoire is obscure. There have been cases in which children have shown an unwavering dislike of a certain food consistent with the past-life personality, a phobia related to the cause of their alleged previous death, and even a penchant for alcohol. Some of these children also show confusion about their surroundings, and their own homes suddenly seem unfamiliar.

On the other hand, subjects normally speak in the language of their current personality, even when the language of the alleged past life personality was different. Proponents of the reincarnation hypothesis argue that memories can be experienced in a variety of ways – emotionally or visually – not only verbally. As Badham (1982: 105) points out, however, "what we see and experience is intimately linked with the language we use to report such experiences." Language is such a central part of an individual that it is unusual that it would not surface in a genuine past personality even as other cultural traits do. The few cases of xenoglossy, in which subjects speak in a language unknown to their current selves, are possible exceptions though very few are compelling (Stevenson 1984).

In any case, if super-psi can be ruled out, three possible explanations remain: genuine reincarnation memories, spirit possession (which is arguably less rational, less scientific, and less parsimonious than a reincarnation hypothesis), or what C. D. Broad called the "psychic factor." According to this idea, after death an individual's memories become detached fragments of personality – residua no longer associated with the former consciousness – which somehow find their way into the mind of a child (Badham 1982: 108). In a limited way, this recalls the Buddhist conception of *skandas*, or sets of elements that make up an individual. However, if such a random process does occur, it is difficult to imagine how all those combined elements could survive in a coherent whole, manifest through a living child, and reconstruct an entire past personality within that child. Being merely a set of memories without an associated conscious being, the result would essentially be a "personality" with no associated "person." A perspective that allows for the survival of *personality* after death but not of *person* seems less intelligible than the reincarnation hypothesis. As with super-psi, nor is it clear how this model could explain a child's recognition of individuals associated with their past life, and the subsequent appropriate emotions involved during "reunions" with the past personality's family and friends.

The philosopher Paul Edwards (1996: 140, 255-56) called Stevenson "deluded," and his work "absurd nonsense." This stance, both extreme and unwarranted, is based mainly upon (a) Edwards's own self-described "presumptions against reincarnation"; (b) the absurd tautological claim that because reincarnation is impossible it cannot occur; (c) unfounded assumptions of fraud on the part of the subjects or their families; and (d) methodological issues which were mostly beyond Stevenson's investigative control, such as not enough interview time, interviews taking place long after the fact, and the families of past-life personalities and present "incarnations" having met prior to investigation. Edwards's first two criticisms are based upon his own culturally situated and scientifically unproven personal philosophy. The third is based upon his unsubstantiated sweeping suspicions rather than particular facts in the cases. The fourth does nothing to disprove a reincarnation hypothesis – it merely stresses research difficulties that were acknowledged by Stevenson himself.

Edwards (1996: 252) also stated that the notion of intermediate states is intrinsically absurd, and if a subject who reports past-life memories also reports having experienced such a state, "this is sufficient to undermine the trustworthiness" of the entire case. This is not an argument, or science, or even philosophy, but merely an opinion. As with many of Edwards's other beliefs and opinions which he characterized as categorical fact, it lacks reason, logic, and objectivity, while also displaying unfamiliarity with conflicting evidence and competing hypotheses.

In addition to the cases investigated by researchers at University of Virginia and elsewhere, there are also historical examples from Burma, China, and Japan. There are also a number of accounts from Native American societies as found in anthropological literature of the 19th and 20th centuries. They will be discussed below alongside the research cases under the relevant regional headings.

Burma

Spontaneous cases with intermission memories appear to be more common in Burma than elsewhere. A historical example involves two male twins named Maung Gyi and Maung Nge, born in 1886. When they learned to talk, they began calling each other by the names of a husband and wife who had died in the area around the time the boys were born. The parents of the boys decided to test their knowledge of their previous life, and found that they were able to identify roads, houses, people, and even their former clothing. They also recalled specific incidents unknown to the parents. At the age of six, the children were interviewed by British official Harold Fielding (1898: 328-29), who noted that one of the boys – the ostensible reincarnation of the woman – was "more like a girl than a boy."

> The boys described their intermission memories to Fielding: "After they died they said they lived for some time without a body at all, wandering in the air and hiding in the trees. This was for their sins. Then, after some months, they were born again as twin boys. 'It used,' said the elder boy, 'to be so clear, I could remember everything; but it is getting duller and duller, and I cannot now remember as I used to do.'"

Another young Burmese boy told Fielding (1898: 338)

> that he passed three months between his death and his next incarnation without a body. This was because he had once accidentally killed a fowl. Had he killed it on purpose, he would have been punished very much more severely. Most of this three months he spent dwelling in

the hollow shell of a palm-fruit. The nuisance was, he explained, that this shell was close to the cattle-path, and that the lads as they drove the cattle afield in the early morning would bang with a stick against the shell. This made things very uncomfortable for him inside.

Later Burmese cases have been researched by medical student Poonam Sharma & psychiatrist Jim Tucker (2004: 107ff). They unfortunately did not provide full descriptions of any accounts, but instead highlighted the most commonly recurring features from the 35 cases they collected. They found that the children often remembered being out of their previous body and seeing the preparations for their funeral. Some recalled attempting to communicate with living relatives but finding that they were unable to do so. The souls were then "directed by an elder or an old man dressed in white" to some earthly place, such as a tree or a pagoda, though some remained near the body or walked along a path.

The children also frequently reported encountering the souls of other deceased people, and over half recalled "choosing parents for the next life." Some followed their new parents home, while others were directed to them by the elder figure. Some recalled entering their new mother, usually being ingested into her body after "transforming into a grain of rice or speck of dust in the water." Sometimes the water would be discarded before being drunk, or guardian spirits would prevent the new soul from entering, and the soul would have to try again.

A girl name Ma Par recalled having been a British pilot who died following a crash in Burma. Her soul went to see her family back in England, but the "King of Death" made her reincarnate in Burma (Stevenson 1997: 1812).

Thailand

Buddhists in Thailand claim to have experienced intermediate states comparatively frequently, though usually remember nothing about them. Those who do most often recall an OBE in which they witnessed their own funeral, and seeing a "man in white" – a sage who welcomes and guides souls, and helps them to decide upon their next birth. The deceased are often given food, usually fruit, which causes them to forget their previous life. Those who claim to remember the experiences say they did not eat the fruit (Stevenson 1983: 6-7). A Thai man named Bongkuch Promsin, born in 1962, remembered that prior to his reincarnation, his soul lived for seven years in a tree before following his new father home on a bus.

A girl named Ampan Petcherat, who began speaking of past-life memories at only one year old, reported that a man took her to the realm of the dead and "introduced her to the 'head man.'" She then went "up a ladder to heaven" with another man, where she met yet another – a kind man "of large size and black complexion who was dressed in white." The girl claimed to be the reincarnation of a four-year-old boy and displayed traits of a male child that age, making thirty-three verified statements of recognition. Another girl, Ratana Wongsombat, began talking about a previous life at the age of eleven months. She described an intermediate state with "many levels of heaven." She was taken to the highest level where she encountered the Buddha's relics (ibid. table 4, 12, 56-66, 69).

Additional investigations into Thai spontaneous cases were made by Stevenson's colleague, Francis Story (1975: 169-70). A soldier recalled an OBE from his previous life, during which he saw his body below before being drawn into the womb of his new mother. Another soldier described similar experiences, adding that he had powers of mental teleportation and passing through solid objects.

A Buddhist monk, born in 1908, also recalled a past life OBE and seeing his own body being cremated. He claimed that his state of awareness was such that he could "see in all directions" at once. He left the other realm spinning and falling, then lost consciousness before finding himself in his new body. Story also mentioned "many" reports of deceased individuals being met by a guide who assists in the transition to a new birth – in numerous cases an old bearded man dressed in white. There are also "several" cases involving the deceased being offered the "fruit of forgetfulness" (ibid. 184-5, 197, 199).

India

In 1930, at the age of four, an Indian girl named Shanti Devi began to talk to her parents about her past life, and her longing to visit her previous home. Studying the case documents in the 1970s and 80s, Ian Stevenson found that Shanti Devi had made 24 verified statements about her previous life. In 1936, aged 10, she recounted her intermission memories:

"Just before death I felt a profound darkness and after death I saw a dazzling light. Then and there I knew I had come out of my body in a vaporous form and that I was moving upwards." She was met by four teenage males dressed in bright saffron robes. They had a rectangular vessel about ten inches in diameter into which they placed Shanti Devi's soul and took her to the third plane. They told her that "those who aspired for a higher life sincerely, but who had committed fleshly wrong in this life, were dipped in the river before moving any higher." They then proceeded to the fourth plane where "all is open space" and "full of light ... very mild, and smoothing and enlivening light." There she saw "still more saints, brighter in appearance than those on the third plane." With them was the deity Krishna, who "was showing each person a record of his activities on earth, good and bad, and accordingly what would be his condition in the future." Though Shanti Devi did not recall much of his words, she did hear him read out "House Number 565," which was her address in her new identity. The four saffron-robed saints then took Shanti Devi "to a place like a staircase where it was very bright." After sitting there for a long period, she "was taken to a dark room, from all sides of which a very bad smell was coming out. I was made to lie down in a clean place there. ... I did not feel any pain. I simply passed into a state of unconsciousness, and at that very moment I saw very brilliant light" (Rawat & Rivas 2005).

Much of Shanti Devi's account is similar to the intermission memories of Santosh Sukla, whose case was investigated by Stevenson. She also recalled being taken to the other world by four people, though she was dipped in the river which made her cry. They then took her to a village where many people ate fruit from numerous trees in gardens. A man dressed in yellow sat on a bed. Santosh leaned against a pillar for a period, and eventually ate some of the fruit that was offered to her. After a year in this place, she was reincarnated (Stevenson 1997: 556).

Sri Lanka

One of Stevenson's (1997: 77ff, 88-102, 105-06, 113-14) most compelling cases is that of the five-year-old Sri Lankan girl, Disna Samarasinghe. She displayed personality traits of the woman she claimed to be, including tastes in particular foods and skills in household chores she had not been taught. She knew the route to her former personality's house though she had never been there. She correctly identified the family members, and knew the layout and contents of the house. Stevenson listed fifty-four confirmed statements of recognition made by the child, most of which could not have been obtained by normal means. He concluded that the only explanations were advanced telepathy or genuine reincarnation memories. Disna recalled leaving her previous body and flying to a realm reserved for the morally good. There she met a kingly figure in reddish-colored clothes which never became dirty. He wore pointed shoes and lived in a glass palace with "beautiful reed beds." Disna wore similar clothes, but of gold, and spent her time playing and materializing food which did not need to be consumed to satisfy her hunger. The king figure then decided that she should be reborn.

A Sri Lankan woman named Purnima Ekanayake remembered mourners weeping at her funeral, floating in darkness, then "going to the light to come to her new family" (Sharma & Tucker 2004: 108). A girl named Sunita Khandelwal described her intermission memory after falling from a balcony in her previous life: "I went up. There was a baba (holy man) with a long beard. They checked my record and said, 'Send her back.' There are some rooms there. I have seen God's house. It is very nice. You do not know everything that is there." (Tucker 2005: 280).

China

In an account from 8th century China, a man recalled that when his previous self died, his "soul hovered about in an uncertain state without leaving the house." He observed his father, Huang Ku, reciting a verse of mourning he had written for his son. Moved by this, the boy decided, "I will again become a son in the Ku family." He then felt himself "seized and sent before an Official of the Underworld," who decreed that his rebirth would indeed be with his previous family. After a period of unconsciousness, the boy woke up in his new body, and though he recognized his relatives, he did not remember anything about his previous life. At the age of seven, however, he began to refer to his older brother as his *younger* brother, for in his previous life *he* had been the eldest; and that apparently triggered full past-life recall (Willoughby-Meade 1928: 76; Matlock 2017: 231-32).

Japan

A well-documented Japanese historical case concerns a boy named Katsugoro, born in 1815 in a village called Nakano, near Tokyo. Though most discussions of the case have used the writer Lafcadio Hearn's translation of a book called *Chinsetsu Shuki* (Collection of Strange Stories), Ohkado Masayuki (2021) has recently analyzed the case using earlier and more reliable primary sources. His source for the intermission memories is an 1823 investigation by the famous Japanese scholar of philology and philosophy, Hirata Atsutane.

Katsugoro began talking about his past life when he was eight years old, and many of the statements he made about it were verified. He recalled that his soul left his previous body just as it was being placed into his coffin. He sat on the shroud covering the body, then went back home. On the way he tried to speak to people but they couldn't hear him.

> An old man appeared with long white hair wearing a black kimono, saying, "Come here." I followed, going up to a place which I didn't know where it was. Then, I was in a beautiful field and played. Flowers were in full bloom, and when I tried to break off a twig, a small crow appeared and threatened me greatly. When I recall this, I still feel scared.

As he played in the other world, he could hear sounds from Earth – his parents talking and monks reciting a sutra. He could also smell their food, though could not eat it. He was even able to visit his previous home.

The old man then pointed out his future home and told him he would be reborn there. Katsugoro left the old man "and stayed under a persimmon tree in the yard" for three days, then entered the house through a window and stayed in the stove for three more days. He heard his mother talking about the possibility of leaving to work in the city, and this conversation was later verified. She canceled the trip when she discovered that she was pregnant, and Katsugoro was born 10 months later. The boy only vaguely remembered entering his mother's womb. He concluded that he was "not afraid of my death." When asked why, he replied,

> I realized I was dead because other people said so. At the time of my death, I didn't see my body, and I didn't think I was dead. The moment of death was not as agonizing as it may have appeared to others. After I died, I didn't become hungry, didn't feel hot nor cold. It was not very dark, even at night. No matter how long I walked, I didn't get tired. When I was with the old man, I was afraid of nothing. People say I was born after six years, but I felt it was just a short time.

The deity Mitake-sama also told him, "You don't have to be afraid of death."

Katsugoro's statement that he did not see his body is interesting in light of the fact that he knew he was leaving his body as it was being placed in its coffin, and he *did* see the coffin at his funeral and even sat on his own shroud. Whether this is an inconsistency in his testimony, or if he was just being literal and specific, or somehow didn't associate the funeral with himself, is not clear.

More recently, a number of unusual Japanese cases have been identified in which children recall only the intermission prior to the present incarnation, without having memories of a previous life at all. One boy, aged six, remembered "flying in the sky, looking for my mother. Looking down. I could see my mother and chose her." A nine-year-old girl recalled being in another realm before her current life, with souls of many other children and "a god, an entity with authority." She described the entity as generous, and said "He was looking after us, like a counselor" (Ohkado & Ikegawa 2014: 477).

A total of 21 such cases were researched, and it was found that most described the other world as "cloud or sky," though others said it was a realm of light, "a wide space where you can see the Earth," "like a star," "where there are a number of levels," "up there," and "in the shape of a long ellipse." It was a peaceful, joyful realm though "difficult to describe." Most met a god or god-like figure who helped them decide on their future parents. Many saw their future siblings, and one described other souls as "light balls." Seeing activities on Earth concerning one's future family was common, and over half remembered the reason for their rebirth, which varied from helping people on Earth to having a better life than their previous one. "One child said he did not remember why he was born because he forgot the reason when he was born in order to find what it is in the current life." Over half the children remembered entering their mother's womb, and three were assisted in the process by a deity, "a shining ball, or an angel-like entity" (ibid. 484).

Turkey

A Turkish Druze boy named Nasir Toksöz began speaking of a former life at the age of two-and-a-half. The boy claimed that prior to his rebirth, he first "went to God and gave an account of his conduct to

Him." Stevenson (1980: 9-10, 324, 335) observed that the experience was comparable to the NDE life review.

Despite its brevity, the account is important because it conflicts with local beliefs. The Druze believe that the soul transmigrates *directly* from one body to the next, meaning that any sort of state between lives is impossible, even including OBEs. Indeed, the issue is so religiously sensitive that it is surprising that the case was reported at all. Druze families have been known to falsify birth and death records in order to make a previous life "correctly" correspond to a present one, *without* any intermediate phase.

Native North America

Numerous Native American cultures held beliefs in reincarnation. Accounts of cases with intermission memories form part of a wider, complex afterlife experience-and-belief system incorporating NDEs, afterlife myths with NDE themes, and shamanic journeys to realms of the dead. It is significant that all of the Native American accounts of intermission memories are found in NDE contexts, and most involved shamans. While there are no examples of research cases like those described above, a number of societies had systems to empirically validate reincarnation claims, including investigating evidential dreams, past-life memories, birthmarks, and personality traits consistent with the earlier personality. These include the Gitksan, Wet'suwet'en, Beaver (Mills 1988: 408), Tillamook (Boas 1923: 12), and Tlingit (De Laguna 1972: 776ff).

Among the Tlingit people of the Pacific Northwest coast, information about the afterlife originated in both NDEs and accounts of intermission experiences prior to reincarnation. It was believed that souls could decide to be reborn on Earth and choose their new parents and sex (Knapp & Childe 1896: 163; De Laguna 1972: 777, 779).

A 19th century account of a shaman named Ky'itl'a'c is found in what at first appears to be an NDE narrative. Ky'itl'a'c committed suicide and his soul ascended a ladder to the realm of the deity Tahit, where he was interrogated by "an old watchman, who was all black, and had curly hair." Ky'itl'a'c was allowed to proceed when he explained that he had killed himself. When he reached the house of Tahit, the deity instructed two spirits to give Ky'itl'a'c a tour of the realm (recalling the otherworld tour accounts discussed in Chapter 2). The spirits took him first to a lake in the Milky Way and gave him a pebble to throw at white geese floating there. The spirits sang when Ky'itl'a'c succeeded, making him laugh and feel like he was being tickled. They then took him "through the cloud door" to see Tahit's daughters. When Ky'itl'a'c saw Earth below he decided to return, so he pulled a blanket over his head and jumped. He made his way to a house where a baby was crying and reincarnated into it. When he grew up he told his people about Tahit and his realm. One of the beliefs that derived from his narrative was that those who had been beheaded in this world "had their eyes between their shoulders in the upper world," something Ky'itl'a'c had apparently seen on his tour of the other realm (Boas 1890: 844– 5; Matlock 2017: 227-28; Shushan 2018: 66).

In an early 20th century Tlingit example, a child revealed that he had recently been a man killed in battle. He taught his people what he had learned during his intermediate experience: that there was a particular realm for those who died by violence, and that spirits of the dead appeared on Earth in the form of St. Elmo's fire when a murder was about to be committed (Swanton 1908: 463; Shushan 2018: 68).

A number of additional Tlingit accounts were collected between 1949-1954. In the first, two men were killed and found themselves walking in a "strange land." One stopped to rest, though the other continued until he came to a river where he sat beneath a tree. Over the course of nine days, the riverbank began to erode and the man could not move. On the tenth night he fell into the river, and woke up in his new body— his sister's baby. His companion was reborn at the same time, and they were raised together (De Laguna 1972: 775; Matlock 2017: 228; Shushan 2018: 68-9).

The second account also features two men dying together. After being shot, they found themselves at a stairway which they ascended. They arrived at a place where the souls of others who had been shot were playing "something like hockey," or "going after water" which was actually the Northern Lights. Another game involved jumping around or through hard rocks known as greenstone. When one of the men jumped onto a sharp stone he was thrown out of the other realm.

> He remembered when he started to fall. And somebody said he was born again. They recognized him. They said his name, and he said something, but they were scared, so they said nothing. When he was born, they find some birthmarks [associated with his previous life]. When he started to talk, he started telling this story, and every time

he started telling the story, there's always something that happens, so he has to stop (De Laguna 1972: 773–774).

A Tlingit man named 'Askadut from the Sitka community died and found himself outside his body, unable to reenter. His family couldn't see or hear him, and he attended his own funeral and cremation. He found that he was unable to leave his ashes "until he began to think of the place where the dead people go." Because he had waited so long, his journey was difficult, plagued by thorn bushes, rain, and sleet. Arriving at a muddy riverbank, he could see people on the other side. He called out but they could not hear him, and it was only when he grew tired and yawned that they heard and came for him. In some versions of the narrative 'Askadut returned to Earth because "he wanted to come back to his family so bad"; though in others it was upon his deceased aunt's instruction. Nine days after his return, he reincarnated as his own wife's baby and she recognized him "by a cut or scar on his foot." As the anthropologist Frederica De Laguna (1972: 767-68) concluded, "So it was from 'Askadut that they learned about the dead, and what to do when people die" (Matlock 2017: 228-30; Shushan 2018: 69).

From the Bering Strait comes a brief Yupik or Inupiat account of a shaman who remembered having died while in a previous incarnation. He visited the land of spirits, then reincarnated on Earth in the body of an unborn child (Nelson 1900: 433- 4).

In his 1909 autobiography, a shaman named Sam Blowsnake (1909: 5– 7) of the Ho-Chunk (Winnebago) people of Wisconsin related intermission memories from *two* previous lives. In the first, Blowsnake (also called Crashing Thunder) recalled how he died on the battlefield. Unaware that he was dead, his spirit traveled back to his home. Ignored by his family, he returned to the battlefield and saw his corpse below. He was then taken to the spirit world in the western horizon, where one can travel anywhere by thought alone. After trying to return home for four years, the chief of the spirit village finally allowed him to be reincarnated so he could take revenge on the enemies who had killed him and his relatives. In his intermission memories from his next incarnation, Blowsnake remembered watching the burial of his body from above, going to a joyful spirit realm, and then to "the place where Earthmaker lived" where he stayed for four years before being reincarnated again (Matlock 2017: 231; Shushan 2018: 34).

Among the Gwich'in (Dene) people of the Canadian far north, a girl named Ruth, born in 1931, began talking about her intermission memories at the age of six. She described to her mother how she had died and

> had gone into the sky up a steep and very narrow trail, [and] had been met at a beautiful big gate by a man in white who identified himself as St. Peter. She had proceeded along a road and had seen a lot of the old people. Finally she came to a big crowd of people and angels, and there was Jesus. She was frightened, but she was taken up to Jesus, who spoke to her kindly and told her, "This is not the time for you." So she turned away and didn't remember anything else. Ruth was born a year later.

Ruth's sister had died a year before, and it was believed that Ruth was her reincarnation (Slobodin 1992: 151). Although the Gwich'in had been fully converted to Christianity, they continued to believe in reincarnation despite the fact that it is not a Christian belief. The authority of the extraordinary experiences of their own people was apparently greater than that of their adopted religion.

One Gwich'in NDE was apparently *almost* an intermission memory. In 1938, a woman who lived near the Peel River in the Northwest Territories recounted how she one day left her body during an illness. Though she did not go to another realm, she recalled seeing from above her whole village and her son. She felt that she had to start searching for a new mother but could think of no pregnant women she knew. She realized she had no choice but to return: "I went down, through the wall of the tent and back into my body, and I woke up here, still sick" (Slobodin 1992: 136-37; Matlock 2017: 231).

The narrative of a Lenape (Delaware) man from 1746 should also be mentioned. It recounts not an experience between lives but one prior to the man's first existence on Earth. He recalled being in a heavenly realm with a "great man" clothed "with the brightest day he ever saw. ... Everything that was beautiful and lovely in the earth was upon him, and might be seen by looking upon him." The man's soul stood apart from his "body," "as lovely as the man himself, and filled all places, and was most agreeable as well as wonderful." The Lenape man was "unspeakably entertained and delighted" in that realm until the great man told him telepathically that he must go to Earth to be born to a particular woman. Although the Lenape man was able to choose his future profession, the great man told him that he would also become a murderer. After the Lenape man's rebirth, the great man would sometimes appear to him in dreams and guide his actions. On some occasions the great man would appear as "all light, and not only light himself, but it was light all around him, so that he could see though men, and knew the thoughts of their hearts" (Edwards & Dwight 1822: 348-50).

United States

Among the statements of children with past-life memories in Tucker's (2005: 269, 278) U.S. researches, a boy named Bobby remembered having been in a realm where "people are just happy and never get sick." Lee "remembered deciding to be reborn. He said that other beings helped him with his decision to come down to Earth." William recalled "that he floated up after dying, and he talked about being in heaven, where he saw God as well as animals."

A fuller account was given by a boy named Sam Taylor, who remembered being his own grandfather. Sam made several accurate statements about his previous life that he could not have known in his current one, and was able to identify "himself" (his grandfather) from old photos. He described how "his body shot up to heaven when he died." He met an uncle there, and also met God, who gave him a card that had green arrows on it, which would allow him to be reincarnated (ibid. 232-35, 238).

Past-Life Regression

Alleged memories from PLR have not been investigated to a scientific standard. This is partly due to the focus on the phenomenon's therapeutic rather than parapsychological significance. There is a consistent lack of information regarding hypnotic techniques and trance states during regressions, and most researchers do not state whether their subjects were in fact hypnotized or not. Hypnosis is scientifically measurable by electro encephalograph, though no researchers have reported performing the requisite tests in PLR cases (Moss & Keeton 1981: 27). This includes Newton (1994: 4) who nonetheless argued that PLRs cannot be hallucinations because hallucinations do not occur in a deep hypnotic state, and that subjects "cannot lie" when under hypnosis (though they can "misinterpret" their subconscious). Nor have there been any controlled experiments in which historians have questioned subjects, or when evidential data was deliberately sought and verified (Badham 1982: 106).

The British hypnotherapist Arnall Bloxham made audio recordings of over 400 regressions over a period of twenty years. While he did not report intermission memories, Bloxham's claims of evidentiality make his work relevant here. He stated that most of the past-life personalities were coherent, stable, and largely consistent with known individuals and the historical facts of their times (Iverson 1977: 15-6). When his cases are studied in depth, however, Bloxham's claims do not hold up. Jane Evans, for example, one of his most celebrated cases, possessed obscure knowledge of six different historical periods of her past personalities. The sources of her information, however – including specific historical inaccuracies and other mistakes made by Evans – have been traced to novels and popular history books (Carroll 2004). Nor is there evidence that her past personalities actually existed (though there is, of course, none that they *didn't* exist, either).

Another of Bloxham's subjects described Vikings with horned helmets, though Vikings never actually wore such helmets (Wilson 1981: 254). Similarly, one of Wambach's (1978: 139) subjects who claimed to be a late 5th century BCE Egyptian "remembered" buying clothes with small gold coins, though coinage was not introduced in Egypt until over a century later. Other alleged evidence such as "period handwriting" and previously unknown accents have been similarly explained away, while cases of xenoglossy are invariably restricted to a limited number of common words and little or no knowledge of grammar and syntax (Wilson 1981: 110).

PLR narratives also differ by researcher, indicating that the therapists themselves impact the reports in specific ways. For example, while Bloxham's subjects range widely over times and places, hypnotherapist Joe Keeton's British subjects remain British in all their transmigrations, and go back no further than the 16th century (Wilson 1981: 13). Popular history writer Ian Wilson (1981: 157-8) suggested that multiple personality disorder could be a possible explanation for PLR phenomena, which could account for "changes of accent, handwriting, facial expressions, body image," and so on. On the other hand, Gauld (1982: 165) argued that they are merely displays of "creative imagination." While few parapsychologists lend them much credence, many hypnotherapists have found their subjects' PLRs to be compelling, including Fiore (1978: 4), Moss & Keeton (1981: 17), Woolger (1987: 33, 70), and Newton (1994: 4).

While it is possible to investigate claims of past-life memories by attempting to validate details about alleged former personalities, there is no way to investigate statements regarding memories of dying and intermediate experiences other than by comparison with other extraordinary experiences of the afterlife. As will be seen, the similarities between PLR afterlife descriptions and those found in NDE and mediumship reports are significant enough that they require explanation.

Edith Fiore

The American psychologist Edith Fiore (1978: 216-217, 219, 224-5, 229-30, 238) has stated that "all" the afterlife descriptions of her "many" subjects conform to the "typical" NDE as described by Moody. These include feelings of joy and peace, OBE and seeing one's body, moving upwards through darkness towards a bright light, and meeting guides and deceased loved ones. Guides are described as wearing robes, and loved ones appear in renewed "bodies" of light, sometimes in familiar clothes. Subjects are often profoundly affected by the experience, and many find it to be life-changing. Even skeptics who originally underwent hypnosis for purely therapeutic reasons become convinced of their previous death and rebirth after the experience.

Helen Wambach

Another American psychologist, Helen Wambach (1979: 89, 139) attempted to confirm historical details in her subjects' past-life memories, and claimed great success at doing so.

Rather than researching individual cases in depth, Wambach took a novel approach to the problem by amassing large numbers of accounts and comparing key features between them (adopting a quantitative rather than qualitative method).

Of more relevance here, she also asked her subjects to describe the death of their previous personality, specifically in order to test if they were consistent with Moody's NDE schema. Realizing that she could neither confirm nor deny descriptions of the death-and-rebirth experiences her subjects reported, she sought to determine if there would be consistencies among the thousands of cases she gathered. In order to facilitate this approach, Wambach "hypnotized" her participants in large "group hypnotic workshops." While she did outline the technique that she used (ibid. 9ff) – a combination of relaxation and visualization exercises – she did not provide scientific evidence that her subjects were indeed in a medically identifiable hypnotic state. Her stated goal was to induce "a brainwave amplitude of five cycles per second" in her subjects, though she did not actually undertake EEG measurements to confirm that this was achieved (see also, Moore 1981: 193).

In any case, Wambach (1978: 67, 43ff) did indeed find that the death and intermission memories of many of her subjects corresponded to the main features of NDEs as outlined by Moody. In varying percentages, these included OBE and seeing one's own "corpse," a sense of release, entering a tunnel and traveling through darkness, moving upwards towards light, encountering deceased friends and relatives, and feelings of peace and joy. While acknowledging that some of her subjects might have read Moody, because of her large sample size she believed that many would have been unfamiliar with his work. Although Wambach stated that she did not suggest the features of light, tunnel, or meeting deceased friends and relatives, part of her induction script involved telling subjects that they would not experience fear, that they had a "cloud" they could return to, and that their "spirit is leaving the body" (ibid. 89).

In addition to the NDE elements, Wambach's subjects also described an afterlife council in the otherworld as having "ancient customs" and sitting on wooden chairs. Guides are like "large beams of light," and time in the other world is spent in education and helping others. Only 0.1% reported encountering deities. Some mentioned going to a "land of light" prior to rebirth. As with Fiore's subjects, groups of individuals are reborn together. Most of Wambach's subjects remembered a helpful figure assisting them in choosing their rebirth, and determining the new sex, time period, and location. A Council of Twelve sometimes fulfilled this function, though more often it was a friend or relative. The choice is determined by the need for experience and spiritual growth (Wambach 1978: 23-4, 28-31, 38, 43, 62, 82, 85, 97, 150). It is unclear what being "spiritual" means in this context, begging the question of how and why a spirit can be more or less spiritual.

Bruce Goldberg

Bruce Goldberg (1982: 91-2), an American dentist and hypnotherapist, is perhaps the only past-life therapist to state outright that his subjects were in a genuine hypnotic state, and to acknowledge the need for empirically measuring such states. His scientific credibility is compromised, however, by his acceptance of a subject's historically absurd claims concerning a past life in ancient Egypt. The subject claimed to have witnessed the building of the Great Pyramid which was overseen by "the directors" who are eight feet tall, with "large heads and long fingers" and teleportation powers. They controlled the workers by means of telepathy, and a battery-powered crane was used to lift the stone blocks.

Goldberg (1982: 171, 174) wrote that there are no cross-cultural differences between the intermediate states reported by Jews, Christians, Muslims, or "any other belief," though he provided no details on how he reached that conclusion. In fact, the claim is flatly contradicted by one of his own subjects, who described a mind-dependent state in which souls have the experiences they would expect. One, for example, saw "haloed angels" playing harps. Goldberg (1982: 5-6) noted similarities between PLR and NDE narratives, and stated that the consistencies suggest "more than coincidences." Communication is telepathic and all minds are open. Souls have the choice of whether or not to enter the light, though they cannot spiritually progress otherwise. Many recall a loud buzzing or roaring sound. There are bright colors which change with one's "vibrational rate," and some reported entering a tunnel (after Goldberg suggested it to them).

Some descriptions were unique to Goldberg's subjects. A skeptic who allegedly had no interest in the afterlife, and had never read anything about reincarnation, described an intermission memory in which he was lying on a table under a dome, surrounded by bright light. Individuals around him were "evaluating" his life. While a dome was described by some of Goldberg's other subjects, it has not been reported by other PLR therapists (although see Newton's "cones" below). Likewise, Goldberg stated that a silver cord connecting the astral body with the physical body was "constantly reported," though it is conspicuously absent in other PLR reports (ibid. 169-70, 172).

Roger Woolger

British psychologist Roger Woolger (1987: 38, 92, 284, 294, 299) claimed that NDEs are described in "thousands of past-life regressions," though it is doubtful that his simple creative visualization method resulted in actual hypnotic states. When I personally attended one of Woolger's workshops in London in 2004, I experienced only my own imagination using his technique. Nor did I see anything that would lead me to believe that other participants were describing genuine past-life memories, or that they were even in altered states of consciousness. Woolger himself described his subjects' "memories" as "psychodrama created by deliberate intervention."

Some of his subjects reported "a state of lucidity ... where visions of great luminosity and great spiritual beauty spontaneously manifest." Others saw only darkness, and some had hellish experiences. One woman was tormented by people she had killed in a previous life, and was then isolated until she had been sufficiently punished. Another reported sitting in a sparse room for a long period, thinking about her selfishness before being permitted to be reborn.

Eighty percent of Woolger's (1987: 115, 296-97, 302) subjects said that they quickly passed into another body, while only 20% saw spiritual beings in another realm – often friends and family, or a figure robed in white radiating "love and wisdom." This figure assists the deceased in self judgement and deciding on the next phase of existence. One subject reported a "celestial temple" in which all her previous lives were recorded, while another saw all her lives woven into a tapestry. Others reported feelings of oneness, wholeness, and complete understanding. None reported tunnel-like experiences.

Joel L. Whitton

Taking a somewhat more methodical approach, Canadian neuropsychiatrist Joel L. Whitton (1986: 3, 28) compared the descriptions of intermediate states of six subjects from differing religious backgrounds. In total, he collected over thirty cases with somewhat consistent reports. Whitton believed he was communicating with his subjects' "higher self," or *atman*, though unfortunately he made no attempts to validate the historical details of the claimed past lives.

With the exception of Goldberg's idiosyncratic dome and silver cord, Whitton's cases feature all the elements familiar from the other studies, alongside additional details. Some reported a tunnel, and some were assisted by guides on the journey to the other realm. More often, however, souls were alone before "merging with a multitude of strangers at the end of the journey" (ibid. 11). Souls must make deliberate attempts to *think* in order to "realize our own individuality." Increased levels of consciousness bring about spiritual advancement.

The other realm is nonmaterial, though a soul's subconscious creates comprehensible symbols experienced as reality. Subjects reported beaches, palaces, gardens, and all manner of idealized mirror-images of Earth. One man reported being in a cave from which he could see Earth in one direction, and the "interlife" realm in the other – a place of Mediterranean-style whitewashed buildings and luminous hills. Many "found themselves hard at work in vast halls of learning equipped with libraries and seminar rooms." Doctors, lawyers, and physicists spoke of "studying their respective disciplines," while others spoke of more metaphysical pursuits. A scientist gained profound knowledge of the workings of the universe and a musician heard rapturous music (ibid. 31, 33-34, 48).

It is a world of light and love with colors beyond our spectrum, where souls communicate in an unknown, unpronounceable language. They experience total understanding, which one subject said was "like going into the sun and being absorbed without any sensation of heat." Cleansed of "fear and negativity," the "soul is reabsorbed into the undifferentiated oneness of existence." It is not explained how the soul then re-integrates in order to be reincarnated (ibid. 33, 37).

The "animal emotions" – such as anger, desire, jealousy, and sadness – disappear with the loss of the physical body. The "cognitive emotions" – "love, guilt, ecstasy, admiration, remorse, loss, dread" – continue with the astral body (ibid. 38).

The "Council" consists of "three wise figures," and while Whitton claimed that a trinity of judges is consistent in afterlife beliefs cross-culturally, this is not supported by my research. Some of Whitton's subjects said there were four, and others seven (but not twelve as in Wambach). After a life review and judgement, some enter a sleep-like state before waking up in a new body. Those burdened by guilt and remorse have distressing experiences, feeling all the pain and suffering they caused in their previous life. A man who had murdered his wife appeared before the tribunal "with his own throat slashed." Most souls, however, describe the judges as benevolent, healing, and encouraging. They do not actually judge, but offer "retrospective counselling," and help to put the past life into the context of the entire span of the soul's existence (ibid. 12, 20, 38, 42, 48).

The period between lives varies from ten months to eight-hundred years, though "cosmic pressure" ensures that all will reincarnate eventually. Returning to Earth, souls pass through the "etheric barrier" – a sort of cosmic river of forgetfulness. This ensures that lives remain clearly distinct, and that individuals do not become homesick for the interlife state and thus fail to engage fully in the new incarnation (ibid. 52-53).

Whitton's statement that a soul "loses all sense of personality by merging into existence itself" (Whitton & Fisher 1986: 7-8) recalls Buddhist beliefs about *nirvana*, though it also conflicts with the testimonies of Whitton's own subjects and would seem to preclude further incarnations as is the case in Buddhism.

Brian Weiss

Though formerly a skeptic, American psychiatrist Brian Weiss (1988: 10, 29, 201) became convinced of the validity of PLR following the regression of one of his patients. Weiss was impressed by her apparent ability to communicate with "evolved 'spirit entities'" who taught her about the afterlife. Weiss's "clinical mind" told him that his subject was not inventing her stories. The scientific method apparently deserted him, however, for instead of investigating the historical validity of his cases, Weiss instead chose to have them validated by a psychic. Weiss was also impressed by the woman's apparent telepathic abilities, knowing, for example about his deceased son's rare heart condition, his father's Hebrew name, and that his daughter was named after him (ibid. 56). While these things could prove telepathy, however, they do not validate PLR.

As far as historical accuracy and evidentiality go, the case that so impressed Weiss is rather poor. One of the subject's past personalities claimed to be speaking from the year "1863 BC," despite the impossibility of a personality who lived nearly two-thousand years before Christ measuring time by the Christian calendar. She also claimed to be a blonde ancient Egyptian, which is highly unlikely, and described a corpse being embalmed in brine rather than in natron which is what the Egyptians actually used. She had almost no knowledge of what was ostensibly her own religion, being unable to correctly recall the name "Osiris" and referring to him as a goddess. She stated that Hathor was a male deity represented by a phoenix, rather than a female deity associated with the cow (ibid. 27, 38, 110-11).

According to Weiss, the woman had never read anything about NDEs or Tibetan Buddhism, but described an afterlife experience consistent with them. Through her intermission memories, she learned that we exist and are reborn to learn, and to teach others, and that "there are many gods, for God is in each of us." There are seven different planes of consciousness corresponding to stages of spiritual development, and each plane has many levels. One is the plane of recollection, where life reviews occur. Those at higher levels "are allowed to see history," while the rest can only see their own lives. At the plane of transition, souls wait for the traits of their next incarnation to be determined. This is followed by the plane of choice. After the seventh plane we are reincarnated, except for the morally bad who suffer and find no peace. Some of the testimony is muddled and contradictory, for the woman seems to say both that we choose our own reincarnations, and that we have no choice (ibid. 46, 53-54, 70, 76, 171).

Michael Newton

The American psychologist Michael Newton (1994: 274) conducted a ten-year study of intermediate states in PLR cases, though without any explicit empirical method. While he found the descriptions "too real and connected to be ignored," he admitted that "there is no scientific foundation to prove the statements of these subjects."

Though the information in his books is convoluted and diffuse, the picture of the afterlife presented by Newton is consistent with earlier studies, though adding much more detail. Some of his subjects reported arriving in a cloudy place, sometimes referred to as "home," from which Earth cannot be seen. In what Newton believed is a mind-dependent subjective creation, one individual found himself in a "cattlemen's bar" in Oklahoma (ibid. 18-19, 56).

The more spiritually evolved are not met by friends and relatives, for they do not require such comforts. Those who do then proceed to have their souls healed by bathing in light "like a stream of liquid energy." During this "orientation stage," the soul undergoes counselling with a guide in "small and intimate conference areas." An appearance "before a panel of superior beings" follows – a "Council of Masters or Elders" who conduct a "soul evaluation conference." Souls are then sent to the "staging area," "like the hub of a great wagon wheel, where we are transported from a center along the spokes to our designated places." One subject described "rivers" of souls which flow into seas of souls. The afterlife world appears to be spherical, and it "never gets crowded" (ibid. 28, 53-4, 70, 73-4, 84, 206).

The soul is described as being like a "whirling" mass of light, and depending on the level of spiritual development it is either white, blue, red, yellow, or purple for "Level IV Ascended Masters." Souls adopt "male and female impressions toward other entities as a form of identity preference," but all are truly androgynous. They can also assume the identity of any of their previous personalities (ibid. 33, 40-41, 99).

Each soul has a group-soul to which it returns with every death, "like a community support group" or "lily pads in one pond." The groups are surrounded by bright cones "above and all around us," funneling energy "as a waterfall in a spreading circle." They allow souls "to concentrate our mental sameness as a group ... we can feel all our thoughts being expanded ... then drawn up ... and returned back ... with more knowledge added" (ibid. 138).

There are eight different types of groups, each with particular characteristics, such as "fun-loving, humorous risk-takers," and "patient, steady, perceptive." Souls cannot enter other groups, though they can communicate with them. Each group has a library of "life books," which are crystals showing the member's lives and "future possibilities" in multi-dimensional moving pictures. Souls spend time "studying" and "doing homework" in schools or Greek temples. Rather than merging completely with their groups as in mediumship narratives, "group cluster activity is considerably reduced past Level II" (ibid. 76, 82, 87, 93-4, 96, 142, 145).

Like "a circus master – a stage manager," a group's guide will appear during "heated debates." One such guide is a wizard "in long, sapphire-blue robes with a tall pointed hat [and] flowing white beard ... an oriental Merlin." Another is "a kindly, nurturing Native American woman called Quinn ... dressed in a deerskin sheath." Contradicting these gender designations, guides are also said to be sexless, with "oval faces, high cheekbones, no hair, and smallish features" and unusual, often unpronounceable names. Spirits themselves have such science fictional-sounding names as Allum, Trinian, Nyala, and Nenthum, who in his higher state is called Mulcatgil (ibid. 115, 139, 141, 148, 261).

Souls engage in leisure pursuits such as playing pranks and hide-and-seek. Groups receive visits from guests, such as a loveable character called "Humor" who makes "them laugh with all his antics." Some souls are tested on their "imagination, creativity, and ingenuity" by entities known as the Watchers. The tests involve "simple energy projects" such as putting together "multidimensional geometric puzzles." "The Maker" creates the matter with which souls work (ibid. 96, 143, 165).

There are numerous levels, stages, and worlds. Levels I and II are beginner levels. Level III has four different worlds: "The World Without Ego" where new souls acquire identity; "The World of All Knowing" which is "the ultimate mental world of planning and design" and "the final destination of all thought"; "The World of Altered Time" which is a replica of the subjects' previous world, where they can alter past events in order to study alternative outcomes resulting from their actions; and "The World of Creation and Non-Creation," similar to Earth but further from the sun, beyond the Milky Way, colder and with fewer bodies of water. It is an Eden-like idealized mirror-image of Earth inhabited by small intelligent animals, without conflict, suffering or strife. Souls enjoy the world "as free spirits," and can become anything, even rocks, for example, in order to "capture the essence of density." In a nonsensical contradiction recalling "Myers's" description of the levels of Summerland, the subject describing the World of All Knowing was on Level II, though it allegedly can only be experienced by those above Level IV, even though it is itself on Level III (ibid. 122-3, 157-62).

Little is said of Level IV, except that the cryptically-named Old Ones live there (presumably unconnected with H.P. Lovecraft's fictional race of malignant ancient alien deities), and that most Level IV souls do not return to Earth for they have no more lessons to learn (ibid. 122-3, 176).

Overall, despite extensive bureaucracy and discipline there is no discernable system of progression or purpose – and much to strain the credulity of even the most sympathetic reader. Some exceptionally ridiculous descriptions include space-time portals that look like railway arches leading to "low-density mental colonies"; a world called Arnth where beings like balls of cotton candy float on "waves of gas" in a swirling motion which is "very orgasmic"; and a volcanic realm called Jesta where souls "can experience the physical and emotional stimulation of becoming intelligent molecules of flame." Subjects also reported becoming or encountering mythical beings including elves, giants, and mermaids with such vividness that Newton suspected that they were authentic (ibid. 168, 218).

Eventually, souls undergo "preparatory exit interviews by spiritual advisors to determine our readiness for rebirth," though the decision is ultimately up to the individual. At "the place of life selection" souls decide the circumstances into which they will be reborn, seeing possible futures as different people. In the "Ring of Destiny" they float inside an energy bubble watching "banks of screens" which they control by telepathically operating a panel like an airplane cockpit. Souls can even enter the prospective new personality for a test-drive and "the soul in residence is put on hold for a moment." Why the body would already have a soul is not explained, and what would happen to that soul if the "new" soul were to choose its body is a mystery. Newton rightly asked one subject why there is a Ring of Destiny if souls choose their own rebirth, and the meaningless reply was, "Oh there is destiny, all right. The life cycles are in place. It's just that there are so many alternatives which are unclear" (ibid. 203, 206, 211-12, 215).

At the "Place of Recognition," floating in "a circular auditorium with a raised dais in the middle" (presumably unconnected with "Carousel" in the 1976 science fiction film *Logan's Run*), souls learn how to find their soulmates back on Earth, and even pre-arrange meetings. This is despite the fact that memory is wiped clean before rebirth because, obscurely, "learning from a blank slate is better than knowing in advance what could happen to you because of what you did before." A speaker floats around the auditorium "pointing a finger at each of us and saying we must pay attention." After one more piece of authoritarian bureaucracy – an "exit interview" with one's guide – souls are escorted by the guide at high speed through "pillows of whiteness" before "sliding down … into a long, dark tube" and entering the womb of the new mother (ibid. 67, 252-3, 265).

Newton's (2001: xiii, 144-5, 230-1, 290, 304) second study added yet more details, though he admitted that many of its subjects had read his earlier book and therefore knew the type of afterlife he was expecting. New descriptions included a star-shaped building with classrooms, and souls that "float around as water nymphs," play music, do gymnastics, and "soul-dancing" which is "like a mating dance" involving changing one's normal "pear-shaped energy" to a "curved crescent" (sic). Newton also reproduced illustrations of medallions worn by guides, featuring occult symbols, a woman riding a horse, an eagle, a deer, and a large cat being stabbed in the throat by a human hand holding a knife.

Spontaneous Cases and Near-Death Experiences

Comparing intermission memories in spontaneous cases around the world, Sharma and Tucker (2004: 108) concluded that "While the specific imagery may be culture-specific, preliminary study suggests that the phases seem to be universally applicable." They also found similarities between the Burmese descriptions in particular and NDEs in both Asia and the West. Common futures include OBEs, meeting other spirits and entities, being in other realms, and "a subjective sense of being dead." Two Burmese subjects remembered feelings of peace and joy, and most were distressed at seeing their relatives mourning them. Interestingly, none reported entering darkness or encountering bright light, which are two of the most common features of NDEs across cultures. None reported a life review, though one was scolded by the underworld deity for failing in her religious duties. Perhaps unsurprisingly, no subjects described reaching a border or barrier from which they had to return, for their return to Earth was in a new incarnation (ibid. 109-110). In any case, the similarities were enough for Sharma & Tucker (2004: 116) to conclude:

> While the differences in the reports should not be glossed over, the similarities indicate that the intermission reports by children claiming to remember previous lives may need to be considered as part of the same overall phenomenon – reports of the afterlife – that encompasses NDEs.

Furthermore, they made a startling discovery: that those who recall intermission states "tend to make more verified statements about the previous life they claim to remember than do other subjects of reincarnation type cases, and they tend to recall more names from that life." This combination of apparently evidential anomalous information retrieval and memories of NDE-like experience between lives might lend credence to the accounts (ibid. 101). This is an important contrast to the mediumistic reports in which veridical cases rarely accompanied descriptions of the afterlife.

The psychologist Titus Rivas et. al. (2015: 104) also noted "a striking similarity" between intermission memories and NDEs, including "the existence of a 'heavenly' realm of light and love, the decision to return to earth, and communication with other discarnate spirit beings." They argued that combined with the evidence from NDEs, these descriptions alongside the "paranormal" aspects of reincarnation cases – in which children knew information that could not have been known by normal means – indicates that "these memories and NDEs are clearly related and convergent, and they collectively point to the reality of conscious discarnate existence."

The anthropologist James Matlock and lawyer Iris Geisler-Petersen (2016) compared 58 Asian and 27 Western spontaneous cases with intermission memories, confirming that they are markedly similar across cultures, and that "most of the differences may be traced to cultural expectations and interpretations." The most frequently reported elements were encountering deceased relatives and "nonhuman spirit entities," with the identity of the latter predictably varying according to cultural background – Asian subjects encountered Yama, while Western subjects met the Christian god or Jesus. The key difference was that the Asian subjects described an earthly or Earth-like environment, while the Western subjects described a heavenly one. This echoes NDE reports in indigenous societies, in which experiencers report walking along a path or road to an Earth-like otherworld (Shushan 2018: 166, 221, 242). Matlock (2019: 462) also found that spontaneous cases "are more similar to NDEs than to regression accounts in their depiction of postmortem consciousness."

Comparing the Burmese cases with their Japanese counterparts, Ohkado and Ikegawa (2014: 484-5) noted that a tree, pagoda, and remaining near the body were most common in Burma, while going to the sky, light, or elsewhere were more common in Japan. They concluded that the Burmese examples were influenced by local Buddhist beliefs, in which the soul might be given a duty to perform between lives, such as guarding a temple. Most of the Japanese cases, in contrast, were from non-religious families.

Stevenson (1975: 50) wrote that when subjects reported memories of intermediate states, they were clearly grounded in "local mythology" and were essentially "culture-bound fantasies." While it was important to note the differences between accounts, as with NDEs, the similarities indicate that the intermission memories cannot have resulted purely from cultural imagination. They must have some cross-cultural (if not universal) foundational experiential elements upon which the cultural and individual interpretations are overlaid. The fact that a Druze case included intermission memories – a notion anathema to local beliefs – further demonstrates that these phenomena cannot be due solely to religion or culture.

The Problem of Past-Life Regression

In some general thematic ways, the PLR narratives also conform to the modern western idea of NDEs. While there had been PLR investigations prior to Moody's popularization of NDEs in 1975 – such as those by Albert de Rochas in the 19th century, A.R. Martin in 1942, and the Bridey Murphy case in 1954 – it is undoubtedly significant that only in post-1975 cases do we find descriptions of intermission states. As seen, those descriptions invariably feature such common NDE elements as OBE (see Wade 1998), light, spiritual beings, other realms, transformation, and so on. Both NDEs and PLR are staples of New Age spiritualities, and indeed all the PLR accounts were generated from within popular therapeutic practices usually associated with such spiritual orientations. Individuals interested in PLR would likely also be interested in NDEs, and the descriptions of their "regressions" were almost certainly influenced by them.

Nor is it a coincidence that the descriptions of intermediate states became increasingly detailed and complex with each PLR study – more systematized, bureaucratized, and merit-based, reaching a zenith in Newton's two volumes. The otherworld he depicts is clearly a white Anglo-American New Age fantasy, no less culturally situated than the Buddhist, Hindu, and Native American themes in the spontaneous cases. Its invasive, authoritarian nature combined with regimented fun and frivolity are reminiscent of a Western nursing home in which elders are treated like children. These somewhat embarrassingly childish aspects of Newton's afterlife bear similarities to some of the mediumship reports, though are absent in NDEs and spontaneous cases. In addition, the life review is not only much more prominent and regularly reported in PLR than in NDEs, it occurs after a tribunal experience which is not a common NDE feature.

This is not to suggest that the PLR subjects are deliberately inventing stories. The psychiatrist Andrew Powell (2001: 2-3) suggested that regression narratives stem from an uncontrolled "active imagination" drawing upon the archetypes of the collective unconscious. As such, they are objective experiences with an external origin, though filtered through the psychology and emotions of the subjects. Those who recall intermission states may be drawing them from a well of memories of past personalities, reminiscent of the super-psi hypothesis only involving free-floating data rather than other consciousnesses. This recalls C. D. Broad's notion of a "psychic factor," discussed above.

Whitton (1986: 27, 30) suggested that PLR descriptions of intermission states are symbolic of an otherwise ineffable but real experience. This could conceivably account for the similarities and differences with the other extraordinary experiences. That is, as with NDEs the unconscious mind might be using symbols to express universal experience types in forms that make sense to the experiencer. Therefore, reasons Whitton, preexisting afterlife beliefs, state of mind, and level of spiritual advancement will all affect the experience. However, afterlife skeptics reportedly had PLR experiences consistent with those of believers (Fiore 1978: 38, Newton 1994: 4) rather than no experience at all, as would be expected if Whitton were correct. Others expressed disappointment at *not* having the experience they expected, such as meeting Jesus (Whitton 1986: 36). The idea also begs the question of what exactly would be objective about the afterlife experience, other than the fact that it happens.

In any case, the obvious influences from NDE accounts, mediumship narratives, and New Age spirituality seem to make these kinds of theories unnecessary. In addition, Wilson (1981: 98-9) noted that a subject's PLR memories reflect the expectations of their hypnotist, which was actually confirmed by Newton in his second study. All this means that ultimately, both Powell's and Whitton's explanations for PLR narratives seem more complex than required. More than any other type of extraordinary experience discussed in this book, PLR narratives are most easily and convincingly explained by mundane factors.

The alternative explanation is that the similarities of PLR narratives to NDEs, mediumship reports, and spontaneous past-life cases indicate that all these experience types reflect a genuine afterlife reality, reinforcing the evidential value of each other in the process.

PLR memories would then be explained in similar terms as NDEs: a combination of universal, cultural, and individual elements. One might also adapt the "excuse" used in mediumship research in order to explain the inconsistencies and absurdities in these "memories": that the past-life personality is compromised by the mind of the current personality (and perhaps that of the therapist as well), coloring all the descriptions and making them collaborative and therefore unreliable.

However, between the universally poor quality of research, a lack of evidentially persuasive cases, some evidence of cryptomnesia, and the absurdities of so much of the content, such a hypothesis is unwarranted. While it cannot be stated categorically that they are all subconscious fantasies, most PLR accounts give that impression. As with the evidence from mediumship, however, they are interesting as *possible* visionary experiences which could involve intimations of an actual afterlife being accessed by the subconscious mind, as described by Jung (1999: 314; see Shushan 2009: 163). At the very least, they demonstrate the ways in which subconscious minds of certain 20th century white New Age Anglo-Americans model (imaginary) next worlds.

In the afterlife beliefs of most religious traditions in the world, the soul passes through various intermediate states prior to reincarnation, or to reaching the final spiritual home (Shushan 2009, 2018). Such descriptions are conceptually consistent with the notion of intermission memories. This could support the experiential source hypothesis for the spontaneous cases, and perhaps even the PLR cases as well. As argued earlier, the notion that afterlife beliefs are grounded in extraordinary experiences is not predicated on those experiences being genuinely metaphysical. Even if the experiences proved to have mundane explanations, like dreams they can still result in new beliefs.

7

WHAT KIND OF AFTERLIFE?
CULTURE, INDIVIDUAL, AND THE
SURVIVAL HYPOTHESIS

Whether arguing for or against the survival hypothesis, most scholarly and scientific discussions of NDEs treat them either as a universal human experience type, or as an entirely culturally-constructed one. Few see them as both, taking differences as well as similarities into account. Fewer still discuss the implications for the survival hypothesis of historical and cross-cultural NDEs in all their diversity and continuity. This is surprising because the relationship between the apparently universally occurring NDE, and the varying ways in which it is individually experienced and culturally expressed, has serious implications for *any* theory that attempts to make ontological sense of the phenomenon – whether materialist or metaphysical.

It is clear that the similarities between accounts indicate that NDEs cannot be due entirely to cultural expectation. Although afterlife beliefs vary widely around the world, individuals in most if not all cultures not only experience NDEs but also attach the same afterlife-related meanings to them. The default belief cross-culturally is that they are actual experiences of a life after death, rather than simply dreams or hallucinations. This apparent universality – both of occurrence and interpretation – could support arguments that they are indeed genuine afterlife experiences. If there is an afterlife, it would presumably be accessible to the souls of all humans after death. At the same time, however, the similarities could alternatively support a materialist hypothesis, for if human neurophysiology or cognitive processes are universal we would expect the same kind of experience and interpretation from biologically similar brains.

Differences could be used to challenge the materialist interpretation, however, on the grounds that individual and cultural uniqueness suggests that NDEs are not "all in the brain." However, differences could be *incorporated* into a materialist hypothesis, by positing that culture and individuality overlay the universal neurophysiological or cognitive experience. Meanwhile, precisely the same argument might be used to support the survival hypothesis: that NDEs are a genuine glimpse of an afterlife state, though one that is filtered through cultural and individual idiosyncrasies.

These dynamics have created an underlying tension in the debate over the ultimate nature of NDEs, further exacerbated by the fact that so few researchers take the historical and cross-cultural evidence fully into account.

Some critics fall back on Karl Popper's concept of "promissory materialism," maintaining that whatever might eventually be revealed by cross-cultural NDEs, it will inevitably reinforce a scientific materialist explanation (Greyson 2007: 142). This is exemplified by Keith Augustine's (2007: 116) statement that if NDEs prove to be universal, they "would be best explained in neuroscientific terms." However, as seen above, the mere fact of universality specifies neither a metaphysical nor a neuroscientific conclusion. Furthermore, as Greyson (2007: 142) noted, models of NDEs as either hallucinatory *or* transcendental create a false dichotomy: "some NDE features may well be linked to physiological events, some to sociopsychological belief, and others to no known materialist cause."

The combination of worldwide thematic and interpretative *consistency* with culturally idiosyncratic *variation* indicates that NDEs can be neither entirely culturally constructed, nor entirely neurophysiological *or* metaphysical. Any cohesive theory of NDEs must therefore take into account a number of universal, cultural, and individual factors. While not the most parsimonious approach, as Greyson (2007: 142) stated, "a model is not preferable if it achieves parsimony only by ignoring what it cannot explain." It is unsurprising that complex, multifaceted phenomena would require a complex, multifaceted explanatory model.

Veridical Observations During NDEs

As seen in earlier chapters, reports in which information obtained during an NDE was later verified are common worldwide. As mentioned in Chapter 1, in recent Western examples, numerous individuals have accurately described events they claim to have witnessed while out-of-body during an NDE (Holden 2009). In Chapter 2 we saw how people across cultures have reported the "Peak-in-Darien" phenomenon during NDEs, in which they met deceased individuals not known to have died at the time of the experience (Greyson 2010). These kinds of anomalous information retrieval often convince NDErs, and those around them, of the genuineness of the experience. Validating the OBE or the encounter with the previously deceased person also validates the reality of the NDE itself.

Descriptions of many kinds of clairvoyance can be found in NDEs around the world and throughout history. A 5th century CE Italian boy named Armentarius returned from his visit to the otherworld with the ability to speak all languages (Gregory the Great trans. 1911: 208-09). During his 1858 NDE, the Sioux warrior White Bull learned of the specific medicinal roots that would cure his illness after his return to life (Vestal 1934: 12-5, 249-50). In an early 19th century Native American account from British Columbia, a Dakelh NDEr returned from the otherworld with information about Christ – despite having had no prior knowledge of Christianity. Similarly, in southern Africa, a Sotho NDEr learned about baptism on a near-death visit to heaven; and another returned from his NDE miraculously able to read after the Christian god bestowed literacy upon him (Keable 1921: 522-23, 527-29).

Accurate precognitive information was obtained in the other world by a Chaga (Tanzania) NDEr concerning her future husband (Werner 1933: 93). The impending deaths of particular individuals were revealed during a Mbundu (Angola) NDE (Chatelain 1894: 225-27), and in that of a medieval English knight named Boso in 1093 (Simeon of Durham trans. 1955: 707-09). During an NDE visit to the otherworld, a Tswana woman was correctly told that she would die later in the evening after her return to her body (Willoughby: 1928, 101-2). In 1861, a French minister named L. J. Bertrand had an NDE while mountain-climbing in Switzerland, and saw specific, accurate details during an OBE: the guide stealing food and wine, and his wife many miles away boarding a different train than the one she had planned (Myers 1892: 195-200).

Of course, historical anecdotal accounts cannot be considered airtight *proof* that any of these extraordinary events actually occurred. It is significant, however, that they share such claims with modern NDE accounts, as well as with further historical examples as widely dispersed as ancient China, medieval Europe, and indigenous societies.

As also discussed in Chapter 2, however, some prophecies ostensibly received during NDEs have gone unfulfilled, and there are additional cross-cultural examples. In the late 19th century, a Papua New Guinea man named Tokeri claimed to have obtained in the otherworld prophetic information about a giant destructive wave that would hit the area, though it failed to appear (Seligman 1910: 656). In 1805, the Shawnee prophet Tenskwatawa returned from his NDE promising his people that if they rejected European lifestyles and returned to indigenous ways, he would reward them with the return of their deceased loved ones (Mooney 1896: 672-4) – a promise that was clearly not possible to keep. More tragically, according to various Native American NDEs, it was prophesied that the indigenous people would enter a new Golden Age after either cooperating with the European invaders or rebelling against them (Shushan 2016). As with the studies of prophetic NDEs in the U.S. and U.K. (Ring 1982, Grey 1985), the contents of such prophecies were due to both universal human anxieties about death and disaster, and the political and social anxieties of their particular times in history.

The Subjectivity of Spiritual Transformation

One of the most common features of NDEs is the individual becoming more spiritually minded, more charitable, or simply a kinder person as a result of the experience. Indeed, this phenomenon is sometimes cited as evidence that the experience is genuine, recalling the famous statement from William James (1902: 20) that religious experiences should be judged "by their fruits."

It must be noted, however, that "fruits" are relative depending on social and cultural contexts, for some claims about NDEs have clearly not arisen from a standpoint of spiritual enlightenment. A perhaps extreme example is that of William Dudley Pelley (1929), who wrote that his NDE gave him a new understanding of how "vast and fine and high and beautiful" life was. He claimed to have been positively transformed by the experience, spiritually, mentally, and physically, and that it had "launched me into a wholly different universe that seems filled with naught but love, harmony, health, good humor, and prosperity." Pelley, however, was not only a convicted conman and fraudster, he was also tried for treason as a Nazi sympathizer who aspired to become "America's Hitler." Notably, it was *after* his NDE that Pelley's fascist and treasonous activities accelerated. This included publishing alleged communications with the "Great Souls" he had met during his NDE, who told him, he claimed, that Jewish and Black people are at the bottom of the spiritual hierarchy, and that they are enemies of white people whose souls are more developed. He also founded a college to teach courses such as "Spiritual Eugenics," lending a chilling tone to a remark in his NDE account that there are "no misfits" or "physical handicaps" in the afterlife (reminiscent of some of the Victorian mediumistic descriptions discussed in Chapter 5).

As with inaccurate prophecies and certain mediumship descriptions, such accounts create problems for those who believe that NDEs are evidence of life after death. One must accept either that (a) postmortem spirits in other worlds can continue to promote racism, eugenics, and other forms of intolerance and oppression, and that the spiritual transformation of an NDEr does not preclude founding a paramilitary group to bring Nazism to the United States; or (b) that Pelley was partly delusional but nevertheless had a genuine NDE, and that the experience is not a universal spiritual panacea. Otherwise, it might be argued that such accounts, clearly lacking in positive "fruits," are fabricated. In this case, Pelley's criminal lack of ethics might support the notion that he invented his NDE as a tool of both propaganda and profit.

Likewise, in PLR accounts spiritual enlightenment did not prevent souls from willingly embarking on a new life that would cause suffering to themselves or others. The system of choosing one's own rebirth with full knowledge of future events is morally problematic. Whitton (1986: 50), for example, explained how a woman's "karmic script" dictated that she "make herself vulnerable to a random personal tragedy" in order to facilitate a change in her "entire soul-complex," and she was thus raped in her next life.

Such a system would justify and even sanction any form of abuse or murder on the grounds that both victim and perpetrator are merely playing out their "karmic scripts" to mutual benefit. In essence, victims have chosen to be victimized, and rape and murder are means of spiritual progression. One murderer was counselled by the "judges" to be reborn as a *potential* murderer in order to overcome his violent tendencies. But if the man no longer recalls the experiences of his former life, and does not possess the psychological tools to overcome his murderous instincts – and indeed is not even aware that he is undergoing a self-imposed test – the entire situation is morally and philosophically unintelligible.

Choosing one's own rebirth contradicts traditional Indian religious-philosophical reincarnation beliefs. The principle of *karma* is the retributive determining factor that dictates the nature of a soul's new incarnation. Within certain forms of Buddhism, a choice of rebirths is believed to be possible, though only the most enlightened individuals are able to make such a decision, and only in order to benefit other living beings. In Plato's Myth of Er, it is said that souls can choose their new incarnation, though they do so based upon disappointments in their previous lives. In hopes that the new life will be simpler and more pleasant, they often chose to be reborn as an animal rather than as another human.

Next Worlds: Near-Death Experiences and a Plurality of Afterlives

If few NDE studies engage with both similarities and differences in relation to survival *per se*, fewer still attempt to construct a reasonable model of what *kind* of afterlife might be philosophically conceivable if we were to accept cross-cultural NDEs as genuine afterlife experiences.

In fact, accepting NDE accounts at face value poses challenges for philosophical ideas of what the afterlife could possibly be like. Once again, the problem is reconciling the cross-cultural differences and similarities – specifically, whether the concept of a panhuman afterlife is intelligible in light of all the cultural and individual diversity of NDEs.

Critics such as Keith Augustine (2007: 116-7) and philosopher Sam Harris (2012) find cross-cultural difference to be fatally problematic for the survival hypothesis, and believe that in order to be philosophically coherent, any actual afterlife must be the same for everyone. Harris, for example, wrote that "unfortunately," NDEs "vary across cultures .... One would think that if a nonphysical domain were truly being explored, some universal characteristics would stand out. Hindus and Christians would not substantially disagree—and one certainly wouldn't expect the after-death state of South Indians to diverge from that of North Indians, as has been reported." Leaving aside the fact of the vast diversity of cultures and religions between North and South India, Harris's reasons for this supposition are unclear. One might instead ask, given the cross-cultural and individual differences between people across the world – religious, linguistic, social, environmental, and so on – why should anyone expect a single afterlife that would be the same for all humanity?

Likewise, Augustine (2007: 109, 117) stated that variability between NDEs "certainly undermines a survivalist interpretation of NDEs." This is because, he claims, "different people would naturally be expected to report similar experiences if they were traveling to the same afterlife environment." He did not explain, however, why he believes that everyone in fact would go "to the same afterlife environment." His attempt to clarify only muddies things further: "NDErs would not be expected to take different journeys to different places after death merely because of where and when they lived while on Earth" (ibid. 121). Not only is this merely a statement of a subjective personal stance ("expected" by whom, other than Augustine?), it actually underplays the role of culture and individual influences on NDEs. Arguing against the notion that NDErs in different cultures actually have the same kinds of experiences but simply interpret them differently (for example, a Hindu and a Christian identifying the same being as Yama or Jesus, respectively), Augustine stated that "the most straightforward interpretation of apparent diversity is actual diversity." He did not, however, extend this principle to the possibility that such diverse experiences might be of diverse genuine afterlife states. In other words, Augustine is willing to take seriously cross-cultural descriptions of NDEs because he believes they undermine the survival hypothesis. He is not willing, however, to take seriously the nearly universal cross-cultural interpretations of those same NDEs: that they are experiences of an actual afterlife (Kellehear 2007: 151).

As the psychologist Harvey J. Irwin (2007: 161) countered, "it entails too great a leap in logic to conclude that, because NDEs show some diversity, all such experiences must be wholly hallucinatory." In this context, Irwin raised the possibility of "the existence of multiple 'afterlife realities.'" As Kellehear (2007: 151) similarly wrote, "I do not believe that diversity of NDEs of itself makes the arguments for survival, for whoever wants to make them, less convincing. Perhaps there really are several 'otherworlds'; there are several 'worlds' here, so why not there?"

In fact, the evidence that NDEs combine thematic similarities with cultural and individual differences does much to resolve the concerns raised by Harris and Augustine. From Western philosophy, the model best suited to address the problem remains that of the Welsh philosopher H. H. Price (1953: 5, 11). He posited a world of mental images, a mind-dependent reality that to the disembodied spirit would seem as real as life on Earth. This would include the impression of having a quasi-physical presence complete with "bodily" senses. Indeed, on an experiential, sensory level spiritual existence might be so similar to physical existence that individuals "would have considerable difficulty in realizing they were dead" – a theme reflected in some NDE and intermission memory accounts as well as in afterlife-related myths. Disembodied spirits would appear to each other as "telepathic apparitions," and also communicate telepathically.

Rather than being a solipsistic otherworld in which all is merely personal illusion created by the self, Price (1953: 16-17) postulated that it would be an "intersubjective" shared afterlife: an experience actually created by the deceased individual in conjunction with the minds of other human spirits. Like-minded individuals – with, for example, similar memories, ideas, values, or culture – would collectively create their surroundings, with each soul contributing to the group-afterlife while also bringing personal, idiosyncratic features into being. Rather than a single universal *afterlife*, Price's model suggests a plurality of *afterlives*: numerous different communal worlds formed by the collective consciousness of each like-minded group member. The way these worlds manifest would be determined by the "memories and desires" of the co-creators, meaning that a person's cultural background and individual psychology would be given form within the experience. This means that while the afterlife exists beyond any single group member, each person can have a different experience.

The individual, retaining free will and the capacity for subjective observation, both consciously and unconsciously contributes to the creation of the shared elements of the group-afterlife, but also creates individual, personal elements. If the barriers between the conscious and unconscious minds dissolve after death (ibid. 22), repressed fears, wish-fulfilment, and self-perception would all play a role in the formation of these otherworlds. This could lead to experiences characterized by states of mind both positive (love, harmony, unity, wish-fulfillment) and negative (guilt, fear, anger, resentment). Such a scenario corresponds to the NDE theme of evaluation of one's earthly life (as in the life review), as well as to reports of distressing NDEs. Both also have parallels in afterlife beliefs across cultures, in the form of judgments, heavens, and hells.

Because souls of the dead – and NDErs – remain conscious with the ability to understand and evaluate the experience in progress, the analogy of lucid dreaming is apt. During lucid dreams, individuals become aware that they are dreaming, though this does not immediately or necessarily alter the dream overall – the landscape, situation, or other individuals involved can all remain stable. Lucid dreamers may, however, achieve a state in which it is possible to change or create their dream content. While such control is rare and normally achieved only through practices such as Tibetan dream yoga (*milam*) or techniques developed in Western psychology, without the confines of the physical brain and the five senses, it is conceivable that disembodied consciousness would be comparable to the creatively interactive state of the advanced lucid dreamer (Badham 1982: 120; Shushan 2009: 186-7).

In Price's (1953: 7-8) model, individuals become aware that they are dead as a result of discovering the "rather peculiar causal laws" of the postmortem state, such as the ability to appear in a particular place by thought alone. Similarly, experiences such as being out of the body, the inability to interact with the living, communicating with other spirits telepathically, and encountering deceased relatives often cause NDErs to realize they are "dead" (Shushan 2009: 144-45). These themes also occur in some of the intermission memory cases, and in the afterlife journey myths across cultures. The psychologist J. Timothy Green (1995: 53-4) also compared the lucid dream state to NDEs, citing common elements such as OBE, darkness, light, feelings of intense clarity, euphoria, and transcendence.

A recent proponent of the hypothesis in relation to NDEs and intermission memories is reincarnation researcher Jim Tucker (2013: 216) who wrote that the NDE is essentially "a transition dream, involving an awareness of dying and moving on to another kind of existence." The dream starts "at the point of death, and the nature of the dream can vary from person to person," and leads to a shared-dream otherworld.

Nor is the hypothesis by any means exclusive to 20th century Western thought. While Price (1953: 3) was aware that similar beliefs could also be found in Mahayana Buddhism, the Buddhism scholar Carl Becker (1993a: 82-3, 179-80) explored the connection in depth. He saw parallels between Price's theories, NDEs, and "both scriptural and experiential accounts" in the Mahayana tradition of Pure Land Buddhism. In 16th century Chinese Pure Land Buddhist texts the afterlife is mind-dependent, though "the fact that everyone at death seems to report essentially similar imagery demonstrates that the Pure Land is indeed intersubjective and substantial rather than hallucinatory or illusory" (Becker 1984: 61, 115). Becker concluded that the similarities reflect "common religious experience, pointing to a reality envisioned in the West as well: an idealist life after death." Finding this notion to be the most reasonable, he summarized, "Since it is the mind or consciousness whose survival we are considering, it need not surprise us that the realms of which it is conscious after the decease of the physical body are also mind dependent."

The *Bardo Thödol* (*Tibetan Book of the Dead*, c. eighth century CE) describes how souls undergo an expected set of intermediate postmortem experiences, though their character is determined by cultural and individual expectation. These involve leaving the body, an encounter with a bright light, having a "karmic body" formed by one's "own past and deeds," encounters with good and evil entities (including beings of light), darkness, fear, judgment, and punishment followed by rebirth. Afterlife images are mind-dependent manifestations of personal hopes, fears, desires and so on (Evans-Wentz 1927: 94; Hick 1976: 414, 400-3).

There are also parallels in the Vedas, which describe the heavenly realm (Svargaloka) as "a projection of the mind" and an intermediate state to be transcended by achieving *moksha*, or liberation (Panikkar 1977: 633). It is reached by traveling in a "chariot of the mind" according to the *Rig Veda*, or "by means of the mind" in the *Upanishads*. Indeed, the *Upanishads* characterize dreaming and lucid dreaming as analogous to the afterlife state, with the *atman* described as "that person who, as one sleeps, roams about in dreams." The afterlife world of the fathers, *Pitaraloka*, is also analogous to the dream-state. The goal of understanding that *atman* is *brahman* (sometimes associated with the sun, a being of light) is essentially the transcendence of illusory separateness – a realization of universal oneness, analogous to the idea of lucidity within a co-creating group-soul. In Egypt, the concept of the *ba* and *ka* – microcosms of Osiris and Re – being reconciled as an *akh*, or divinized spirit, is also relevant here. The *akh* then becomes one with multiple deities yet personal identity remains.

The Lacandon Maya believe in an illusory afterlife which tests the readiness of the deceased to transcend it (Bierhorst 2002: 155), reminiscent of Tibetan Buddhism. The Aztec notion that souls of the dead are fragments of the sun, and that reunification with the sun is the afterlife goal, is conceptually similar to the group-soul idea. Associations between dreams and the afterlife also occur in Mesopotamia where the dream-god Sissig "lights up" the netherworld;

and the dream-goddess Nanshe is the wife of underworld deity Niminur. In China, the conception of Shangdi as "an amalgam of the deceased of the ruling clan" (Paper 2005: 64) recalls the conception of the group soul. The concept of a mind-dependent afterlife can also be found in Zoroastrian, Jewish, Sikh, Christian, and Sufi traditions (Badham 1990: 18; 1995: 119, 121; see also Shushan 2009: 188-90; Shushan 2018: 234).

In general, the afterlife beliefs found in the ancient texts discussed in Chapter 3 facilitate a mind-dependent or collective lucid dream interpretation when we consider the recurring importance placed upon themes of (a) self-awareness and realization of the reality of the spiritual self; and (b) souls of the dead being continually associated with the divine – notably including *creator*-deities – while still retaining their discrete identities. Even where it involves becoming one with the divine, "death may represent the end of all personal limits and boundaries, without necessarily being the end of conscious experience" (Becker 1993a: 185). This reflects NDE reports in which individuals describe the experience as happening to their own individual conscious self, despite feelings of transcendent oneness. Both concept and experience involve the transformation (or realization) of the self as a microcosmic part of the macrocosmic whole, rather than being totally subsumed into a greater identityless, impersonal whole.

The concept of group souls is also found in indigenous societies. The idea of a post-mortem collective merging with the ancestors or other spirit beings was common in Oceania, for example (Oliver 1989: 771), including among Aboriginal Australians. In Hawaii it was believed that souls of the dead were "united in thought and all joined together ... in harmony" with relatives, friends, and acquaintances (Kamakau 1866–71: 49–51). In the Cook Islands there was a belief in groups of souls ascending together with the sun-god (Gill 1876: 159). In Melanesia, the Kiwai believed that people from the same villages lived together in the spirit world.

The Wyandot, Ojibwe, and other Algonquian peoples believed in culturally divided afterlife realms for indigenous people and Europeans, while the Wyandot also believed in afterlife divisions based on social groupings. For the Pawnee, each family had their own afterlife village (Shushan 2018: 24, 30, 56).

In Africa, the idea of transcending individuality into "collective immortality" in the spirit world was common (Mbiti 1990: 160). It is typified by the Lango concept of "Orongo," which is "the universal spirit from which the individual *tipo* [soul] derives its separate, though not entirely independent, origin." Orongo itself is a manifestation of the divinity Jok, though they are associated with one another as two aspects of the same divine principle. Thus, the soul is a part of the universal collective spirit, which itself a part of the divine. The soul is sometimes referred to as Jok Orongo, though after death it is called simply *jok*, indicating that it becomes one with the universal divine. In shamanic practices, shamans sent their souls to Orongo in order to gain information from Jok (Driberg 1923: 220, 229; Shushan 2018: 234). Beliefs in reincarnation were also common in many African traditional religions. As with the Hindu and Buddhist concepts of *moksha* and *nirvana*, when a soul achieved collective immortality the cycle of rebirths ended (Mbiti 1990: 160).

Beliefs in a mind-dependent afterlife are also found in traditional indigenous cultures around the world. According to one native of New Britain, the otherworld can be seen "if our eyes were turned so that what is inside the head were now outside." This seems to suggest a self-created afterlife (Brown 1910: 192– 6, 210). For people on Maewo island in Vanuatu, a "stone of thought" was encountered on the afterlife journey, causing the deceased's presence of mind and control of memories to determine whether they would continue to the spirit world or return to Earth.

A Plains Cree NDEr could not cross the river to the other world when he recalled his bad deeds, and a Tlingit NDEr could only proceed to the other world when he thought about it. A Ho-Chunk Native American shaman recounted the ability to travel anywhere at will by thought alone (Radin 1923: 267). According to Ho-Chunk beliefs, the spirit must be free of fear and doubt when undergoing afterlife trials, indicating that psychological and emotional factors shaped the nature of the experience. As Kalweit (1984: 64, 66-7) explained, the barriers and perils the soul encountered were considered "culturally conditioned visions of an ego which is still caught in the grip of social and cultural models of the imagination and has not yet learned to adapt to the new environment" and "our primordial consciousness confronted by our thoughts." These experiences of the soul were "an attempt to make the surviving consciousness aware of the fact that it itself constitutes the world of the Beyond" (Shushan 2018: 234).

As acknowledged by Price (1953: 3), there are parallels between his hypothesis and the ideas of the British parapsychologist Whately Carrington, and those of the French philosopher C. J. Ducasse (1951: 486-88). The latter suggested that a "dream consciousness" form of survival could account for the differences between the various mediumistic descriptions of the afterlife. On the one hand it would explain the frequent accounts of idealized mirror-images of Earth, for they would simply be products of like-minded souls who desired such realms. On the other it would also account "for the fact that some of the reports deny what some others confirm; for where wish is architect and playwright, diversity of scenery and of drama is naturally to be expected from diversity of persons."

Furthermore, Ducasse argued, the "afterlife-as-dream" hypothesis would also account for the absurdities in the accounts, and for "the lack of firmness and precision" in the descriptions conveyed by mediums. In other words, rather than being due to communication issues or "overshadowing," inaccuracies and uncertainties about the otherworld would reflect the spirit's own mind-dependent perceptions, which may sometimes be hazy and imprecise. Individuals might be fully aware of the fact that they are creating the other world, a possibility Ducasse termed "critically controlled creative imagination." He described this process as "the purposively critical activity characteristic of mental creativity or discovery, whether poetic, pictorial, musical, mathematical, dramatic, philosophical, or other."

Price noted similar concepts in some of the mediumship accounts, such as those communicated by Leonard and Cummins. He found these descriptions to be "coherent and well presented ... detailed and intelligent" and worthy of "respect" (Price 1953: 16, 21-22). This is perhaps unsurprising considering that the concepts are highly similar to his own, though the degree to which they actually influenced his hypothesis is unknown.

Price's model, however, actually makes less philosophical sense when applied to much of the mediumistic descriptions of the otherworld than when applied to cross-cultural afterlife beliefs, NDEs, and intermission memories in spontaneous reincarnation cases. For example, if like-minded souls are drawn together to form groups, there should be different afterlives based upon belief or culture, including Hindu groups, Muslim groups, and so on. These groups would not create or willingly participate in a world in which they are merely converted Christians in-waiting, making their own religions and cultures irrelevant while also portraying them as immoral and bad. Other mediumistic descriptions, however, are more in line with Price's model, such as the claim by "Helen" via Mrs. Leonard that culture-specific realms are temporary familiar comforts until souls are ready to progress beyond their own earthly conditioning (Thomas 1945: 63). The more recent accounts by mediums such as John Edward are also exceptions.

Mind-dependent, group-soul, and inclusive afterlife concepts are also reflected in the writings of Robert Monroe (1994: 248-50), a pioneer in experimentation with deliberately induced out-of-body experiences. Following his own OBEs in which he claimed to have traveled into afterlife dimensions, he described the various levels and stages that souls pass through. The first is for those who are unaware that they are "dead," or are unable to let go of their earthly ties. This is followed by the "Belief System Territories," occupied by souls "from all periods and areas who have accepted and subscribed to various [particular] premises and concepts," including "religious and philosophical beliefs that postulate some sort of post-physical existence." Souls then advance to what Monroe called "the Reception Center or the Park":

> This is an artificial synthesis created by human minds, a way station designed to ease the trauma and shock of the transition out of physical reality. It takes on the form of various earth environments in order to be acceptable to the enormously wide variety of new comers.

Souls may also create their own "personal and special place" within this realm, which results in areas "that are as varied and unique as the participants themselves, ranging for example from log cabins by quiet streams to clumps of trees, South Sea islands, palaces of crystal, and corners of one's heart." Souls may also assist those at the previous level who are finding it difficult to accept their physical death. The state of being above the Park level is "beyond not only space-time but human thought," making it perhaps analogous to *nirvana* or *moksha*. Traveling there "limits any return to a physical body."

The mind-dependent group soul notion could account for descriptions of rarefied parochial Englands, if we consider that the particular spirit communicators conveying such descriptions belonged to a white middle class Edwardian Spiritualist-Christian group. It does not, however, explain conflicting statements about institutional post-mortem racial segregation, class hierarchies, and ultimate white Christian supremacy. In other words, while the group that these communicators belonged to may have created a whites-only Christian world, the mind-dependence hypothesis itself makes unintelligible their claims about the metaphysical place *per se* of anyone who is neither Christian nor white. Again we are left with the impression that such mediumship accounts are more culturally immersed than NDEs and intermission memories, if not wholly derived from preexisting ideas found in Theosophical and Spiritualist literature. Mrs. Leonard's communications with "Helen" are again a notable exception, explaining the system in a way that is very similar to Monroe's descriptions ostensibly derived from his own OBE journeys.

A mind-dependent afterlife and group souls are also prominent in the PLR accounts, particularly those of Whitton (1986) and Newton (1994), though as argued in Chapter 6 such similarities are likely entirely a result of influence from a variety of New Age and paranormal literature sources.

The Projection Model: A Variation on Mind-Dependence

There are further limitations to Price's hypothesis. One is that it necessitates an extreme form of relativism which circumvents critical challenge: because the subjective essentially becomes objective in the otherworld – the imaginary becomes "real" – we must regard any description of the afterlife as "true." This includes the acceptance of all statements about racial, religious, and class superiority, as well as the numerous flatly contradictory statements that are especially typical of the mediumship and PLR accounts. We must accept that there are monkeys in the sun, cats that behave like dogs in the otherworld, a pharaonic Egyptian Muslim Lucifer who has forgotten his native language, and that souls can time-travel to see dinosaurs, meet figures from Arthurian legend, and fight "Ancient Egyptian crocodile-headed monsters" (as per a spirit communication through medium J. S. M. Ward writing in 1920, Ferguson 2012: 93).

The degree to which a place or thing is *self*-created and perceived or *group*-created and perceived is also obscure. This is illustrated by an example from one of Leonard's scripts, in which a family argued about the design of a garden and enlisted a spirit gardener to resolve the matter (Thomas 1936: 77). If anything can be materialized by thought alone, it is unclear why each family member didn't simply create their own individual perceptions of a garden in their own mind-dependent ways. This point applies to all descriptions of apparently permanent, objective elements of the afterlife, such as social organization, bureaucracy, and the system of post-mortem judgement, as well as quasi-physical features.

Furthermore, it is unclear how and why several levels of mind-dependent but increasingly idealized Earths would exist; and why the most spiritually enlightened individuals in the highest spheres would not only continue creating the familiar material comforts of increasingly rarefied Englands, but also continue to participate in a social system rooted in various forms of apartheid and oppression. As with the argument about enlightenment above, it is difficult to reconcile claims of spiritual progression with the notion of a mind-dependent (that is, conscious and deliberate) maintenance of such a system.

A proposed modification to Price's theory by the British theologian John Hick (1976: 270-1) does little to resolve the problem. He suggested that rather than many shared group-worlds, the minds of souls "are pooled to produce a common environment . . . by the cancelling out and mutual reinforcements of the multitude of individual desires," resulting in "a single post-mortem world, formed by the memories and desires of all the human beings who have died since man began." The realm would develop over time, "as new sets of memories are contributed to the common stock" and "the prevailing pattern of human desires changes." Such a scenario, however, might not account for the cultural and individual differences between NDEs. Furthermore, the idea that there could ever be a universal "prevailing pattern of human desires" seems unlikely. One might argue that in a sense all living human beings have a hand in creating the reality of the present world, so perhaps the next world is governed by similar dynamics. If so, however, it would hardly be a realm of oneness, joy, infinite love and transcendence.

An alternate modification to Price's hypothesis is that the otherworld is as objective as this one, but that things there are only *perceived* differently according to the individual. Or, more accurately, the individual actually "projects" specific forms onto a general background structural experience. The generic otherworld features are "clothed" with coherent imagery by the psyche of the person having the experience. The otherworld and a soul's experiences there are thus not *generated* by culture and individual, but nor are they *separable* from culture and individual. A person's stock of images, memories, creativity, and ideas overlay the mostly featureless background experiences, bringing them to life, making them comprehensible and indeed *experienceable*.

As outlined earlier, the combination of cross-cultural diversity and similarity of NDEs indicates different perceptions of the same phenomena. In the next world, it might likewise be a case of subjective interpretations being mentally projected onto the structural, thematic environment. For example, everyone may travel to the same spirit village, but the dwellings would be perceived variously as wood-and-straw huts, adobe houses, skyscraper apartments, tipis, stone cottages, and so on.

This brings us back to the *Bardo Thödol* as discussed in Chapter 1, in which the "Clear Light" in the otherworld is experienced by the soul as a culturally relevant identity, whether the Buddha, Vishnu, Jesus, Muhammad, or a generic "being of light."

These perceptions – or projections, rather – could also be shared or intermingled. As Becker (1993a: 121) described: "While some of the scenery and images perceived in such states will be unique to each individual, other features may be intersubjectively perceived by many consciousnesses." The afterlife thus "shares certain intersubjective features for all its 'inhabitants,' has various regions suited to various types of consciousness, and responds in its minor events to the thoughts and wills of its 'inhabitants' or experimenter/creators." As in Pure Land Buddhism, deceased relatives and other spirits would be real identities rather than illusory, and only certain details could be altered by individual souls (Becker 1984: 61, 65-6). Only objects, not people, are mind-dependent, and individuals retain consciousness and free-will. For example, if multiple individuals simultaneously desire to see the same person, that person cannot be forced to appear to any of them. The Pure Land tradition even addresses problems regarding conflicting wills and wishes of the co-creators, such as Leonard's family of gardening enthusiasts: there would be an objective, generic otherworldly garden, but each family member would project their own ideals upon it, and perceive it according to their personal preferences.

Becker (1993a: 121) found this model to be the best way to account for both NDEs and Mahayana Buddhist meditation accounts, and it is consistent with the evidence that NDEs themselves are composed of cross-culturally thematically stable features, experienced in culture- and individual-specific ways. Such a model is also compatible with the many reports of feelings of transcendent unity, becoming divine, or having divine-like abilities during NDEs (Shushan 2009: 186-91).

This "projection model" variation of the mind-dependent hypothesis is, in fact, often the conclusion reached by scholars who explore the problem from multiple angles, and who actually engage with both differences and similarities. Osis and Haraldsson (1986: 182), for example, hypothesized that scenes of idealized earthly beauty are "symbolizations" of the feelings of joy, peace, and calm typically reported by NDErs. The diversity of otherworldly landscapes is merely a reflection of the idealized local environment of the NDEr. Likewise, Greyson (2007: 139) pointed out that cross-cultural diversity of NDEs could indicate different perceptions of the same phenomena.

Mind-dependent afterlife models overcome Augustine's (2007: 117) claim that "the greater the diversity between different NDE accounts, the less credible the NDE consistency argument for survival." As with Harris (2012), Augustine's (2007: 120-1) objection is based on his own particular preconception of what an afterlife must or should be like, and the rules that must govern it: that it would be the same for everyone by virtue of our "common humanity" irrespective of cultural diversity. There is, however, simply no reason to believe that disembodied individuals would cease to process their experiences in their own idiosyncratic modes, including the use of personal and cultural memory, imagination, and visual metaphor. A metaphysical interpretation of NDEs is not predicated on the negation of cross-cultural or individual difference (Irwin 2007: 160-1; Kellehear 2007: 151). Put another way, given the nearly infinite diversity of human life experiences on Earth according to individual, environmental, geographic, economic, racial, cultural, biological, historical, social, and familial circumstances, it seems inconceivable that such diversity would simply cease to exist in an afterlife.

It is also the case that Harris (2012) severely downplayed any similarities between NDEs across cultures, misleadingly giving only generalized and unsourced cursory examples. Augustine (2007: 173-4) similarly characterized them as being far less consonant than they actually are, sharing only "broadly defined elements that we would expect to see among those who feel that they are dying." This claim inaccurately assumes that end-of-life concerns are universal. Widespread beliefs in Africa about the continued presence of ancestors on Earth, for example, would not prompt an NDE involving going to another realm and meeting deceased relatives, though such accounts have been reported from Africa (Shushan 2017, 2018).

Furthermore, Augustine asserted that NDE elements such as "feelings of peace, OBEs, passages through a tunnel or darkness toward light, and life reviews . . . are strikingly absent from most extant nonWestern NDE accounts." Though life reviews *per se* are rare cross-culturally, they are at least attested, as are thematic equivalents. The other four elements are some of the most common. Indeed, Augustine's assertion is so wildly insupportable that one questions his familiarity with the cross-cultural NDE literature. While that literature was not as extensive in 2007 as it is today, there had certainly been a number of relevant works prior to that date, including Abramovitch, Badham, Bailey, Becker, Campany, Counts, Green, Groth-Marnet, Kellehear, McClenon, Pasricha, Schorer, Shiels, Wade, and Zhi-ying & Jian-xun. As with the many scientists who are culturally and historically uninformed, unsubstantiated and incorrect presuppositions can only lead to error and unconvincing conclusions. One cannot construct useful generalizing theories about human beings *per se* based primarily upon knowledge of a single Western society, with only superficial consideration of the rest of the world.

In summary, just as we dream in symbols – giving form and apparent "reality" to fears, desires, worries, hopes, and other abstract concepts without conscious intent or deliberation – it is conceivable that we manifest our afterlife experiences in the same way. NDEs are apparently universal on contextual, thematic, and interpretative levels. They also share highly specific cross-cultural similarities on the symbolic and narrative levels. The most common features can therefore give us some idea of what the afterlife experience could be like, including OBE, darkness, light, heightened awareness and emotions, meeting spirits of the dead, personal evaluation, and so on – all given specific form by our individual and cultural particularities. Such features also regularly occur in the mediumistic and PLR accounts, though the reports of intermission states in spontaneous reincarnation memories appear to be more closely aligned with NDEs and without such extensive elaboration and idiosyncrasies.

The modified "projection model" of Price's mind-dependent afterlife hypothesis demonstrates that it is possible to accommodate the cross-cultural and cross-experiential evidence with a reasonable, philosophically coherent idea of what the next world(s) might be like. This, however, is very different from claiming that the cross-cultural data actively supports such a hypothesis. While veridical information resulting from NDEs – such as Peak-in-Darien experiences and observations while out of the body – appear to support the survival hypothesis, arguments that the reality of NDEs is demonstrated by associated prophetic or transformative phenomena are more problematic. Even if such phenomena are veridical, they do not necessarily point to an actual afterlife, technically proving only the possibility of precognition and transformation resulting from near-death states.

In any case, if we grant that NDEs are evidence for survival after death, that evidence tells us about a transitional period rather than about any ultimate fate. In other words, even if consciousness does survive death and leaves the body, it is possible that it would not persist beyond the stages that NDErs have experienced. Survival itself might be temporary or perhaps even extremely brief. Likewise, a mind-dependent afterlife could be merely an intermediate phase prior to some other state of being (Price 1953: 25) or even annihilation, or a *nirvana*-like impersonal merging beyond consciousness.

It is also conceivable that different postmortem fates await different people, whether determined by culture, belief, or some unknown factor. Some may enter a mind-dependent state influenced by their state of mind and awareness at the moment of death. Others may find themselves in heavenly or hellish realms according to their actions and thoughts in this life (whether mind-dependent or otherwise). Some may remain on Earth in ghostly form, while others may reincarnate and perhaps eventually achieve a transcendent, transpersonal state. And some may simply die with the body (Becker 1993a: 120-1). This kind of wide diversity of post-mortem possibilities could conceivably explain why up to 90% of those who come close to death do not report NDEs – perhaps some other fate awaited them.

There are grounds to believe in the veridicality of NDEs, reincarnation, and perhaps mediumship, and therefore there are reasonable grounds to believe in an afterlife. There is also a coherent philosophical model that can accommodate individual and cultural diversity, making belief even more reasonable than the evidence alone. Furthermore, there has been no cogent purely biological explanation for NDEs in all their diversity and similarity. Nevertheless, the ultimate nature of NDEs and the possibility of survival after death remain matters of personal belief – and that includes materialist models of NDEs and *disbelief* in an afterlife.

APPENDIX I

EXTRAORDINARY EXPERIENCES OR CULTURAL IMAGINATION: "ALL IN THE BRAIN" REVISITED

Many readers who are interested in NDEs will be familiar with the criticisms of skeptical materialist scientists who argue that the phenomenon is not proof of an afterlife. As touched upon in Chapter 1, they propose a number of possible physical explanations to suggest that NDEs are essentially hallucinations of a compromised brain.

Many readers will not, however, be familiar with the ways in which skeptics within the humanities seek to deny not only the validity and significance of NDEs, but in a very real sense their actual existence. This may seem absurd given the mass of evidence in this book and others, but it is nevertheless the case.

Though arguing from quite a different stance from skeptics within the sciences, and for very different reasons, the result of this denial of extraordinary experiences in the humanities is very much the same. Regardless of their "mainstream" credentials, background, and standing in the scientific community, those who reach conclusions in favor of a survival hypothesis (or other non-physicalist theories) are immediately relegated to the "fringe." In the humanities – specifically in the secular study of religions – regardless of any prestigious academic background, research history, publication record, or other accomplishments, scholars who challenge the dominant paradigms face ostracization, ridicule, and lack of employment opportunities, career advancement, or other meaningful support.

This dual onslaught has unreasonably and pointlessly stunted the study of important and fascinating pan-human phenomena. In the sciences, it has hindered progress into our understanding of the ultimate nature of NDEs and other extraordinary experiences. In the humanities it has limited our knowledge of the origins and development of religious and ritual systems, and therefore of human cultural development *per se*.

Because the main research and debates surrounding NDEs has concerned the survival hypothesis, they have been largely confined to the sciences. Attitudes towards NDEs in the humanities are largely unknown to even the most dedicated NDE reader. Some may therefore be interested in reading about some of the scholarly dynamics (and challenges) that have formed the backdrop to the research in this book. This appendix will show how the academic study of religions has sought to invalidate research into NDEs and other extraordinary experiences, thereby silencing those who have them, and marginalizing those who study them. This has ensured that the field progresses no further than the myopic parameters it has imposed upon itself.

A Culture of Disbelief

The study of religions is a field rather than a discipline. As such, its scholars follow no particular methodology. Our methodologies are the same as those used by scholars of anthropology, sociology, psychology, cognitive science, or whatever other approach is taken to conduct a given study. One of the strengths of the field, in fact, is that scholars are free to adopt interdisciplinary approaches to their subject, drawing upon ideas from multiple disciplines rather than feeling confined to one. Scholars in the field also derive their theoretical concerns, debates, and lessons from these other areas of study.

In an effort to distinguish itself from the faith-based field of theology, the secular study of religions proceeds from a default position of neutrality – at least in theory. As in the closely aligned discipline of anthropology, we are to avoid judgment of the beliefs and practices of "the Other." At the same time, we are expected to cultivate self-awareness concerning our own possible biases, and to make explicit any religious commitments that might impact our thinking.

Because it is a secular field, again in contrast to theology, scholars in the study of religions do not engage with questions of truth claims in the religious and spiritual beliefs we study. We examine the beliefs themselves, their historical foundations and social functions, their expressions in text, art, or music; and we study the people who believe them and create them. But in theory, at least, we do not question whether a particular culture's deities really exist, if their rituals are effective, or if their cosmological or metaphysical beliefs measure up to our own version of reality.

In practice, however, the default stance is that the statements of our subjects are considered patently untrue when they conflict with our own philosophical commitments. This serves to keep Western academics in a position of power over the people we study.

There is not only an inherent bias in the field, but also an inherent hypocrisy: we are able to remain neutral only when our own beliefs are not challenged.

One result of this refusal to take seriously the claims of those we study has been a backlash against comparing religions, for seeking cross-cultural commonalities might reveal, for example, a kind of extraordinary experience or spiritual belief that could conceivably be "true." This, many scholars fear, is a dangerous path that could lead to "cryptotheology" – metaphysical interpretations of religious phenomena by allegedly secular scholars. Rather than risk discovering commonalities that might undermine preconceived notions in the field, it is best not to compare at all. Do not seek because you might find. Such is the fear of similarity that the very name of the field was changed, for it used to be known as "comparative religion."

There are some undoubtedly sound reasons for being critical of cross-cultural comparisons. Certain scholars of the past – James Frazer, Carl Jung, Aldous Huxley, Mircea Eliade, and Joseph Campbell to name only a few – had a habit of overgeneralizing similarities and neglecting difference, resulting in the romantic notion that all religions are "the same" and that they point to a single divine reality. This is not only clearly inaccurate, it also served to deny individuality of the Other and subsume the beliefs of other cultures into a Western construct (Shushan 2009, 2013).

The reaction, however, has been extreme, and along with comparison itself, the study of extraordinary experiences has been another casualty.

This is because experiences that are considered to be religious or spiritual by those who have them are a threat to the currently dominating paradigm: namely, that any religious experience cannot be independent of its cultural or linguistic context, and indeed that experience *per se* is literally and entirely *constructed* by language and/or culture. Because languages, cultures, and religions differ (the argument goes), there can be no such thing as an experience type that can by definition be considered "religious" or "spiritual." Therefore, extraordinary experiences such as NDEs have no place in explaining religious beliefs. On the contrary, religious beliefs explain religious experiences.

Although such notions lack empirical validation and are thus more accurately seen as speculative philosophical stances, they are nevertheless treated by many scholars as axiomatic (e.g., Proudfoot 1985; Cupitt 1998; Sharf 1998; Bocking 2006). Near-death and out-of-body experiences present serious challenges to these ways of thinking and indeed may be seen as the tools that dismantle the philosophical houses of cards upon which the axioms are built.

The first of these axioms is that we cannot separate an account of an experience from the experience itself; and moreover, that there *is* no actual experience underlying the description of it. The Buddhism scholar Robert Sharf (1998: 286) considers it a "mistake" to treat "representations" of experiences "as if they referred back to something other than themselves" – that is, to the kind of experience which they purport to describe. At the same time, Sharf does not deny subjective experience, although nor does he explain how a person can have such an experience but be intrinsically unable to accurately "represent" or "refer" to it in narrative form.

It is absurdly obvious that any narrative will not be the *same* as the actual experience it attempts to describe (Rennie 2000: 108). Different cognitive functions are employed in *having* an experience, which involves the actual occurrence, and *recounting* it, which involves memories of that occurrence. To anyone who has any kind of experience – meaning literally everyone – the experience itself and relating it are obviously not the same. Implying that certain individuals – by virtue of the fact that they claim to have had an extraordinary experience – cannot make such distinctions, or are unable to differentiate between experience types, or lack the critical faculties to interpret rationally their experiences, is both groundless and demeaning.

Aside from that, some individuals will embellish more than others, while descriptions, symbols, similes, and interpretations will vary widely by one's culture, individuality, and preexisting beliefs. This does not, however, indicate that individuals do not have something like the kinds of experiences they describe. This is demonstrated by the existence of specific, identifiable, extraordinary experience types such as NDEs and OBEs. As seen throughout this book, despite cultural and individual idiosyncrasies, NDEs share many general thematic similarities: apparently dying, leaving the body and traveling to another realm, encountering supernatural beings and deceased relatives, being instructed to return, and coming back to life followed by a subsequent spiritual or other positive transformation. It is important to stress again that not only do NDEs have cross-culturally similar content, *they also share cross-culturally consistent, locally-ascribed interpretations*: that the individual really died, left the body, had a variety of unusual experiences, and returned to the body.

Sharf (1998: 280-82) further questions whether there is any reason to assume that reports of mystical experiences are "credible" as "phenomenological descriptions" – that is, descriptions of what the individual subjectively experienced, apart from any interpretation of it. In other words, Sharf is not simply objecting to the idea that a person would interpret an experience as "mystical" – he is objecting to the claim that there was ever any experience at all. But is there any reason to assume such descriptions are *not* credible? Categories of specific experience types are identified through observation and comparison. Terms such as "near-death experience" are possible because similar *types* of narratives of experiences have been identified and generically categorized in consistent ways by numerous and diverse scholars. Searches for articles and books concerning NDEs and OBEs on PubMed, ScienceDirect, or Google Scholar yield thousands of results. How could this cross-disciplinary subject of study even exist if the descriptions of NDEs were not "credible" to some degree?

It is obvious that certain narratives of experiences that occur in return-from-death or near-death contexts contain a particular set of similarities that leads to their identification as NDEs. Similarities across cultures and throughout history are evidence that the narratives share some descriptive credibility, despite cultural and individual variation. This shows that there is such a pan-human experience type as the NDE. Conversely, it is difficult to imagine what kind of proof there could ever be that the masses of descriptions of NDEs and OBEs found cross-culturally do not actually refer to any experiences.

Again, these observations exist regardless of what we choose to believe about the ultimate nature of NDEs. They apply whether we subscribe to a psychological, neurophysiological, or metaphysical explanation of the nature of the phenomena. All attempts to explain NDEs in materialist terms involve *physical* events, such as REM intrusion, anoxia, hypercarbia, and other epiphenomena of a compromised brain. These events cause experiences with identifiable, predictable, and consistent features, enabling critics of the veridicality of NDEs to formulate theories predicated on their universality. NDEs also share a similar phenomenology with the effects of the drug ketamine, according to individuals who have had experiences of both (Jansen 2001). This similarity demonstrates that there are objectively stable features of two experience types. To accept one on the grounds that it has medically identifiable origins (ketamine) and not the other on the grounds that some claim it does not (NDE) would be an example of cognitive dissonance and an anti-scientific privileging of philosophical commitments over evidence.

Obviously, the empirical study of NDEs and OBEs would not be possible if there were no such experiences to fit these categories. Research has measured neurological data while NDEs are in progress and pinpointed the timing of their occurrence, as well as the ostensible observations during them (Parnia et. al. 2014). There have been experiments in OBE induction (Blanke et. al. 2003; Metzinger 2005: 76), and survey- and fieldwork-based studies on the relationship between experiences and beliefs (Shiels 1978; McClenon 1994, 2002; Yao & Badham 2007). All this demonstrates that these experiences are temporal, finite, actual *occurrences* (Davis 1989: 19-22) that can be referred to and described like any other.

Critics (Katz 1978; Proudfoot 1985; Sharf 1998) also argue that our particular terms for experience types may not have counterparts in other languages, which means that the phenomenon we term "near-death experience," for example, may be unknown in a given society. The lack of a term in a given language for a particular experience type, however, plainly does not indicate that the experience itself is unknown to speakers of that language. Taken to its illogical extreme, this line of thought would imply that speakers of Malayalam or Russian, for example, do not experience having hands on the grounds that they have no separate word for "hand" (it is considered a part of the "arm"). Put simply, linguistic differences do not negate the possibility of common human experiences (Forman 1990: 18). The notion that the existence of terms is somehow equivalent to that to which they refer is unsupportable. Put another way, the existence of an experience type is not predicated on the existence of a term for it.

Concepts, objects, and experiences are all expressible between different languages and cultures, even if translation from one to another can never be 100% exact. Individuals in contemporary China have extraordinary experiences (including NDEs) that are consistent with those known elsewhere, and they commonly associate them with religious ideas and beliefs (Yao & Badham 2007: 28ff). And although Tibetans consider everything to be part of the natural order and do not have a term for "supernatural," they nevertheless "consider certain phenomena as beyond normal consciousness, outside the realm of ordinary experience" (McClenon 1994: 1). The fact that experiences are often described and interpreted in similar ways across cultures indicates that it is more a question of how people negotiate these experiences within their cultural and linguistic contexts rather than whether or not they actually have them. As we have seen, despite the fact that NDEs were only formally named in 1975, and OBEs in 1943 (by mathematician and physicist George N. M. Tyrrell), we have many accounts prior to those dates of experiences that correspond to those that came to be called "NDEs" and "OBEs" – and they should therefore be properly considered as such.

Philosopher of religion Wayne Proudfoot (1985) argues that the concept of religious experience can be traced only as far back as the German Lutheran theologian Friedrich Schleiermacher (1799). Thus, Sharf (1998: 271) reasons, such notions should not be applied earlier because to do so "anachronistically imposes the recent and ideologically laden notion of 'religious experience' on our interpretations of premodern phenomena." However, NDEs and OBEs are clearly described in pre-Schleiermacher *religious contexts* around the world, confirming that they are neither late nor exclusively Western, and that they are regularly interpreted in religious terms cross-culturally.

As we have seen, many religious texts relating to life after death show an awareness of the concepts of NDEs and OBEs and involve an individual's soul temporarily traveling to afterlife realms. Such texts are often intended to prepare the reader for what to expect after death, providing instructions about behaviour types that will ensure a positive fate. This indicates that they were believed to be based on first-hand knowledge and actual experiences. This, in fact, does seem to be the case with the continuous strand of otherworld-journey narratives spanning the range of Vedic literature as described in Chapter 3, and is overtly the case with the Tibetan *Bardo Thödol*. There is an important, perhaps foundational connection between NDEs and Pure Land Buddhism in China and Japan, with many prominent figures in the traditions reporting them (McClenon 1994: 182). Much shamanic poetry and other narratives from ancient China contain descriptions of OBE journeys to other realms. In light of these and many other examples, it is clear that NDEs and OBEs were part of human experience long before they were named by Western researchers, and were seen in religious terms long before Schleiermacher.

Nor is there is there any psychological, neurophysiological, or anthropological evidence to support the notion that experience is dependent upon language. On the contrary, there is evidence that both emotions and cognition (which are kinds of experience) can *precede* language (Downey 2010; McClenon 2002: 161). If some experience types can precede language, it is logical to assume that others can as well.

Furthermore, it is objectionable to characterize those who claim to have had extraordinary experiences as uncritical products of their belief systems at best (Barnard 1992) or liars at worst. To adopt the stance that "we are not obliged to accept" their testimonies (Sharf: 1998: 283; see also Cupitt 1998: 33) creates a culture of disbelief that places critics in an unwarranted superior position to those they study. To question the credibility of accounts of religious experience is to question the credibility of the individuals relating them, and to effectively stigmatize them. Furthermore, it privileges specific western scholarly interpretations over those of the individuals who provide us with our data in the first place, while also deflecting attention away from the very phenomena we are studying.

Language and the Mediation of Experiences

The fact that OBEs and NDEs are often characterized as being ineffable by those who have them creates further problems for the notion that these experiences are linguistically "constructed." The philosopher and NDE writer Mark Fox (2003: 134-35) raises a highly pertinent question: if language is the primary factor in the creation of such experiences, why is it that experiencers often do not have the "language" to describe them? As with mystical experiences described as Pure Consciousness Events, with NDEs there is often a "disjunction" between the event and the later attempt to describe it. It is this disjunction that the experiencer refers to as "ineffable" – inexpressible because it is non-linguistic (Forman 1990: 41). Humanities professor Larry Short (1995:

665, 668, 670) sees mystical practices as techniques to "interfere with language use" and "disassociate sound from meaning, signifier from signified," resulting in a non-linguistic state.

This does not necessarily mean that the experience is unmediated – only that the mediator is not predominantly language. Language is important in making sense of the experience, however, and of course in relating it. As Fox (2003: 134-35) concludes, "Far from being a product of language and/or cultural-linguistic expectation," the core elements of the NDE "stand prior to and independently of their culturally acquired expectations of what death might be like."

The inadequacy of language to express OBEs and NDEs suggests that the experience originated prior to the attempt to put it into language, while the existence of cross-cultural similarities indicates that they originate in phenomena that are independent of culture. Diffusion or intertextuality cannot explain the structurally similar narratives describing contextually stable experiences from such different times, places, and cultural-linguistic backgrounds (Shushan 2009: ch. 2).

The idea of a pre-cultural, pre-linguistic origin of NDEs is supported by two further considerations. The first is that the experiences often conflict with the expectations and cultural-religious background of experiencers (Fox 2003: 115-16). The second is that they are spontaneous, with no associated religious practice, no expectation, and indeed often with total ignorance of the phenomenon. An experience cannot conform to expectation if one does not expect it. An early twentieth-century Zuni Native American NDE, for example, included encounters with deceased relatives and bright light – motifs that are inconsistent with Zuni afterlife conceptions (Wade 2003: 94–5; Shushan 2018: 48). Medieval Chinese, Japanese, and European NDE narratives often conflicted with the theological conventions of their times and places (McClenon 1994: ch. 9), and atheists have NDEs generally consistent with those of theists.

Conversely, certain themes that we might expect to find in the NDEs of religious individuals are rarely reported, regardless of their religion. For example, neither salvation, physical resurrection, nor reincarnation commonly feature in NDE reports at all, whether from Buddhists, Christians, Hindus, Jews, or Muslims. Significantly, while NDErs report a number of sub-experiences from a recognized repertoire, variability between accounts is often attributable to specific, identifiable cultural and individual factors (Shushan 2009: 39-50) (and perhaps to the duration of the experience – see Stevenson and Greyson [1996: 203-04]).

All this means that NDEs can conflict with the expectations even of those *with* prior knowledge of the phenomenon, who may wonder, for example, why they did not go through a tunnel, have a life review, or meet the relative or deity they'd hoped to meet.

This is not to suggest that language and culture play no role in mediating NDEs and OBEs. Related by individuals from within their own cultures, narratives of experiences are obviously culturally embedded just like any other narrative. However, accepting that experience is culturally *mediated* is not the same as accepting that it is entirely culturally *fabricated*. Mediation is often seen as being at odds with true mystical experiences and thus enlisted as proof that they cannot occur, as if the only type of experience that could be accepted as mystical must be a pure-consciousness event wholly transcending culture and individual. Short (1995: 661-64), however, argues that mediation actually *enables* experience, and is a central component to the process of understanding it. Indeed, as human beings, "we come with given physical, perceptual, and neurological equipment," as well as common experiences of "time, space, and causality" – all pre-linguistic mediators that filter our experiences. This indicates a degree of commonality of all human perception, and thus of the ways in which we experience.

This is precisely the model for NDEs that has been suggested in this book. The possibility of NDEs and OBEs having pre-cultural origins is not predicated on their being wholly unmediated "pure" cultureless experiences. Rather, it is more productive to see such experiences as having interconnected universal, individual, and cultural layers: universal "events" which are experienced by enculturated individuals who give them specific form. These individuals subsequently attempt to make sense of the experience according to their socio-cultural-religious situation, or indeed by innovating away from it (King 1988).

As universally human beings we have universal experience types, and as enculturated human beings we process and express those experiences according to our specific cultural-linguistic modes. As a self-conscious, analytical species, we have the ability to discern one experience from another, to generalize about them in order to construct categories of experience types, and to analyze, interpret, and describe them in culturally and individually diverse ways.

Nor does acknowledging cultural and individual idiosyncrasies in NDEs indicate that truly unmediated experience is impossible. Fox (2003: 125-26) emphasizes that mystical experiences are typically described as "a state which bypasses normal modes of sense and apprehension." Exceptional experiences such as apparently being out of the body and traveling to another realm are commonly regarded by those who have them as occurring beyond the physical senses and therefore not subject to physical laws, and thus beyond our ability to understand through our usual constraining modes of materialist analysis and interpretation. In other words, while unmediated experience is not *normally* possible, it is at least philosophically conceivable that in certain exceptional states it is (Evans 1988: 54-55).

Although claims of the total narrative construction of experience are without empirical validation, they are nevertheless widely accepted in the study of religions. The study that Proudfoot cited in support of his arguments (Schachter & Singer 1962) has been highly criticized and effectively refuted by half a century of further research (Barnard 1992: 234-35; McClenon 2002: 161-63). While Proudfoot (1993: 793) later clarified that his argument is not dependent upon that article's conclusions, he provided no further empirical evidence to support his claims. Without evidential underpinnings, such claims should more correctly be regarded as philosophical stance rather than scientific fact. Ultimately, there is no rational justification for giving default primacy to language and culture over experience.

NDEs, OBEs, and the Experiential Source Hypothesis

If there were no such things as universal experience types that people around the world widely consider to be religious, it would be pointless to look for some kind of religious experience that might help us account for the origins of religious beliefs. Buddhism scholar Brian Bocking (2006), for example, believes that Sharf's argument that such experiences are merely cultural-linguistic inventions "is, or should be, unsettling for anyone who naively thinks that religious beliefs are grounded in religious experiences." Note his denigrating use of "naively" for those who choose to take seriously the testimonies of experiencers.

However, among the range of experiences humans have, are ones that *within their cultural contexts* are commonly considered religious, mystical, or otherwise extraordinary, and inexplicable without reference to some supernatural, metaphysical, or divine cause or agency. Cross-culturally, presumably universally, NDEs and OBEs are considered exceptional within the contexts in which they occur, and they are given special, often elevated status. I know of no narrative from any time or place in which an NDE is accepted casually or seen to be a common everyday occurrence. There is clearly a difference between the quotidian sensations of one's awareness being in the body and interacting with other tangible human beings, and non-quotidian sensations of one's awareness being out of the body and interacting with spiritual beings. Regardless of whether or not these things veridically occur, people around the world have been reporting them throughout recorded history and regarding them as being in a separate category to everyday occurrences. This pattern of consistent ascription is an important indicator of the cross-cultural stability of such experiences.

There are certain types of human experience that are obviously most relevant to certain types of beliefs, and as such they are logical candidates to help us explain the origins of those beliefs. As we have seen, there is direct evidence in the form of historical, ethnographic, and contemporary personal testimony that people around the world regularly base beliefs concerning an afterlife upon specific NDEs undergone by real individuals. People also often change their beliefs following their own NDE. Notably, that includes atheists who neither believed in an afterlife nor expected to have an NDE.

As a single, discrete experience (as opposed to the composite NDE), OBEs are perhaps even more problematic for cultural-linguistic constructivist beliefs. In whatever culture it occurs, the OBE is by definition always and unambiguously considered a dualistic state in which consciousness is separated from the body. While Sharf (1998: 277) may be correct that Western perceptions and assumptions about religious experience lie in Descartes' "notion of mind as an 'immaterial substance,'" what is being described in all OBE reports is a *kind* of mind-body dualism. The clear, consistent descriptions of the phenomenon make it irrelevant whether the OBE is understood in philosophically Cartesian, Upanishadic, or Salteaux terms. Cultural views of mind-body dualism need not be identical in order to be grounded in the same experience type.

Not only are explicit descriptions of OBEs found in Eastern and Western narratives throughout history, but mind-body dualism, often exemplified by descriptions of OBEs, is a common element of nearly every branch of Egyptian, Ancient Near Eastern, Zoroastrian, Græco-Roman, Hindu, Jewish, Christian, Muslim, Buddhist, and numerous other theologies (see, for example, Badham 1997, Bremmer 1983, Couliano 1991, Metzinger 2005, Pilch 2011, Zaleski 1987). Dean

Shiels (1978: 699) found that of the 67 small-scale indigenous societies he reviewed, 95 percent believed in OBEs, and they were consistently described in remarkably similar ways. He concluded that the most likely explanation for this wide cross-cultural occurrence of OBE belief was that it "results from a common experience of this happening" (Shiels 1978: 699). McClenon's fieldwork (1994, 2002: 106-31) provides a mass of cross-cultural evidence that demonstrates that NDEs and OBEs often lead directly to beliefs in an afterlife and in mind-body dualism.

From a neuroscientific perspective, Thomas Metzinger (2005: 57) also theorizes that dualistic beliefs cross-culturally originate in OBEs. He stresses that OBEs "can be undergone by every human being and seem to possess a culturally invariant cluster of functional and phenomenal core properties." They "almost inevitably lead the experiencing subject to conclude that conscious experience can, as a matter of fact, take place independently of the brain and the body." Metzinger (2005: 78 n.8) cites other studies that support his hypothesis, including one (Osis 1979) in which 73% of survey respondents claimed that their beliefs had changed as a result of their OBEs, and another (Gabbard and Twemlow 1984) in which 66% claimed that their OBEs caused them to adopt a belief in life after death. Metzinger concludes:

> Although many OBE reports are certainly colored by the interpretational schemes ordered by the metaphysical ideologies available to experiencing subjects in their time and culture, the experiences as such must be taken seriously. Although their conceptual and ontological interpretations are often seriously misguided, the truthfulness of centuries of reports about ecstatic states, soul-travel and second bodies as such can hardly be doubted. (Metzinger 2005: 78 n.8)

Perhaps unsurprisingly, NDEs and OBEs have been largely ignored by most constructivist critics of religious experience. One exception is Carol Zaleski (1987: 190), whose work is marked by logical inconsistencies that appear to result from adherence to a preconceived constructivist interpretation, even when it conflicts with her own data. For example, as mentioned in Chapter 1, she carefully draws parallels between modern and medieval NDE narratives, but because similarities are problematic for her conclusion that the NDE is wholly imaginative, they are left unexplained in order to focus on the differences. Considering her argument that NDE researchers deny the testimonies of experiencers by using the neutral term "being of light" (p. 22, above), it is ironic that

Zaleski (1987: 127) herself denies insider testimony comprehensively and deliberately by concluding that NDEs are imaginary.

In his discussion of John Wren-Lewis's NDE (see Chapter 2), Bocking (2006) writes that the author differentiates the experience he had from an NDE because it "had none of the classic NDE features of tunnel, light etc." and because "it stayed with him permanently." However, while Wren-Lewis (1995) was indeed puzzled by elements that he believed were inconsistent with so-called "classic" NDEs, he himself referred to his experience *as* an NDE. Furthermore, his description actually does feature some typical elements of NDEs, including the fact that "it stayed with him permanently": NDEs commonly remain vivid long after the experience and have lasting positive aftereffects, such as loss of a fear of death and increased spiritual orientation (Noyes et. al. 2009) – both of which Wren-Lewis described. Other common NDE elements found in Wren-Lewis's account include time slowing down, indescribable bliss and joy, universal understanding and feelings of unity, returning to a home or origin state of being, ineffability, being "pure consciousness" beyond space and time, and dramatic impressions of light and darkness – an "almost palpable blackness that was yet somehow radiant." While NDEs are not central to Bocking's paper, he nevertheless employs a straw man methodology by selecting an isolated example of an NDE allegedly inconsistent with other NDEs in order to imply that consistencies do not exist in general, while (similar to Zaleski) also ignoring consistencies actually found within that example. Wren-Lewis's change of beliefs concerning mysticism as a direct result of his NDE is ignored, even though it directly challenges Bocking's assertion that beliefs cannot be grounded in experiences.

NDEs and OBEs are specific, stable pan-human experience types, and their basic consistent interpretations cross-culturally have been attested, helping to explain certain structurally common themes found in religious beliefs in diverse societies around the world. The generalizations being made here about these phenomena are contextually relevant to the cultures that produce the narratives of the experiences: they are seen locally as being related to consciousness leaving the body and/or surviving physical death.

As discussed, the experiential source hypothesis does not in itself attempt to define the ontological status of the experience and can be used to support both theological and reductionist interpretations (as evidenced by Metzinger, above). We do not necessarily need to believe that the person genuinely did leave the body in order to respect and take seriously his or her account of the experience. Whatever their ultimate nature, individuals have experiences that *seem* like they leave the body and travel to another realm, and such experiences can alter their pre-existing beliefs.

The Challenge of Near-Death and Out-of-Body Experiences

For a variety of reasons, NDEs and OBEs present major challenges to the types of criticisms discussed above:

(1) A great deal of empirical and social scientific research on these phenomena has been undertaken, and they are widely accepted as pan-human experiences by researchers from the most reductionist to the most theological of orientations. Narratives of NDEs and OBEs are found throughout history and in all parts of the world. Their occurrence is not in general dispute, only their origins and meanings. This demonstrates that they are classifiable and distinguishable as a particular type of experience.

(2) NDEs typically occur under similar, generally physical circumstances: an individual is close to death, apparently dies, subsequently revives, and reports having undergone unusual experiences. A particular originating event (being near death) is thus a common catalyst for generating the effects of NDEs. This means they have an objectively, cross-culturally stable context which indicates a pre-cultural origin. They are not created by the "cultural imagination."

(3) The fundamental interpretation of NDEs appears to be universal – not only in general religious, mystical, or otherwise supernatural terms, but specifically in the belief that *this is what happens when we die.*

If there is no common experience underpinning narratives of religious experiences, cross-culturally consistent narratives of these specific extraordinary experience types should not exist, and certainly should not have the same apparently universally ascribed basic meanings.

Cultural-linguistic constructivist perspectives rely on a number of mutually reliant unproven axioms. The considerations above reveal how these axioms do not stand up to scrutiny: (1) experience cannot precede language/culture, (2) narratives of experience do not refer to actual experiences, (3) "religious experience" is meaningless as a cross-cultural category, and (4) religious beliefs cannot be grounded in religious experiences (Shushan 2014). All these culturally situated philosophical beliefs are demonstrably wrong.

Constructivist philosophies about religious experience also come with dubious political baggage, especially when seen in the context of Western cultural imperialism and colonialist thinking. For example, certain Christian missionaries refused to accept indigenous claims that local afterlife beliefs stemmed directly from personal NDEs. Chrétien Le Clercq (1691: 207) wrote that Mi'kmaq Native American statements to this effect resulted from "error and imposture." Jean de Brébeuf (1636: 141) was "astounded" that anyone could believe the narratives he heard from the Wyandot. In his exploration of how spiritual experiences have been treated as mental disorders, Hufford (2005: 21-25) pointed to "Enlightenment skeptics such as David Hume who saw supernatural belief as inherently not rational." Furthermore, Protestant and Calvinist theologies after the Middle Ages encouraged negative views of spiritual experiences, which were downplayed in favor of "non-rational" faith.

The contemporary constructivist stances may thus have roots in Catholic missionary ethnocentric justifications of colonialism, Humean skepticism, and Protestant/Calvinist theologies in (a) their culture of disbelief and mistrust of experiencer testimony; (b) their negative judgments about narratives of experience; (c) their portrayal of the Other as untrustworthy, non-rational, and ignorant (inventing narratives of experience, being unable to understand or distinguish between experience types, and being uncritical products of belief systems); and (d) their unscientific privileging of their own philosophical commitments over evidence. Finally, the denial of cross-cultural similarities and the emphasis on difference can be divisive and potentially foster ethnocentrism.

Rather than being comprehensive explanations in and of themselves, language and culture are more productively seen as contributing factors in the formation, processing, and expression of extraordinary experiences. To recognize and engage intellectually with the cross-cultural occurrence of NDEs and OBEs is little different from doing so with any other type of human experience. Grief at the loss of loved ones, for example, is universal although culturally expressed (Stroebe and Stroebe 1987: 53-54). People who ascribe to certain experiences religious, spiritual, or otherwise supernatural meanings should be taken seriously rather than stigmatized – regardless of the ultimate nature of those experiences.

APPENDIX II

THE NEAR-DEATH EXPERIENCE OF

MRS. LEONORA PIPER

In February of 1896, the medium Leonora Piper (see Chapter 5) underwent hernia surgery. Two days later she recounted her NDE:

The first experience I had was as though I was being raised from my bed while still in my body, that is to all intents and purposes I was in my body. Then I felt a strong hand clasping my arm on the left; it seemed like the hand of a man. On my right I was being lifted apparently without any contact.

I saw a man with long wavy hair and stoop-over shoulders. I think it was Phinuit. I saw George also. It was he who seemed to be holding me up.

Then I heard voices saying, "Come, we wish to take you with us; we wish to give you a rest from your tired body," and without further sound I was raised. There was a break between my hearing the voices and my being lifted or raised above my bed. I was conscious of not being on my bed. Then I was carried in space until we came to a delicate blue drapery hanging in folds as though blowing in the breeze. It seemed to be immovable until we passed through when it parted, and I was not conscious of there being any sides to it; I then heard a rustling sound as of people approaching, but I didn't hear the footsteps. It was like the rustling of garments, and then I saw a light as though all space—the whole earth was aglow—such a light! —I never saw anything like it before.

Then I heard children's voices as though singing, and a chorus like young ladies' voices; I was surrounded by them; they were everywhere and they then seemed to form a ring around me. They were all very beautiful, and passing around from one to the other was what seemed to be a silken banner or sash which they seemed to be holding. It was soft and silky and entwined about with flowers, and it was held from one to the other so that the silken band helped to form a ring. They had beautifully sandalled feet. I heard the rustling of their garments (something like the rustling of tissue paper) —loose, Greek, flowing garments. They danced about as they formed the ring; then the ring seemed to separate and they dispersed. I felt it was a sort of greeting to me as it were, that is, the ring and their dancing and singing.

We passed on along a smooth walk hedged on either side with flowers. We came to pillars—they looked like real pillars, but were not solid-looking, almost transparent. The pillars seemed to be an entrance to what seemed to be a large building. It seemed as though one whole side of the building was open, the pillars forming the entrance. Inside the building as we passed, I saw a long bench or table around which many men were writing; they were each one sitting back one to the other and did not seem to pay any attention to me. It seemed as though some sort of educational work was being carried on. I looked into their faces as we passed the building; their faces were smooth and devoid of all wrinkles,—they had very clear complexions.

I suddenly saw an elderly gentleman. He was gray-haired and had bluish-gray eyes, heavy moustache—no beard—distinguished looking,—face rather small. He said he was not lame now; he took hold of his robe and began to dance, saying, "See, I am not lame now." A young lady was with him; she was very lovely. She had dark hair combed back away from her forehead, pompadour fashion—large eyes and intelligent, sweet face.

Then I saw an elderly gentleman with hair white and a full white beard—clear eyes—intelligent—large distinguished nose. He resembled Mr. Hodgson, but Mr. Hodgson has more dreamy and spiritual expression about the eyes. I said to Mr. Hodgson: "I could take that gentleman to be your father."

I also saw a dark-complexioned gentleman with pointed beard—very intelligent looking—but rather small. He approached George. I saw them shake hands and heard them say, "Hulloa, old fellow," or something of the kind. They discussed, but I could not hear what they were discussing. All seemed so happy: I also saw an aunt of mine who died of cancer and also a cousin who died of consumption. I got along so easily and did not seem to walk, but made progress without stepping—I stood erect.

I saw two of Mrs. Thaw's children. I was conscious that they were hers but did not see Mrs. Thaw's mother.

A thin-faced young man came to me who was anxious about a friend of his; he wanted information which I could not give him. He was about 30 or 35. He may have been Dr. Thaw's brother. He was perhaps looking for his wife—This was my impression.

I think I saw Mr. D. ... I saw Mrs. S.'s husband and her son and her aunt, and she seemed to be doing something with her hands as though she were picking something to pieces. I seemed to see every-one I had ever known who has died.

I saw a very tall gentleman; he was extremely tall. They called him Charles.

As I was beginning to see a great number of people approaching, I felt as though some one had stabbed me in the back. When I was first being taken up, I seemed to follow a streak of light; it seemed to be a ray of light, similar to a ray of light from the sun through a knot hole, and we followed that light. When I felt the stab, I felt that the same light was behind me, and it seemed to be a cord or string but nothing tangible, and it seemed to be the same ray of light which led me off away from this sphere. As these people approached me, some one seemed to be pulling on the cord, though I could not say it was a cord—it looked like a light and felt like cord. Someone kept pulling and I was being lowered and taken from my feet—(I had been standing erect)—to a position of lying down, and then I awoke and I had a feeling that I had not been asleep but had been awake and had had this experience while awake—and yet my body was so heavy I could not move—my body seemed so dark and heavy as though it did not belong to me ; I had to struggle for breath. I felt depressed to think that I had got back. I could not move a limb at first (Sidgwick 1915: 377-81).

REFERENCES

～

Abramovitch, H. (1988) "An Israeli account of a near-death experience: A case study of cultural dissonance." *Journal of Near-Death Studies* 6, 175–184.

Allen, J. P. (1988) *Genesis in Ancient Egypt: The Philosophy of Ancient Egyptian Creation Accounts.* New Haven: Yale University Press.

Allen, J. P. (2005) *The Ancient Egyptian Pyramid Texts.* Atlanta: SBL.

Almeder, R. (1987) *Beyond Death: Evidence for Life After Death.* Springfield: Thomas.

Anderson, George (1999) *Lessons from the Light.* New York: Putmans.

Arbuckle, G. (1997) "Chinese religions." In H. Coward (ed.) *Life After Death in World*

Religions. New York: Orbis.

Assman, J. (1984; trans. 2001) *The Search for God in Ancient Egypt.* Ithaca: Cornell University Press.

Assman, J. (2001; trans. 2005) *Death and Salvation in Ancient Egypt.* Ithaca: Cornell University Press.

Athappilly, G., B. Greyson, & I. Stevenson (2006) "Do prevailing societal models influence reports of near-death experiences? A comparison of accounts reported before and after 1975." *Journal of Nervous & Mental Disease* 194, 218-222.

Atherton, Henry (1680), quoted in Selwyn, D.G. (2004) "A 17th century 'near-death' experience." *De Numine: The Newsletter for the Members of the Alister Hardy Society* 35, 5-9.

Augustine, K. (2007) "Psychophysiological and cultural correlates undermining a survivalist interpretation of near-death experiences." *Journal of Near-Death Studies* 26(2) (Winter), 89-125.

Badham, P. (1982) *Immortality or Extinction?* London: SPCK.

Badham, P. (1990) *Near-Death Experiences, Beliefs About Life After Death, and the Tibetan Book of the Dead.* Tokyo: Honganji International Buddhist Study Center.

Badham, P. (1997) "Religious and near-death experience in relation to belief in a future life." *Mortality* 2(1), 7-20.

Bailey, L. W. (2001) "A 'little death': the near-death experience and Tibetan delogs." *Journal of Near-Death Studies* 19(3), 139–59.

Barnard, G. W. (1992) "Explaining the unexplainable: Wayne Proudfoot's 'Religious Experience.'" *Journal of the American Academy of Religion* 60.2, 231-56.

Beard, P. (1980) *Living On: A Study of Altering Consciousness After Death.* London: Allen & Unwin.

Becker, C. B. (1984) "The Pure Land revisited: Sino-Japanese meditations and near-death experiences of the next world." *Anabiosis* 4, 51-68.

Becker, C. B. (1985) "Views from Tibet: near-death experiences and the Book of the Dead." *Anabiosis* 5(1), 3-20.

Becker, C. B. (1993a) *Breaking the Circle: Death and the Afterlife in Buddhism.* Carbondale: Southern Illinois University Press.

Becker, C. B. (1993b) *Paranormal Experience and Survival of Death.* Albany: SUNY.

Beckwith, M. (1940, rpt. 1970) *Hawaiian Mythology.* Honolulu: University of Hawaii Press.

Belanti, J., M. Perera, and K. Jagadheesan (2008) "Phenomenology of near-death experiences: a cross-cultural perspective." *Transcultural Psychiatry* 45(1), 121–33.

Bell, F. L. S. (1937) "Death in Tanga." *Oceania,* 7(3), 316–339.

Berndt, R. M., & Berndt, C. H. (1964) *The World of the First Australians.* London: Angus Robertson.

Best, E. (1900) "Spiritual concepts of the Maori, Part I." *Journal of the Polynesian Society* 9(4), 173–199.

Best, E. (1901) "Spiritual concepts of the Maori, Part II." *Journal of the Polynesian Society* 10(1), 1–20.

Best, E. (1905) "Maori eschatology." *Transactions and Proceedings of the New Zealand Institute* 38, 148–239.

Bierhorst, J. (1992) *History and Mythology of the Aztecs: The Codex Chimalpopoca.* Tucson: University of Arizona Press.

Bierhorst, J. (2002, rev. ed.) *The Mythology of Mexico and Central America.* Oxford: Oxford University Press.

Black, J. A., G. Cunningham, E. Robson, and G. Zólyomi (eds) (2004) *The Literature of Ancient Sumer.* Oxford: Oxford University Press.

Blackmore, S. J. (1993) *Dying to Live: Near-Death Experiences.* London: Grafton.

Blanke, O., T. Landis, L. Spinelli, & M. Seeck (2003) "Out-of-body experience and autoscopy of neurological origin." *Brain* 127.2, 243-58.

Blowsnake, S. (1909; ed. P. Radin 1920) *Crashing Thunder: The Autobiography of an American Indian*. New York: Appleton.

Boas, F. (1890) "First general report on the Indians of British Columbia." In *Fifth report of the Committee on the Northwest Tribes of Canada*. In *Report of the 59th Meeting of the British Association for the Advancement of Science*, 801– 893. London: Murray.

Boas, F. (1923) *Notes on the Tillamook*. University of California Publications in American Archaeology and Ethnology 20. Berkeley: University of California Press.

Bocking, B. (2006) "Mysticism: no experience necessary?" *DISKUS* 7. http://jbasr.com/basr/diskus/diskus7/bocking.htm (accessed 20 Oct. 2021).

Bodewitz, H. W. (trans.) (1973) *Jaiminiya Brahmana* 1, 1–63. Leiden: Brill.

Bodewitz, H. W. (1991) *Light, Soul and Visions in the Veda*. Professor P.D. Gune Memorial Lectures 5th Series. Poona: Bhandarkar Oriental Research Institute.

Bodewitz, H. W. (2002) "The dark and deep underworld of the Vedas." *Journal of the American Oriental Society* 122(2), April–June, 213–24.

Braude, S. (2003) *Immortal Remains*. Lanham: Rowman Littlefield.

Bremmer, J. (1983) *The Early Greek Concept of the Soul*. Princeton: Princeton University Press.

Broad, C. D. (1962) *Lectures on Psychical Research*. London: Routledge & Kegan Paul.

Brown, G. (1910) *Melanesians and Polynesians: Their Life-Histories Described and Compared*. London: Macmillan.

Bush, N. E. (2009) "Veridical perception in near-death experiences." In J. M. Holden, B. Greyson, & D. James (Eds.) *The Handbook of near-death experiences: thirty years of investigation*. Santa Barbara: Praeger/ABC- CLIO, 63–86.

Butzenberger, K. (1996) "Ancient Indian conceptions on man's destiny after death: the beginnings and the early development of the doctrine of transmigration I." *Berliner Indologische Studien* 9, 55–118.

Campany, R. F. (1990) "Return-from-death narratives in early medieval China." *Journal of Chinese Religions* 18, 90–125.

Campany, R. F. (1995) "To hell and back: death, near-death, and other worldly journeys in early medieval China." In J.J. Collins and M. Fishbane *Death, Ecstasy and Other Worldly Journeys* 343-60. Albany: SUNY Press.

Carroll, R. T. (ed.) (2004) "Reader comments: past-life regression." *The Skeptic's Dictionary*. Online edition, retrieved 3 Oct. 2021. http://skepdic.com/comments/pastlifecom.html

Chan, W. (1963) (trans.) *A Sourcebook in Chinese Philosophy*. Princeton: Princeton University Press.

Chapman, J. W. (1912) "The happy hunting-ground of the Ten'a." *Journal of American Folklore* 25(95), 66–71.

Chatelain, H. (1894) *Folk-Tales of Angola*. Memoirs of the American Folklore Society, 1. Boston: Houghton Mifflin.

Ching, J. (1993) *Chinese Religions*. London: Macmillan.

Codrington, R. H. (1880) "Notes on the customs of Mota, Banks Islands." *Transactions of the Royal Society of Victoria* 16, 119–144.

Codrington, R. H. (1881) "Religious practices and beliefs in Melanesia." *Journal of the Anthropological Institute of Great Britain and Ireland* 10, 261–316.

Codrington, R. H. (1891) *The Melanesians: Studies in their Anthropology and Folklore*. Oxford: Clarendon.

Coe, M. (1989) "The Hero Twins: myth and image." In J. Kerr (ed.) *The Maya Vase Book*. vol. 1, 161–84. New York: Kerr.

Couliano, I. P. (1991) *Out of This World: Otherworldly Journeys from Gilgamesh to Albert Einstein*. Boston: Shambhala.

Counts, D. A. (1983) "Near-death and out-of-body experiences in a Melanesian society." *Anabiosis* 3, 115–35.

Crookall, R. (1961) *The Supreme Adventure*. London: Clarke.

Cummins, G. (1932) *The Road to Immortality*. London: Nicholson.

Cummins, G. (1935) *Beyond Human Personality*. London: Nicholson & Watson.

Cupitt, D. (1998) *Mysticism After Modernity*. Oxford: Blackwell.

Davis, C. F. (1989) *The Evidential Force of Religious Experience*. Oxford: Oxford University Press.

Dawson, J. (1881) *Australian Aborigines*. Melbourne: Robertson.

De Brébeuf, J. (1636; trans. 1897) *Relation of What Occurred in the Country of the Hurons in the Year 1636*. Travels and Explorations of the Jesuit Missionaries in New France, vol. X, ed. R. Gold Thwaites, trans. J. M. Hunter. Cleveland: Burrows Brothers.

De Groot, J. J. M. (1892) *The Religious System of China*, I. Leyden: Brill.

Delacour, J. B. (1973; trans. 1974) *Glimpses of the Beyond: The Extraordinary Experiences of People Who have Crossed the Brink of Death and Returned*. New York: Dell.

De Laguna, F. (1972) *Under Mount Saint Elias: The History and Culture of the Yakutat Tlingit.* Washington, DC: Smithsonian Institution Press.

Dieffenbach, E. (1843) *Travels in New Zealand.* London: Murray.

Dingwall, E. (1985) "The need for responsibility in parapsychology: my sixty years in psychical research." In Paul Kurtz (ed.) *A Skeptic's Handbook of Parapsychology,* 161–174. New York: Prometheus.

Dobbin, J., & Hezel, F. X. (2011) *Summoning the Powers Beyond: Traditional Religions in Micronesia.* Honolulu: University of Hawai'i Press.

Dodds, E. R. (1934) "Why I do not believe in survival." *Proceedings of the Society for Psychical Research* 42, 147-72.

Downey, G. (2010) "Life without language." *Neuroanthropology* blog, July 21, 2010 entry. http://neuroanthropology.net/2010/07/21/life-without-language/

Driberg, J. H. (1923) *The Lango: A Nilotic Tribe of Uganda.* London: Unwin.

Ducasse. C. J. (1951) *Nature, Mind, and Death.* La Salle, IL: Open Court.

Edward, J. (1998) *One Last Time.* London: Piatkus.

Edward, J. (2003) *After Life.* Seattle: Hay.

Edwards, J. & S. E. Dwight (eds.) (1822) *Memoirs of the Rev. David Brainerd; Missionary to the Indians.* New Haven: S. Converse.

Edwards, P. (1996) *Reincarnation.* New York: Prometheus.

Eggeling, J. (trans./ed.) (1882–1900) *Satapatha Brahmana.* 5 vols. (Sacred Books of the East) XII, XXVI, XLI, XLIII, XLIV. Oxford: Clarendon.

Ehrsson, H. H. (2007) "The experimental induction of out-of-body experiences." *Science* 317: 1048.

Eliade, M. (1973) *Australian Religions.* Ithaca: Cornell University Press.

Elkin, A. P. (1945) *Aboriginal Men of High Degree.* Sydney: Australian Publishing.

Ellis, W. (1823, rpt. 1917) *A Narrative of a Tour Through Hawaii.* Honolulu: Hawaiian Gazette.

Emerson, J. S. (1902) "Hawaiian beliefs regarding spirits." *Ninth Annual Report of the Hawaiian Historical Society,* 10–17.

Erkes, E. (1940) "The god of death in ancient China." *T'oung Pao* 35, 185-210.

Ernst, M. & A. Anisi (2016) "The historical development of Christianity in Oceania." In L. Sanneh & M. J. McClymond (eds.) *The Wiley Blackwell Companion to World Christianity,* 588- 604. Chichester: Wiley Blackwell.

Evans, D. (1988) "Can philosophers limit what mystics can do?" *Religious Studies* 25, 53-60.

Evans-Wentz, W. Y. (1927, 3rd ed.) *The Tibetan Book of the Dead*. Oxford: Oxford University Press.

Eyre, E. J. (ed. 1845) *Journals of Expeditions of Discovery into Central Australia*, vol. 2. London: Boone.

Faulkner, O. (1973, 1977, 1978) *The Ancient Egyptian Coffin Texts*. 3 vols. Warminster: Aris and Philips.

Fenwick, P. (2005) "Science and spirituality: a challenge for the 21st century." *Journal of Near-Death Studies* 23(3), 131-57.

Fenwick, P., and E. Fenwick (1995) *The Truth in the Light: An Investigation of Over 300 Near-Death Experiences*. London: Headline.

Ferguson, C. (2012) *Determined Spirits*. Edinburgh: Edinburgh University Press.

Fielding, H. (1898) *The Soul of a People*. London: Macmillan.

Fiore, E. (1978) *You Have Been Here Before*. London: Sphere.

Flint, L. (1971) *Voices in the Dark*. London: MacMillan.

Foges, P. (2010) "An atheist meets the masters of the universe." *Lapham's Quarterly*. http://www.laphamsquarterly.org/roundtable/roundtable/an-atheist-meets-the-masters-of-the-universe.php (accessed 06 June, 2013).

Forman, R. K. C. (1990) "Mysticism, constructivism, and forgetting." In *The Problem of Pure Consciousness*, ed. R. K. C. Forman, 3-49. Oxford: Oxford University Press.

Fornander, A. (1918–19) *Collection of Hawaiian Antiquities and Folk-Lore* (2nd series). Honolulu: Bishop Museum Press.

Fortune, R. F. (1963) *Sorcerers of Dobu* (2nd ed.) London: Routledge and Kegan Paul.

Fox, M. (2003) *Religion, Spirituality and the Near-Death Experience*. London: Routledge.

Frazer, J. G. (1913, 1922, 1924) *The Belief in Immortality and the Worship of the Dead*, vols. 1-3. London: MacMillan.

Friedlaender, J. S., Friedlaender, F. R., Reed, F. A., Kidd, K. K., Kidd, J. R., Chamber, G. K., ... Weber, J. L. (2008) "The genetic structure of Pacific Islanders." *PLOS Genetics*. Retrieved from https://journals.plos.org/plosgenetics/article?id=10.1371/journal.pgen.0040019

Furness, W. H. (1910) *The Island of Stone Money*. Philadelphia: Lippincott.

Gabbard, G. O. & S. W. Twemlow (1984) *With the Eyes of the Mind: An Empirical Analysis of Out-of-Body States*. New York: Praeger.

Gardiner, Eileen (ed. 1989) *Visions of Heaven and Hell Before Dante.* New York: Italica.

Gauld, A. (1982) *Mediumship and Survival.* London: Paladin.

George, A. (2003, rev. ed.) *The Epic of Gilgamesh.* London: Penguin.

Gibbes, E. B. (1932) "Introduction." In Cummins (1932).

Gifford, W. W. (1924) *Tongan Myths and Tales* (Bulletin 8). Honolulu: Bernice P. Bishop Museum.

Gill, W. W. (1876) *Myths and Songs from the South Pacific.* London: King.

Gill, W. W. (1877) "On the origin of the South Sea Islanders, and on some traditions of the Hervey Islands." *Journal of the Anthropological Institute* 6, 2–5.

Goldberg, B. (1982) *Past Lives, Future Lives.* North Hollywood: Newcastle.

Goldie, W. H. (1904) "Maori medical lore." *Transactions and Proceedings of the Royal Society of New Zealand* 37, 1–120.

Goodenough, W. H. (2002) *Under Heaven's Brow: Pre-Christian Religious Tradition in Chuuk.* Philadelphia: American Philosophical Society.

Green, J. T. (1984) "Near-death experience in a Chammorro culture." *Vital Signs,* 4(1/ 2), 6–7.

Green, J. T. (1995) "Lucid dreams as one method of replicating components of the near-death experience in a laboratory setting." *Journal of Near-Death Studies* 14(1) (Fall), 49-59.

Green, L. C., & Beckwith, M. W. (1926) "Hawaiian customs and beliefs relating to sickness and death." *American Anthropologist,* 28(1), 176–208.

Gregory the Great (593) *Dialogues,* 4.XXXI. Trans. "P.W." (1608), ed. Edmund G. Gardner (1911) London: Philip Lee Warner, pp. 214-5.

Grey, M. (1985) *Return from Death: An Exploration of the Near-Death Experience.* London: Arkana.

Greyson, B. (1983) "The near-death experience scale: construction, reliability, and validity." *Journal of Nervous and Mental Disease* 171/6, 369-75.

Greyson, B. (1999) "Defining near-death experiences." *Mortality* 4/1, 7-19.

Greyson, B. (2006) "Near-death experiences and spirituality." *Zygon: Journal of Religion & Science* 41, 393-414.

Greyson, B. (2007) "Commentary on 'Psychophysiological and cultural correlates undermining a survivalist interpretation of near-death experiences.'" *Journal of Near-Death Studies* 26(2), 127– 45.

Greyson, B. (2010) "Seeing people not known to have died: 'Peak in Darien' experiences." *Anthropology and Humanism*, 35/2, 159–171.

Greyson, B. & N. E. Bush (1992) "Distressing near-death experiences." *Psychiatry* 55, 95-110.

Greyson, B., Kelly, E. W. and Kelly, E. F. (2009) "Explanatory models for near-death experiences." In Holden, J. M., Greyson, B. and James, D. (eds.) *The Handbook of Near-Death Experiences: Thirty Years of Investigation*, 213–234. Santa Barbara: Praeger/ABC-CLIO.

Greyson, B. & S. Khanna (2014) "Spiritual transformation after near-death experiences." *Spirituality in Clinical Practice* 1/1, 43–55.

Griffiths, J.G. (1986) "Some claims of xenoglossy in the ancient languages." *Numen* 33/1 (June), 141-169.

Groth-Marnet, G. (1994) "Cross-cultural perspectives on the near-death experience." *Australian Parapsychological Review* 19, 7– 11.

Gunson, N. (1962) "An account of the Mamaia or Visionary Heresy of Tahiti, 1826-1841." *Journal of the Polynesian Society* 7/2, 208-43.

Haley, E. N. (1892, rpt. 1907) "A visit to the spirit land; or, the strange experience of a woman in Kona, Hawaii." In T. G. Thrum (Ed.), *Hawaiian Folk Tales*, 58–61. Chicago: McClurg.

Hampe, J. C. (1975, rpt. 2022) *To Die is Gain: Near-Death Experience and the Art of Dying Before We Die*. Surrey: Afterworlds Press.

Handy, E. S. (1927) *Polynesian Religion*. Honolulu: Bernice P. Bishop Museum.

Handy, E. S. (1930) *Marquesan Legends*. Honolulu: Bernice P. Bishop Museum.

Hariot, T. (1588) *A Briefe and True Report of the New Found Land of Virginia*. London: n.p.

Harris, S. (2012) "Science on the brink of death." https://samharris.org/science-on-the-brink-of-death/ Retrieved 15 October, 2021.

Hart, H. (1959) *The Enigma of Survival*. London: Rider.

Hawkes, D. (1985, rev. ed.) *Songs of the South*. Harmondsworth: Penguin.

Hazlegrove, J. (2000) *Spiritualism in British Society Between the Wars*. Manchester: Manchester University Press.

Heidel, A. (1949, 2nd ed.) *The Gilgamesh Epic and Old Testament Parallels*. Chicago: University of Chicago Press.

Henry, T. (ed.), & Orsmond, J. M. (1928, rpt. 1971) *Ancient Tahiti*. New York: Kraus.

Hick, J. (1976) *Death and Eternal Life*. London: Collins.

Hodges, D. (2004 rev. ed.) *Do We Survive Death?* Ashford: Hodges.

Holden, J. M. (2009) "Veridical perception in near-death experiences." In Holden, J. M., Greyson, B. and James, D. (eds.) *The Handbook of Near-Death Experiences: Thirty Years of Investigation*, 185–211. Santa Barbara: Praeger/ABC-CLIO.

Howitt, A. W. (1887) "On Australian medicine men; or, doctors and wizards of some Australian tribes." *Journal of the Anthropological Institute of Great Britain and Ireland* 16, 23–59.

Howitt, A. W. (1904) *The Native Tribes of Southeast Australia*. London: Macmillan.

Hufford, D. (1982) *The Terror That Comes in the Night: An Experience-Centered Study of Supernatural Assault Traditions*. Philadelphia: University of Pennsylvania Press.

Hufford, D. (2005) "Sleep paralysis as spiritual experience." *Transcultural Psychiatry* 42/1, 11-45.

Hultkrantz, Å. (1957, rpt. 2022) *The North American Indian Orpheus Tradition: Native Afterlife Beliefs and their Origins*. Surrey: Afterworlds Press.

Humphreys, C. B. (1926) *The Southern New Hebrides*. Cambridge: Cambridge University Press.

Hyman, R. (2003) "How not to test mediums." *Skeptical Inquirer,* 27/1, 20-30.

Hyslop, J. (1907) "Experiments with Mrs. Piper since Dr. Richard Hodgson's death." *Journal of the American Society for Psychical Research* 1, 93-107.

Irwin, H.J. (2007) "Commentary on Keith Augustine's Paper." *Journal of Near-Death Studies* 26(2) (Winter), 159– 61.

Iverson, J. (1977) *More Lives Than One?* London: Pan.

Jacobsen, T. (1976) *The Treasures of Darkness: A History of Mesopotamian Religion*. New Haven: Yale University Press.

Jacobsen, T. (1987) *The Harps That Once...*. New Haven: Yale University Press.

James, W. (1902) *The Varieties of Religious Experience*. London: Longmans.

Jansen, K. (2001) *Ketamine Dreams and Realities*. Santa Cruz, CA: Multidisciplinary Association for Psychedelic Study.

Jarves, J. J. (1843) *History of the Hawaiian or Sandwich Islands*. Boston: Munroe.

Johnson, R. C. (1957) *Nurslings of Immortality*. London: Hodder & Stoughton.

Jung, C. G. (1961, rev. ed. 1989) *Memories, Dreams, Reflections*. New York: Vintage.

Jung, C. G. (1999 coll.) *Jung On Death and Immortality*. Princeton: Princeton University Press.

Kalakaua, D. (1888) *Legends and Myths of Hawaii*. New York: Webster.

Kalweit, H. (1984, trans. 1988) *Dreamtime and Inner Space: The World of the Shaman*. Boston: Shambhala.

Kalweit, H. (1992) *Shamans, Healers, and Medicine Men*. Boston: Shambhala.

Kamakau, S. M. (1866-71, rpt. 1964) *Ka Po'e Kahiko: The People of Old*. D. Barrére (ed.) & M. K. Pukui (trans.), Honolulu: Bishop Museum Press.

Kamma, F. C. (1954, rpt. 1972) *Koreri: Messianic Movements in the Biak-Numfor Culture Area*.

W. E. Haver Droeze-Hulswit (ed.) & M. J. van da Vathorst-Smit (trans.) The Hague, Netherlands: Nijhoff.

Katz, D. (2003) *The Image of the Netherworld in the Sumerian Sources*. Bethesda MD: CDL.

Katz, S. T. (1978) "Language, epistemology, and mysticism." In S. T. Katz (ed.) *Mysticism and Philosophical Analysis*, 22-74. Oxford: Oxford University Press.

Keable, R. (1921) "A People of dreams." *Hibbert Journal* 19, 522–31.

Keauokalini, Z. K. (1860, rpt. 1932) *Kepelino's Traditions of Hawaii* (Bulletin 95). M. W. Beckwith (trans.) Honolulu: Bernice P. Bishop Museum.

Keen, M., A. Ellison, and D. Fontana (1999) "The Scole report." *Journal of the Society for Psychical Research* 58, 150-452.

Keen, M. & A. Roy (2004) "Correspondence: chance coincidence in the cross-correspondences." *Journal of the Society for Psychical Research* 68, 57-59.

Kellehear, A. (1996) *Experiences Near Death: Beyond Medicine and Religion*. New York and Oxford: Oxford University Press.

Kellehear, A. (2001) "An Hawaiian near-death experience." *Journal of Near-Death Studies* 20(1), 31–5.

Kellehear, A. (2007) "Culture and the near-death experience: comments on Keith Augustine's 'Psychophysiological and cultural correlates undermining a survivalist interpretation of near- death experiences.'" *Journal of Near-Death Studies* 26(2) (Winter), 147– 53.

Kelly, E. F. (2010) "Review: out-of-body and near-death experiences: brain-state phenomena or glimpses of immortality?" *Journal of Scientific Exploration* 24(4), 730.

King, M. (1985) *Being Pakeha: An Encounter with New Zealand and the Maori Renaissance*. Auckland: Hodder and Stoughton.

King, S. B. (1988) "Two epistemological models for the interpretation of mysticism." *Journal of the American Academy of Religion* 41/2, 257-79.

Klemenc-Ketis, Z., J. Kersnik, and S. Grmec (2010) "The effect of carbon dioxide on near-death experiences in out-of-hospital cardiac arrest survivors: a prospective observational study." *Critical Care* 14(2), R56.

Knapp, F. D. & R. L. Childe (1896) *The Thlinkets of Southeastern Alaska.* Chicago: Stone and Kimball.

Landtman, G. (1912) "Wanderings of the dead in the folk-lore of the Kiwai-speaking Pauans." In O. Castrén, Y. Hirn, R. Lagerborg, & A. Wallensköld (eds.), *Festskrift Tillengnad Edvard Westermarck i Anledning av Hans Femtioårsdag den 20 November 1912*, 5980. Helsingfors, Finland: Simelii.

Landtman, G. (1917) *Folk-Tales of the Kiwai Papuans* (Acta Societatis Scientiarum Fennicae, 47). Helsingfors, Finland: Finnish Society for Literature.

Le Clercq, C. (1691, trans. 1910) *New Relation of Gaspesia*, ed. and trans. W. F. Ganong. Toronto, CA: The Champlain Society.

Legge, J. (1879, rpt. 1967) *The Sacred Books of China; The Texts of Confucianism. Part I: The Shu King etc.* (Sacred Books of the East). Delhi: Banarsidass.

Legge, J. (1885, rpt. 1967) *The Sacred Books of China: The Texts of Confucianism. Part III and IV: The Li Ki.* (Sacred Books of the East). Delhi: Banarsidass.

Lodge, O. (1916) *Raymond.* London: Methuen.

Lodge, O. (1932) "Foreword." In Cummins (1932).

Long, J., and J. M. Holden (2007) "Does the arousal system contribute to near-death and out-of-body experiences? A summary and response." *Journal of Near-Death Studies* 25, 135–169.

Lopez Austin, A. (1988) *The Human Body and Ideology: Concepts of the Ancient Nahuas.* Salt Lake City: University of Utah Press.

Lorimer, D. (1984) *Survival: Body, Mind and Death in the Light of Psychic Experience.* London: Routledge & K. Paul.

Lundahl, C. (1993) "Otherworld personal future revelations in near-death experiences." *Journal of Near-Death Studies*, 11(3) Spring, 171-79.

Lundahl, C. (1999) "Parallels between near-death experience prophetic visions and prophecies from the Bible and Mormon holy writ." *Journal of Near-Death Studies*, 17(3) Spring, 193-203.

Lundahl, C. (2001) "Prophetic revelations in near-death experiences." *Journal of Near-Death Studies*, 19(4) Summer, 233-39.

Malinowski, B. (1916, rpt.1928) *Baloma: The Spirits of the Dead in the Trobriand Islands.* London: Faber & West.

Marsh, M. (2010) *Out-of-Body and Near-Death Experiences: Brain-State Phenomena or Glimpse of Immortality?* Oxford: Oxford University Press.

Martin, J. & P. Romanowski (1989) *We Don't Die.* New York: Berkeley.

Matlock, J. G. (2017) "Historical near-death and reincarnation-intermission experiences of the Tlingit Indians: case studies and theoretical reflections." *Journal of Near-Death Studies* 35/4 (Summer), 214-41.

Matlock, J. G. (2019) *Signs of Reincarnation: Exploring Beliefs, Cases, and Theory.* Lanham, MD: Rowman & Littlefield.

Matlock, J. G. & I. Geisler-Petersen (2016) "Asian versus western intermission memories: universal features and cultural variations." *Journal of Near-Death Studies* 35/1 (Fall), 3-29.

Mbiti, J. S. (1990; 2nd ed.) *African Religions and Philosophy.* Oxford: Heinemann.

McClenon, J. (1994) *Wondrous Events: Foundations of Religious Belief.* Philadelphia: University of Pennsylvania Press.

McClenon, J. (2002) *Wondrous Healing: Shamanism, Human Evolution, and the Origin of Religion.* DeKalb: Northern Illinois University Press.

Metzinger, T. (2005) "Out-of-body experiences as the origin of the concept of a 'soul'." *Mind & Matter* 3(1), 57–84.

Mills, A. (1988) "A comparison of Wet'suwet'en cases of the reincarnation type with Gitksan and Beaver." *Journal of Anthropological Research* 44(4), 385–415.

Monroe, R. A. (1994) *Ultimate Journey.* Garden City: Doubleday.

Moody, R. (1975) *Life After Life.* New York: Bantam.

Moody, R. (2010) *Glimpses of Eternity.* Harlan IA: Guideposts.

Mooney, J. (1896) *The Ghost-Dance Religion and the Sioux Outbreak of 1890.* Washington, DC: Government Printing Office.

Moore, B. N. (1981) *The Philosophical Possibilities Beyond Death.* Springfield IL: Thomas.

Moreira-Almeida, A. (2013) "Implications of spiritual experiences to the understanding of mind–brain relationship." *Asian Journal of Psychiatry* 6/6, 585–589.

Moreman, C. M. (2003) "A re-examination of the possibility of chance coincidence as an alternative explanation for mediumistic communications in the cross-correspondences." *Journal of the Society for Psychical Research* 67.4/873, 225-242.

Morse M. L. (1994) "Near-death experiences of children." *Journal of Pediatric Oncology Nursing* 11/4, 139-145.

Moss, P. & J. Keeton (1981) *Encounters with the Past.* Harmondsworth: Penguin.

Moss, R. (1925) *The Life After Death in Oceania and the Malay Archipelago.* Oxford: Oxford University Press.

Myers, F. (1892) "On indications of continued terrene knowledge on the part of phantasms of the dead." *Proceedings of the Society for Psychical Research* 8, 195-200.

Needham, J. (1974) *Science and Civilization in China,* vol. V, pt. II. Cambridge: Cambridge University Press.

Nelson, E.W. (1900) *The Eskimo about Bering Strait.* Washington, DC: Government Printing Office.

Newland, S. (1887–88) "The Parkengees, or Aboriginal tribes on the Darling River." *Papers Read Before the Royal Geographical Society of Australia, South Australian Branch, 3rd Session,* 20–32.

Newton, H. (1914) *In Far New Guinea.* London: Seely, Service.

Newton, M. (1994; rev. ed. 2000) *Journey of Souls.* St. Paul: Llewellyn.

Newton, M. (2001) *Destiny of Souls.* St. Paul: Llewellyn.

Northrup, S. (1996) *The Séance.* New York: Dell.

Noyes, R., P. Fenwick, J. M. Holden, & S. R. Christian (2009) "Aftereffects of pleasurable Western adult near-death experiences." In Holden, J. M., Greyson, B. and James, D. (eds.) *The Handbook of Near-Death Experiences: Thirty Years of Investigation,* 41-62. Santa Barbara: Praeger/ABC-CLIO.

O'Flaherty, W. D. (1981) *The Rig Veda.* London: Penguin.

Ohkado, M. (2021) "Katsugoro (reincarnation case)." *Psi Encyclopedia.* London: The Society for Psychical Research. https://psi-encyclopedia.spr.ac.uk/articles/katsugoro-reincarnation-case. Retrieved 21 September 2021.

Ohkado, M., & Ikegawa, A. (2014) "Children with life-between-life memories." *Journal of Scientific Exploration,* 28/3, 477–490.

Olivelle, P. (trans.) (1999) *The Early Upanishads.* Oxford: Oxford University Press.

Oliver, D. L. (1974) *Ancient Tahitian Society,* vols. 1-3. Honolulu: University of Hawaii Press.

Oliver, D. L. (1989) *Oceania: The Native Cultures of Australia and the Pacific Islands,* vol. 1. Honolulu: University of Hawaii Press.

Oliver, D. L. (2002) *Polynesia in Early Historic Times.* Honolulu: Bess.

Osis, K. (1979) "Insider's view of the OBE: a questionnaire study." In W. G. Roll (ed.) *Research in Parapsychology*, 50-51. Methuen, NJ: Scarecrow Press.

Osis, K. and E. Haraldsson (1986 rev. ed.) *At the Hour of Death*. Mamaroneck, NY: Hastings House.

Owen, A. (1989) *The Darkened Room*. London: Virago.

Panikkar, R. (1977) *The Vedic Experience*. London: Darton, Longman and Todd.

Paper, J. (1995) *The Spirits Are Drunk*. Albany: SUNY Press.

Paper, J. (2005) *The Deities Are Many*. Albany: SUNY Press.

Parmentier, R. J. (1987) *The Sacred Remains: Myth, History and Polity in Belau*. Chicago: University of Chicago Press.

Parnia, S., K. Spearpoint, G. de Vos, P. Fenwick, D. Goldberg, J. Yang, J. Zhu, K. Baker, H. Killingback, P. McLean, M. Wood, A. M. Zafari, N. Dickert, R. Beisteiner, F. Sterz, M. Berger, C. Warlow, S. Bullock, S. Lovett, R. M. McPara, S. Marti-Navarette, P. Cushing, P. Wills, K. Harris, J. Sutton, A. Walmsley, C. D. Deakin, P. Little, M. Farber, B. Greyson, E. R. Schoenfeld (2014) "AWARE – AWAreness during REsuscitation: a prospective study." *Resuscitation* 85(12), 1799–1805.

Parnia, S., K. Spearpoint, and P. Fenwick (2007) "Near death experiences, cognitive function and psychological outcomes of surviving cardiac arrest." *Resuscitation* 74, 215–221.

Pasricha, S. (1992) "Near-death experiences in South India: a systematic survey in Channapatua." *National Institute of Mental Health and Neuro-Sciences Journal* 10, 111–18.

Pasricha, S. (1993) "A systematic survey of near-death experiences in South India." *Journal of Scientific Exploration* 7, 161–71.

Paulson, D. S. (1999) "The near-death experience: an interpretation of cultural, spiritual, and physical processes." *Journal of Near-Death Studies* 18(1), 13-25.

Pelley, W. D. (1929) "Seven minutes in eternity." *The American Magazine* CVII/3 (March), 7-9, 139-44.

Pilch, J. J. (2011) *Flights of the Soul: Visions, Heavenly Journeys, and Peak Experiences in the Biblical World*. Grand Rapids: Eerdmans.

Platthy, J. (1992) *Near-Death Experiences in Antiquity*. Santa Claus, IN.: Federation of International Poetry Associations of UNESCO.

Poo, M. (1998) *In Search of Personal Welfare: A View of Ancient Chinese Religion*. Albany: SUNY.

Potthoff, S. E. (2017) *The Afterlife in Early Christian Carthage: Near-Death Experiences, Ancestor Cult, and the Archaeology of Paradise*. Abingdon: Routledge.

Powell, A. (2001) "Beyond space and time: the unbounded psyche." http://citeseerx.ist.psu.edu/viewdoc/download;jsessionid=9A8204C546607 C20221D82200F9F5A08?doi=10.1.1.580.5921&rep=rep1&type=pdf. Retrieved 4 Oct., 2021.

Price, H. H. (1953) "Survival and the idea of 'another world.'" *Proceedings of the Society for Psychical Research* 50(182), 1-25.

Proudfoot, W. (1985) *Religious Experience*. Berkeley: University of California Press.

Proudfoot, W. (1993) "Response." *Journal of the American Academy of Religion* 61.4, 793-803.

Radin, P. (1923, rpt. 1990) *The Winnebago Tribe*. Lincoln: University of Nebraska Press.

Randall, N. (1975) *Life After Death*. London: Hale.

Rawat, K. S. & T. Rivas (2005) "The life beyond: through the eyes of children who claim to remember previous lives." *Journal of Religion and Psychical Research*, 28/3 (July) 126-136.

Rennie, B. (2000) "Manufacturing McCutcheon: the failure of understanding in the academic study of religion." *Culture and Religion* 1/1, 105-12.

Rice, W. H. (1923) *Hawaiian Legends* (Bulletin 3). Honolulu: Bernice P. Bishop Museum.

Ring, K. (1980) *Life at Death: A Scientific Investigation of the Near-Death Experience*. New York: Coward, McCann, and Geohegan.

Ring, K. (1982) "Precognitive and prophetic visions in near-death experiences." *Anabiosis: The Journal of Near-Death Studies* 2, 47–74.

Ring, K. (1988) "Prophetic visions in 1988: A critical reappraisal." *Journal of Near-Death Studies* 7/1, 4–18.

Ring, K., and S. Cooper (1999) *Mindsight: Near-Death and Out-of-Body Experiences in the Blind*. Palo Alto: William James Centre for Consciousness Studies.

Rivas, T., E.M. Carman, N.J. Carman, & A. Dirven (2015) "Paranormal aspects of pre-existence memories in young children." *Journal of Near-Death Studies* 34/2 (Winter), 84-207.

Robinson, P. (2003) "'As for them who know them, they will find their paths:' speculations on ritual landscapes in the 'Book of Two Ways.'" In D. O'Connor and S. Quirke (eds.) *Mysterious Lands*. London: UCL.

Rousseau, D. (2011) "Physicalism, Christianity and the near-death experience: an essay review of 'Out-of-Body and Near-Death Experiences: Brain-state

Phenomena or Glimpses of Immortality?' by Michael Marsh." *Journal of the Society for Psychical Research* 75.4/905, 225-34.

Ruby, R. H. & J. A. Brown (1989) *Dreamer Prophets of the Columbia Plateau: Smohalla and Skolaskin.* Norman: University of Oklahoma.

Ruby, R. H. & J. A. Brown (1996) *John Slocum and the Indian Shaker Church.* Norman: University of Oklahoma.

Sabom, M. B. (1982) *Recollections of Death: A Medical Investigation.* New York: Harper & Row.

Sabom, M. B. (1998) *Light and Death: One Doctor's Fascinating Account of Near-Death Experiences.* Michigan: Zondervan.

Sage, M. (1903) *Mrs. Piper and the Society for Psychical Research.* London: Johnson.

Sahagun, B. (1547–69; trans. 1973–78) *The Florentine Codex.* Trans. A. I. O. Anderson and C. E. Dibble. 13 vols. Santa Fe: Monographs of the School of American Research.

Sahagun, B. (ed. 1997) *Primeros Memoriales.* Trans. T. D. Sullivan. Norman: University of Oklahoma Press.

Saltmarsh, H.F. (1938) *Evidence of Personal Survival from Cross-Correspondences.* London: Bell.

Sartori, P. (2008) *The Near-Death Experiences of Hospitalized Intensive Care Patients: A Five-Year Clinical Study.* Lewiston, Queenston, Lampeter: Edwin Mellen Press.

Savage, S. (1916) "The period of Iro-nui-ma-oata and Tangiia-nui-ariki." *Journal of the Polynesian Society,* 25(100), 138–149.

Schachter, S. & J. E. Singer (1962) "Cognitive, social, and physiological determinants of emotional state." *Psychological Review* 69, 379-99.

Schleiermacher, F. (1799, trans. 1988) *Speeches on Religion to its Cultured Despisers.* Cambridge: Cambridge University Press.

Schlieter, J. (2018) *What is it Like to be Dead? Near-Death Experiences, Christianity, and the Occult.* New York: Oxford University Press.

Schorer, C. E. (1985) "Two Native North American near-death experiences." *Omega* 16, 111– 3.

Schwartz, G. E. (2002) *Afterlife Experiments.* New York: Simon & Schuster.

Schwartz, G.E. & L. Russek (2001) "Evidence of anomalous information retrieval across two mediums." *Journal of the Society for Psychical Research* 65.4/865, 257-275.

Seligman, C. G. (1910) *The Melanesians of British New Guinea*. Cambridge: Cambridge University Press.

Serdahely, W. J. (1990) "Pediatric near-death experiences." *Journal of Near-Death Studies* 9(1), 33-9.

Serdahely, W. J. (1995) "Variations from the prototypic near-death experience." *Journal of Near-Death Studies* 13(3), 185–196.

Sharf, R. (1998) "Experience." In *Critical Terms in Religious Studies*, ed. M. C. Taylor, 94-115. Chicago: University of Chicago Press. Reprinted as "The rhetoric of experience and the study of religion." *Journal of Consciousness Studies* 7.11/12 (2000): 267–87.

Sharma, P. & J. B. Tucker (2004) "Cases of the reincarnation type with memories from the intermission between lives." *Journal of Near-Death Studies*, 23/2 (Winter), 101-118.

Shiels, D. (1978) "A cross-cultural study of beliefs in out-of-the-body experiences." *Journal of the Society for Psychical Research* 49(775), 697– 741.

Short, L. (1995) "Mysticism, mediation, and the non-lingusitic." *Journal of the American Academy of Religion* 93/4, 659-75.

Shortland, E. (1882) *Maori Religion and Mythology*. London: Longman Brown Green.

Shortland, E. (1856) *Traditions and Superstitions of the New Zealanders* (2nd ed.). London: Longman.

Shushan, G. (2009) *Conceptions of the Afterlife in Early Civilizations: Universalism, Constructivism, and Near-Death Experience*. London: Continuum Bloomsbury.

Shushan, G. (2011) "Afterlife conceptions in the Vedas." *Religion Compass*. June 2011, vol. 5 no. 6, p. 202-13. London: Wiley-Blackwell.

Shushan, G. (2013) "Rehabilitating the neglected 'similar': confronting the issue of cross-cultural similarities in the study of religions." *Paranthropology: Journal of Anthropological Approaches to the Paranormal* 4(2), 48–53.

Shushan, G. (2014) "Extraordinary experiences and religious beliefs: deconstructing some contemporary philosophical axioms." *Method and Theory in the Study of Religion* 26, 1–33.

Shushan, G. (2016) "'The Sun told me I would be restored to life': Native American near-death experiences, shamanism, and religious revitalization movements." *Journal of Near-Death Studies* vol. 34 no. 3 (Spring), p. 127-150.

Shushan, G. (2017) "'He should stay in the grave': Cultural patterns in the interpretation of near-death experiences in indigenous African beliefs.'" *Journal of Near-Death Studies* vol. 35 no.4 (Summer 2017), p. 185-213.

Shushan, G. (2018) *Near-Death Experience in Indigenous Religions*: New York and Oxford: Oxford University Press.

Sidgwick, H. (1915) "A contribution to the study of Mrs. Piper's trance phenomena." *Proceedings of the Society for Psychical Research*, XXVIII.

Simeon of Durham (c. 1096) *History of the Church of Durham*. Trans. Joseph Stevenson (1855) *The Church Historians of England*, vol. III part II. London: Seeleys.

Simpson, W. K. (ed.) (2003, 3rd ed.) *The Literature of Ancient Egypt*. New Haven: Yale University Press.

Slobodin, R. (1970, rev. 1992) "Kutchin concepts of reincarnation." In Mills, A, & R. Slobodin (eds.) *Amerindian Rebirth: Reincarnation Belief among North American Indians and Inuit*. Toronto: University of Toronto Press, 136-155.

Smith, G. (2003) *Spirit Messenger*. London: Hay.

Solomon, G. and J. (1999) *The Scole Experiment*. London: Piatkus.

Somerville, B. T. (1894) "Notes on some islands of the New Hebrides." *Journal of the Anthropological Institute of Great Britain and Ireland*, 23, 2–21.

Spencer, B., & Gillen, F. J. (1927) *The Arunta: A study of a Stone Age people*. London: Macmillan.

Steiger, B. (1968) *The Mind Travellers*. New York: Tandem.

Stevenson, I. (1975, 1977, 1980, 1983) *Cases of the Reincarnation Type*. 4 vols. Charlottesville: University Press of Virginia.

Stevenson, I. (1984) *New Studies in Xenoglossy*. Charlottesville: University Press of Virginia.

Stevenson, I. (1997) *Reincarnation and Biology*. Westport/London: Praeger.

Stevenson, I. & B. Greyson (1996) "Near-death experiences: relevance to the question of survival after death." In Bailey, L. W. & J. Yates (eds.) (1996) *The Near-Death Experience: A Reader*, 199-206. London: Routledge.

Stevenson, I. A. Kellehear, S. Pasricha, & E. W. Cook (1994) "The absence of tunnel sensations in near-death experiences from India." *Journal of Near-Death Studies* 13/2, 109-113.

Stevenson, I., J. E. Owens, & E. W. Cook (1990) "Features of 'near-death experience' in relation to whether or not patients were near death." *The Lancet* 336, 1175-1177.

Stevenson, R. L. (1891, rpt. 1896) *In the South Seas*. New York: Scribner's.

St. Johnston, T. R. (1918) *The Lau Islands (Fiji) and their Fairy Tales and Folklore*. London: Times.

Story, F. (1975) *Rebirth as Doctrine and Experience*. Kandy: Buddhist Publication Society.

Stroebe, W. & M. S. Stroebe (1987) *Bereavement and Health: The Psychological and Physical Consequences of Partner Loss*. Cambridge: Cambridge University Press.

Swanton, J. (1908) "Social condition, beliefs, and linguistic relationship of the Tlingit Indians." *Twenty-Sixth Annual Report of the Bureau of American Ethnology*, 391– 485. Washington, DC: Smithsonian Institution.

Tassell-Matamua, N. (2013) "Phenomenology of near-death experiences: an analysis of a Maori case study." *Journal of Near-Death Studies*, 32, 107–117.

Taylor, R. (1855) *Te Ika a Maui, or New Zealand and its Inhabitants*. London: Wertheim & Macintosh.

Tedlock, D. (1996, rev. ed.) *Popol Vuh*. New York: Simon and Schuster.

Thomas, C. D. (1928) *Life Beyond Death, With Evidence*. London: Collins.

Thomas, C. D. (1936, rpt. 1960) *In the Dawn Beyond Death*. London: Psychic Press.

Thomas, C. D. (1945, rpt. 2018) *From Life to Life*. Surrey: White Crow Books.

Thompson, L. G. (1992, rev. ed.) *Chinese Religion*. Encino: Dickensen.

Thomson, B. (1908) *The Fijians: A Study of the Decay of Custom*. London: Heinemann.

Thornton, J.K. (1998) *The Kongolese Saint Anthony: Dona Beatriz Kimpa Vita and the Antonian Movement, 1684– 1706*. Cambridge: Cambridge University Press.

Tregear, E. (1890) "The Maoris of New Zealand." *Journal of the Anthropological Institute of Great Britain and Ireland*, 19, 96–123.

Trigger, B. G. (1993) *Early Civilizations: Ancient Egypt in Context*. Cairo: American University in Cairo Press.

Tucker, J. B. (2005) *Life Before Life: Children's Memories of Previous Lives*. New York: St. Martin's.

Tucker, J. B. (2013) *Return to Life: Extraordinary Cases of Children Who Remember Past Lives*. New York: St. Martin's.

Turner, G. (1884) *Samoa, A Hundred Years Ago and Long Before*. London: Macmillan.

Vahman, F. (1986) (trans.) *Ardā Wirāz Nāmag: The Iranian 'Divina Commedia.'* London: Curzon.

Van Lommel, P. (2006) "Near-death experience, consciousness, and the brain: a new concept about the continuity of our consciousness based on recent scientific research on near-death experience in survivors of cardiac arrest." *World Futures* 62, 134–151.

Van Lommel, P. (2007) *Conscious Beyond Life: The Science of the Near-Death Experience*. New York: HarperOne.

Van Lommel, P., R. van Wees, V. Meyers, and I. Elfferich (2001) "Near-death experience in survivors of cardiac arrest: a prospective study in the Netherlands." *The Lancet* 358, 2039–2045.

Vestal, S. (1934, rpt. 1984) *Warpath: The True Story of the Fighting Sioux*. Lincoln: University of Nebraska Press.

Wade, J. (1998) "The phenomenology of near-death consciousness in past-life regression therapy: a pilot study." *Journal of Near-Death Studies* 17(1), 31-54.

Wade, J. (2003) "In a sacred manner we died: Native American near-death experiences." *Journal of Near-Death Studies* 22(2), 83–115.

Wambach, H. (1978, rpt. 2021) *Reliving Past Lives*. Surrey: White Crow Books.

Wambach, H. (1979, rpt. 2020) *Life Before Life*. Surrey: White Crow Books.

Warner, W. L. (1937) *Black Civilization*. New York: Harper.

Watson, B. (1963) *Hsün Tzu: Basic Writings*. New York: Columbia University Press.

Weiss, B. (1988) *Many Lives, Many Masters*. London: Piatkus.

Werner, A. (1933) *Myths and Legends of the Bantu*. London: Harrap.

Westervelt, W. D. (1915) *Legends of Gods and Ghosts*. Boston: Ellis.

Wheeler, G. C. (1914) "An account of the death rites and eschatology of the people of the Bougainville Strait (Western Solomon Islands)." *Archiv für Religionswissenschaft, 17*, 64–112.

White, J. (1891) "A chapter from Maori mythology." *Report of the Third Meeting of the Australasian Association for the Advancement of Science, 3*, 359–64. Sydney: The Association.

Whitton, J. L. & J. Fisher (1986) *Life Between Life*. New York: Warner.

Williams, F. E. (1930) *Orokaiva Society*. London: Oxford University Press.

Williams, F. E. (1934) "The Vailala Madness in retrospect." In E. E. Evans-Pritchard, R. Firth, B. Malinowski, & I. Schapera (eds.), *Essays Presented to C. G. Seligman*, 369-380. London: Kegan Paul.

Williams, T. (1860) *Fiji and the Fijians*, vol. I. New York: Appleton.

Williamson, R. W. (1933) *Religious and Cosmic Beliefs of Central Polynesia*, vols. I & II. Cambridge: Cambridge University Press.

Willoughby, W. C. (1928) *The Soul of the Bantu*. London: Student Christian Movement.

Willoughby-Meade, G. (1928) *Chinese Ghouls and Goblins*. London: Constable.

Wilson, I. (1981) *Mind Out of Time?* London: Gollancz.

Witney, W. D. (trans.) (1905) *The Atharva Veda*. Cambridge, MA: Harvard Oriental Series VII–VIII.

Woolger, R. (1987) *Other Lives, Other Selves*. New York: Bantam.

Worsley, P. (1968, 2nd ed.) *The Trumpet Shall Sound*. New York: Schocken.

Wren-Lewis, J. (1995) "The dazzling dark: A near-death experience opens the door to a permanent transformation." *What Is Enlightenment?* 2/4 (Summer). Available at http://www.nonduality.com/dazdark.htm Accessed 16 December, 2019.

Yao, X. & P. Badham (2007) *Religious Experience in Contemporary China*. Cardiff: University of Wales.

Yü, Ying-shih (1987) "O soul, come back: a study of the changing conceptions of the soul and afterlife in pre-Buddhist China." *Harvard Journal of Asiatic Studies* 47, 363–95.

Zaleski, C. (1987) *Otherworld Journeys: Accounts of Near-Death Experiences in Medieval and Modern Times*. Oxford: Oxford University Press.

Zhi-ying, F. and L. Jian-xun (1992) "Near-death experiences among survivors of the 1976 Tangshan earthquake." *Journal of Near-Death Studies* 11(1), 39–48.

Some of the content in this book has been adapted, revised, and expanded from the following previously published articles:

"Near-death experience." In Christopher Moreman (ed.) *The Routledge Companion to Death and Dying*. London: Routledge (2017).

"Near-death experience as divine revelation." In Balázs Mezei, Francesca A. Murphy, and Kenneth Oakes (eds.) *The Oxford Handbook of Divine Revelation*. Oxford: Oxford University Press (2021).

"The afterlife in early civilizations." In Yujin Nagasawa & Benjamin Matheson (eds.) *The Palgrave Handbook of the Afterlife*. London: Palgrave Macmillan (2017).

"Afterlife conceptions in the Vedas." *Religion Compass*. vol. 5 no. 6 (June 2011), 202-13. Wiley-Blackwell.

"'My heart sang within me, and I was glad to be dead': afterlife myths, dreams, and near-death experiences in the cultures of the Pacific." *Journal of Near-Death Studies* vol. 36 no.3 (Spring 2018), 135-169.

"Cultural-linguistic constructivism and the challenge of near-death and out-of-body experience." In Bettina Schmidt (ed.) *The Study of Religious Experience: Approaches and Methodologies.* London: Equinox (2016).

Some of the content in this book has been adapted, revised, and expanded from the following previously published articles:

"Near-death experience." In Christopher Moreman (ed.) *The Routledge Companion to Death and Dying.* London: Routledge (2017).

"Near-death experience as divine revelation." In Balázs Mezei, Francesca A. Murphy and Kenneth Oakes (eds.) *The Oxford Handbook of Divine Revelation,* Oxford University Press (2021).

"The afterlife in early civilizations." In Yujin Nagasawa & Benjamin Matheson (eds.) *The Palgrave Handbook of the Afterlife.* London: Palgrave Macmillan. (2017).

"Afterlife conceptions in the Vedas." *Religion Compass.* vol. 5 no. 6 (June 2011), 202-13. Wiley-Blackwell.

"'My heart sang within me, and I was glad to be dead.': Afterlife myths, dreams, and near-death experiences in the cultures of the Pacific." *Journal of Near-Death Studies* vol. 36 no.3 (Spring 2018), 135-169.

"Cultural-linguistic constructivism and the challenge of near-death and out-of-body experience." In Bettina Schmidt (ed.) *The Study of Religious Experience: Approaches and Methodologies.* London: Equinox (2016).

INDEX